YESTERDAY'S TOMORROWS

YESTERDAY'S TOMORROWS

*A Historical Survey
of Future Societies*

by

W. H. G. ARMYTAGE

London
ROUTLEDGE & KEGAN PAUL

First published 1968
by Routledge & Kegan Paul Ltd
Broadway House, 68–74 Carter Lane
London, E.C.4

Printed in Great Britain
by Richard Clay (The Chaucer Press), Ltd.,
Bungay, Suffolk

CONTENTS

Contents

vii

Contents

viii

PREFACE

News of an unemployed mob hanging the Minister of Transport, dislodging Big Ben by mortar-fire, and setting about the destruction of the B.B.C. so alarmed some English listeners on 16th January 1926 that they turned to the telephone for reassurance. A similar scare in the United States some twelve years later, after a broadcast account of Martians landing on earth, evoked a virtual panic. That the cause of both panics was a predictive fantasy, in the first case by Father Ronald Knox, in the second by H. G. Wells, was an indication of the way in which views of the future reflect collective emotional tensions. A later, if less ostensible outlet for such tensions can be observed in the alleged phenomenon of 'flying saucers'; seen by some as angels sent from advanced technological societies to relieve their distress; or by others as reconnaissance probes from overcrowded planets anxious to colonise earth. Both fantasies mirror the hopes or fears of the 'viewers'.

Further myths and beliefs based on expectancy, whether of redemption or retribution, could be cited.

Panic, evoked by the disorder of the natural world, takes many forms. Indeed the word comes from Pan, who embodies this disorder. 'Quiet panic' might well animate man's wider quest for orientation in a puzzling world, by providing compensatory fantasies to supplement others springing from intellectual adventurousness, or curiosity, or a love of sensation, or even technological dreams. These fantasies or 'mirror worlds' are ideal countries on the other side of the hill, from the Ever-Ever lands of Rabelais to the Erewhon of Butler. Such countries of the imagination have been mapped by enthusiastic meliorists, who seize upon them, as did the fabled explorers in Plato's *Critias*, when the ocean of contemporaneity is clear, since they mirror their own wish-fulfilments, displacements, projections, denials, evasions, and withdrawals.

But, in so doing, these 'visions' can, and do, refresh minds for renewed grappling with the present by arming them with ideas for man's future needs. From the Boolean algebra of Swift's Laputans, the 'radar' in Gernsback's Ralph 124C+, or Wells' myriad 'anticipations', these fantasies might well contribute more than we now recognise to the apprehension of the course of technological invention. Today the process of prediction is attracting increasing attention, the more so as the casting of national and international horoscopes becomes fashionable. Psychologists have also taken up the matter and Professor Hadley Cantril (who investigated the American 'panic' mentioned in the first paragraph) asked 82 Americans on 27th October 1941 to 'write out in a page or two' their general predictions of how things would turn out in the next ten years. Forty replied, and of these he printed twenty-six in the *Clinical Supplement*, Vol. 2. of *The Journal of Abnormal and Social Psychology*, XXXVIII, (1943), 6–47. Subsequently analysed by Hans H. Toch in the light of how things actually did turn out in 1952, these, as he showed in *Public Opinion Quarterly*, XXII, (1958), 57–66, indicated that the two most accurate predictors posed, wherever feasible, several alternative sequences. Ten years later, in 1967, access to ever more copiously stored data banks have enabled normative-relevance-tree-techniques to be devised, trends to be more ingeniously extrapolated, systems to be more exquisitely analysed, and increasingly complex mathematical models to be constructed.

The rise of these 'conflict models' of prediction out of what might otherwise be regarded as a welter of futuristic fantasies is the theme of this book. It tries to show how, out of the long process of preparatory day-dreams, imagined encounters, wish-fulfilments, and compensatory projections, a constructive debate about tomorrow is emerging, providing us with operational models of what tomorrow could, or should, be. This debate (dialogue is perhaps the more fashionable term) is increasingly becoming part of the modern self whereby man is enabled to maintain his equilibrium.

My thanks are due to Reginald Pilkington for friendly criticism and especially for helpful reading of a bad typescript. That a lawyer should find it entertaining, encourages me to hope that others also will.

W. H. G. A.

'The rule is, jam to-morrow and jam yesterday—but never jam *to-day*.'

'It *must* come sometimes to "jam to-day",' Alice objected.

'No, it can't,' said the Queen. 'It's jam every *other* day: to-day isn't any other day, you know.'

'I don't understand you,' said Alice. 'It's dreadfully confusing!'

'That's the effect of living backwards,' the Queen said kindly: 'it always makes one a little giddy at first——'

'Living backwards!' Alice repeated in great astonishment. 'I never heard of such a thing!'

'—but there's one great advantage in it, that one's memory works both ways.'

'I'm sure *mine* only works one way,' Alice remarked. 'I can't remember things before they happen.'

'It's a poor sort of memory that only works backwards,' the Queen remarked.

'What sort of things do *you* remember best?' Alice ventured to ask.

'Oh, things that happened the week after next,' the Queen replied in a careless tone.

LEWIS CARROLL, *Through the Looking Glass, and what Alice Found There* (1872) in *Works*, ed. Roger Lancelyn Green (1965) 161.

Chapter One

THE MANTIC HERITAGE

I SYMBOLS AND ARCHETYPES

Since man began to extricate himself from being engulfed by his environment he has been devising a symbolic language—some call it myth—that both propitiates and accounts for the mysterious forces around him.[1] Perpetual ecdysis, or shedding of the mythical integument, has created from these explanations and propitiations a compost of science, history, and religion. These discarded explanatory and propitiatory myths contain memories of experiences undergone that are for ever evoked by the imagination of the Shaman, and his modern equivalents.[2] These modern equivalents have multiplied with contemporary environmental tensions, perhaps not as crippling as those of Cro-Magnon times. So interest in 'primordial images' or 'archetypes' mounts with the ever more intensive emphasis on planning man's future.

The first real optimistic interest in the future was exhibited by the Jews. Lacking a glorious past, their interest was held by a succession of prophets whose names and stories they cherished long after their death to serve as analogues for others. God, to them, was always unrolling his purpose, was always going to come and inaugurate his Kingdom. Even their history was prophecy in retrospect and the Pentateuch itself looks beyond Moses (*c.* 1200 B.C.), their first prophet, to the day when they would be the holy nation of God.

Their early prophets divined, foresaw, and proclaimed the country's mission (Torah) either individually, or in companies. One such company was led by Miriam, and chanted for victory at the Red Sea. Elijah added a new ethic to prophecy: a stern call to elevation above the animal. To preserve prophecies already made, and to disseminate the word more effectively, prophecy was written down.

The first of these 'literary' prophets was Amos (*c.* 765 B.C.), a shepherd who with Hosea (*c.* 735 B.C.) buoyed up the Israelites by a sense of mission during the Syrian wars. To their religious message Isaiah added a social component: denunciation of land-grabbing and luxury.[3] This curious dialectic of prophecy and fulfilment whereby each fulfilment of the word of God announced a yet more decisive event[4] so imprinted itself on history that, two millennia later, Voltaire could sardonically observe:

> What I most admire in our modern compilers (of history) is the wisdom, the good faith, with which they prove to us that everything that happened anciently in the greatest empires of the world happened in order to afford instruction to the inhabitants of *Palestine*. . . Turks and Arabs came along simply to chastise this worthy people. It must be allowed that they have had an excellent education; never were there so many teachers.[5]

II APOLLO AND THE CHRESMOLOGUES

To descry what lay ahead, early Mediterranean peoples would climb mountains to look for new land, examine entrails to see if animals were diseased, observe the flight of birds for information about the weather, and con the surface of rivers for clues as to up-country vegetation. These practices in time hardened into rituals, which clustered round the real source of illumination: the Sun god, Apollo, who, said Plato, 'sits at the very centre and navel of the earth to instruct the human race'. As the god of prophecy, poetry, and science his advice was invoked by oracles, which though originally independent, came under political influences of various kinds. A later priest of the oracle at Delphi, Plutarch, thought it would continue for ever[6] to help mankind to find their way on this earth in the face of an unknown or threatening future.[7] Sometimes it was not so much finding one's way as in-suring oneself or bouncing one's ideas off an external auditor— a kind of precursor of psychoanalysis.[8] This is why intuitive (*atechnos adidaktos*) was separate from indicative divination (*entechnos technike*).

As house physician at Mount Olympus—if one can so describe the lofty conclave of the Greek gods—Apollo was also the god of healing. This, too, was apt symbolism, as forecasting was accelerated by the rise of medical science.

> I hold [wrote Hippocrates], that it is an excellent thing for a physician to practise forecasting. For if he discover and declare unaided by the side of his patients the present, the past and the future, and fill in the gaps in the account given by the sick, he will be the more believed to understand the cases so that men will confidently entrust themselves to him for treatment. Furthermore, he will carry out the treatment best if he knows beforehand from the present symptoms what will take place later. Now to restore every patient to health is impossible. To do so indeed would have been better even than forecasting the future. But as a matter of fact men do die, some owing to the severity of the disease before they summon the physician, others expiring immediately after calling him in—living one day or a little longer—before the physician by his art can combat each disease. It is necessary, therefore, to learn the natures of such diseases, how much they exceed the strength of men's bodies, and to learn how to forecast them. For in this way you will justly win respect and be an able physician. For the longer time you plan to meet each emergency the greater your power to save those who have a chance of recovery, while you will be blameless if you learn and declare beforehand those who will die and those who will get better.[9]

The most influential seer in Periclean Athens was Lampo, who advised the founder of the New Greek Colony of Thurii and was a sort of political pamphleteer.[10] Other chresmologues were Onomacritus, who advised Xerxes, and Diopithes who tried to prevent Agiesilaus becoming King of Sparta. The most famous of such advisors was Plato, who paid three visits to Syracuse. In the interval he put forward his theory of ideas—that intelligible form of a thing exists outside the sense world of its actuality, and that the supreme idea was that of the Good. A state, quite unlike that under Dionysius in Syracuse, took shape in his *Republic*, one of a series of dramatic dialogues in which he put forth such general ideas in ideological concreteness. Now Plato's theory of forms depended on his mathematics. To him God was a geometer, and his insights into the structure of generations of individuals, indeed his provision of a special relationship between individuals as members of a living organism, suggested to a recent writer that:

> The brilliant development in the physical sciences [in the twentieth century] has tended again unconsciously by its own dialectic to

confirm the Platonic intuition of form and measure everywhere. The building bricks of nature—electrons, neutrons, etc.—are measured, are constant in nature, and this fact indicates cosmic control. The discovery by Moseley of atomic number—a series of atomic forms repeated in nature everywhere—is evidence of the cosmic architecture which would have delighted the soul of Plato. There is now also an indication of a life-number—a radiating pattern of life forms. This order, even more obviously than atomic number, has reference to time.[11]

So side by side with the impetus from medicine and mathematics, legend fostered belief in prediction. Calchas, the wisest soothsayer among the Greeks at Troy, explained how long the war would last, but died, according to one legend, when he was out-prophesied by another soothsayer Mopsus, whose maternal grandfather had prophesied that Thebes would be victorious against the seven. Blind from the age of seven, this grandfather had been given in compensation the power of prophecy which was to last for seven or nine generations. His name, immortalised for us by Tennyson, Swinburne, and T. S. Eliot, was Tiresias.

III   THE SIBYL

So unimaginatively operated was the official soothsaying of the Romans that Cato the Elder imagined a *haruspex* laughing if he met a colleague of the craft. Cato advised readers of his book on agriculture not to consult either a *haruspex* or an *augur*, much less the quacks and Oriental prophets that flooded Rome in his day— the *harioli* and *Chaldeans*.[12] The augurs, however, took themselves seriously. Cicero, speaking as one of the craft, argued:

> . . . that there is no nation, whether the most learned and enlightened or the most grossly barbarous, that does not believe that the future can be revealed, and does not recognise in certain people the power of foretelling it.

> It is an ancient belief [he continued in his *De Divinatione*], that there exists within mankind an undeniable faculty of divination. The Greeks called it *mantike*, the capacity to foresee, to know future events, a sublime and salutary act that raises human nature most nearly to the level of divine power.

Clues to the course of action to be adopted by the state were provided by the book of the Sibyl. This was a collection of rhymes attributed to a wise woman of Cumae, and was believed to have been purchased by King Tarquin. Meticulously preserved, they were invariably consulted by the Quindecemviri before any political move was made. All access to them was only on the order of the Senate, supplemented with the help of two officials with a knowledge of Greek. Destroyed by fire in 83 B.C., the Sibylline books were reconstituted after the Senate had sent special envoys to places possessing Sibylline writings to produce a more authoritative edition. This was then deposited in the vaults of the temple of Jupiter Capitolinus, becoming such a buttress of the established order that conspirators like Lentulus had to manufacture others to confute them. Such 'false' oracles, in acrostics, for safety's sake, had such a wide circulation that Augustus destroyed nearly two thousand volumes of them in 12 B.C. The original official books he had re-copied and deposited in his new temple of the Palatine Apollo. Later a similar inspection and re-editing was ordered by Tiberius.

The spectacle of Apollo dashing from shrine to shrine—Delphi, Colophon, Xanthus, Claros, Delos, or the Branchidae (a family of temple keepers), to give advice on future action to the many who consulted him, amused Lucian. As a result he wrote his *True History*: the inspiration of a new type of mock prophecy or satire: a foretaste of *Gulliver's Travels*.[13]

For by Plutarch's time, *ad hoc* expedients had hardened into meaningless rituals of divination. Indicative divination studied phenomena like birds (ornithomancy), phrases (cledonomancy), entrails (hieromancy), fire (pyromancy), water (hydromancy) mirrors (cataptromancy) or the lot (cleromancy) as manifest by dice or pebbles (astragalomancy), the swing of the pendulum (dactyliomancy), quotations on slips of paper (rhapsodomancy), or use of vessels of water (lecanomancy).[14] Intuitive divination relied on divine possession. *Mantike*, a third category, consisted of the interpretation of dreams (oneiromancy) or evoking the ghosts of the dead (necromancy).

IV VIRGIL THE OPTIMIST

The first Roman to entertain a hopeful or Hebrew view of the
future was Virgil. Before his time it was held that the world was
declining from a gold to a silver, then to a bronze, and then to an
iron age. Thus Horace wrote:

> *Damnosa quid non imminuit dies?*
> *Aetas parentum peior avis tuilit*
> *Nos nequiores, mox daturos*
> *Progeniem vitiosiorem;*

and Juvenal:

> *Nona aetas oritus peioraque saecula ferri*
> *Temporibus, quorum sceleri non invenit ipsa*
> *Nomen et a nullo posuit natura metallo.*

But Virgil held to the Hebrew view that man's true perfection lay
ahead of and not behind him. This led to Virgil's fourth eclogue
being regarded as a prophecy of the coming of Christ:

> *Ultima Cumaei venit iam carminis aetas;*
> *magnus ab integro saeclorum nascitur ordo.*
> *Iam redit et Virgo, redeunt Saturnia regna;*
> *iam nova progenies caelo demittitur alto.*
> *Tu modo nascenti puero, quo ferrea primum*
> *desinet ac toto surget gens aurea mundo,*
> *casta fave Lucina: tuus iam regnat Apollo.*[14]

Though the Christ for whom Virgil was regarded as a prophet,
was himself a prophet, and was presented by his early followers as
such following the day of Pentecost, and though Paul placed prophets immediately after the apostles, yet religious prophecy was
considerably dampened by the establishment of the Christian
Church. Indeed the Revelation of St. John was intended to close
prophecy until Christ's second coming.

So the Christian Church began to conduct itself by reference to
the 'scriptures' as the fountain of divine truths, treating such prophets as arose within it, however inspired, with due reserve.
Reserve grew to mistrust after the Montanist movement of the
second century.[15]

Virgil was brought into the Christian framework in A.D. 313 by the first Roman Emperor to embrace Christianity and during the Middle Ages his role as a Christian herald was authoritatively scripted by Dante who regarded him as a guide sent by Beatrice to light a path from the dark forest of worldly ambitions. Virgil's view of Elysium seemed also to be a prophecy of the role of Rome in the Holy Empire:

> *Excudent alii spirantia mollius aera,—*
> *Credo equidem,—vivos ducent de marmore vultus:*
> *Orabunt causas melius, caelique meatus*
> *Describent radio et surgentia sidera dicent:*
> *Tu regere imperio populos, Romane, memento;*
> *Hae tibi erunt artes, pacisque imponere morem*
> *Parcere subjectis et debellare superbos.*[16]

Other magical powers attributed to him were those of making statues move, speak, and act.[17] Similar compensatory fantasies took shape in the minds of the persecuted Jews in Central Europe, who imagined that a mind-reading entity capable of detecting their enemies and lightening or sharing their labours could be made by writing any one of the names of God on a piece of paper and sticking it on the forehead or mouth of a clay image. Round these *golems* grew legends, as esoteric theosophical doctrines followed the Cabbala. By the sixteenth century Elijah of Chelm was credited with having made a golem that grew so great that its maker feared it would destroy the world. So he extracted the name of God from the forehead of his golem, which returned to dust. Even better known was the golem of Hohe Rabbi Löw. Used as a servant on week-days and rested on the Sabbath, it gave good service until one day he forgot to extract the Shem. Fearing that the golem would desecrate the Sabbath, he chased it and only caught it in front of the synagogue just before the Sabbath began. He hurriedly extracted the Shem and the golem disintegrated.

One golem, said to have been made by Rabbi David Jaffe of Dorhiczyn at the end of the eighteenth century, was created especially to heat the ovens of Jews on Winter Sabbaths, until in error it set a town on fire.[18] The traditions of the golems outlasted the hopes and fears of ghetto Jews in Central Europe, for they became the nucleus of a powerful prophetic drive for energy-slaves behind such expatriate Jews as Charles Proteus Steinmetz, of the General Electric Company of America.

Transmuted by the Czech dramatist Karl Capek in his Play *R.U.R.*, its essence survives as the robot.

V   THE INVENTION OF MERLIN

The English had their Virgil too. He gave them a past (King Arthur) and a future (Merlin). This was twelfth-century Geoffrey of Monmouth[19] who skilfully used history to lead up to prophecy.[20] His view of the future was so useful[21] and his interpretation of the past so attractive[22] that both became myths for centuries. The future was sketched in his *Book of Merlin* and the *Vita Merlini*, the past in the *Historia Regum Britanniæ*. The first reads like space fiction:

> The helmet of Mars shall cast a shadow, and the rage of Mercury shall overpass all bounds. Iron Orion shall bare his sword. Phoebus of the Ocean shall torment his clouds. Jupiter shall trespass beyond his appointed bounds, and Venus forsake the way that hath been ordained unto her. The malignity of Saturn shall fall upon the earth with the rain of heaven, and shall slay mankind as it were with a crooked sickle.[23]

Compounded from Welsh traditions, the second gathered up several earlier prophetic writings, and set the tone for what one commentator has called the 'Galfridan' style.[24] Merlin became a greater prophet than Virgil, since his prophecies, his hopes, and his beliefs ministered to the national pride.[25] His history provided us with, amongst other things, a tradition of the antiquity of Oxford. Geoffrey became the 'Orpheus of Britain',[26] indeed of Europe too. In France his prophecy of the overthrow of the Anglo-Saxons[27] was exploited. In Venice it was used by a scribe between the years 1276 and 1279 to denounce corruption in the Roman church.

In days when warnings were still cast into prophetic forms, and vaticination was still 'an effective vehicle for important pronouncements',[28] Merlin had to be co-opted, as other scribes were, and as Virgil had been before him, into the hagiography, and hailed as a prophet after the manner of Job, Balaam, Cassandra, and the Sibyls.[29] But prophecies could misfire, and be used by the wrong people, as the Crown realised in 1402 when it considered 'divination and lies' spread by Welsh minstrels to be 'the cause of the insurrection and rebellion in Wales'. So further 'false prophecies' predicting the downfall of the Government of 1406 led to the framing of laws against prophecy. Hotspur could well complain of Glendower:

> Sometime he angers me
> With telling me of the moldwarp and the ant,
> Of the dreamer Merlin and his prophecies ...
> And such a deal of skimble-skamble stuff
> As puts me from my faith.[30]

This skimble-skamble stuff became a traditional favourite. *Lytel Tretys* put out by Wynkyn de Worde in 1510 was called for again in 1524 and in 1533. More firm credit was given by 1549 to 'the diverse prophane Prophesies of Merlin' and 'other corrupit vaticinaris' than to 'Isaiah, Ezekiel, Jeremiah or the evangel'. The name of Merlin remained something to conjure with for at least a century: on setting himself up as a prophet in 1644, Lilly entitled his annual almanac *Merlinus Anglicus Junior, the English Merlin Revived*. And he was but one of numerous almanac makers during the Civil War and after.

> To Prophets there be several attributes given, some called prophetae, some vates, others videntes. Vates was a title promiscuously conferred on prophets and poets as belonging to them both ... [wrote Merlin's seventeenth-century biographer as he placed his subject in the tradition]. Of the vatical or prophetical poets among the Greeks were Orpheus, Homer, Hesiod, etc., and amongst the Latins, Publius Virgilius Maro and others.[31]

VI   THE JOACHITE BALANCE OF HOPE AND FEAR

The first man to see the book of Apocalypse both as a continuous description of the history of mankind as well as a forecast of its destiny was the Calabrian mystic Joachim of Flora (*c.* 1131–*c.* 1202). He saw the Old Testament as the age of the Father, of spouses, of patriarchs, of Kings and of slaves; the New Testament as the Age of the Son, of freemen and of priests. The third, the age of the Holy Ghost, was also to be the age of friends and mystics. This third age would be inaugurated in 1260 when the church would collapse, and antichrist would arrive. The subsequent three and a half years would see him struggle to prevent the happy renovation of man.

Dominicans and Franciscans rode on the ground swell of his prophecy that by 1260 two new orders would appear, personified by the raven and the dove. Indeed the great Franciscan English scientist Roger Bacon is credited with the idea of organising the sciences (*naturae et artis*) to defeat the coming of antichrist.[32]

Sharpened by the crusades and prophecies of Islamic emperors who were to awake and take over the empire of the world, Joachite disciples began to see in every opponent an embodiment of the 'beast', 'the red dragon', the creature with 'seven heads and ten horns', or as Satan, 'loosed out of his prison seducing the nations'.

All their pother and ingenuity only emphasised the salient fact that by historicising the eschatological concept of antichrist, Joachim, as Professor Bloomfield points out, 'made the apocalyptic a political and social phenomenon'.[33] He provided the synthesis, so needed in late medieval thought, between the fear that the world's end was imminent, and the hope that it was to be renovated on a grand scale.

His theory enabled both optimists and pessimists to find consolation. Astronomers, who served the expansionist ethic of the surgent class of merchants and embryo industrialists, also made calculations for the advent of antichrist. Their observations of the stars and the political situations led a number of them to settle on the date 1365. Such prophecies were collected and studied by men like John Ergholme, who bequeathed his library to his Augustinian priory at York. He symbolises the way in which Joachism in England was associated with the biblical exegetes and monastic philosophers: a very responsible forum for the consideration of 'futures'. Fortified by such respectable authorities as John of Salisbury and Thomas Aquinas they canvassed the view that history could be understood, and that the Kingdom of God, the perfect state, was ahead. To quote Professor Bloomfield again, 'To some this historical perfectibility has been a heady brew; and when secularised, it has led to much Utopian thinking, not all of it bad'.[34]

This secularisation, fostered by voyages to other non-Christian lands, was to lead to further descants on destiny, and to these wanderers outside prescribed limits we now turn.

Chapter Two

EXTRAVAGANCE TO EXTRAPOLATION

I   THE ORPHIC CYCLE

The heady influence of Ovid's *Metamorphoses* with its stories of men and women, even Gods and Goddesses, being transmuted into flowers and trees through the Orphean cycles of time and eternity (*Cuncta fluunt omnisque vagans formatur image*) exerted a powerful influence on an age of travellers.[1] For Orpheus was a pilgrim, and all medieval pilgrimages were conflations of fact and symbol. Thus Jean de Hauteville's *The Man of Many Sorrows* (*c.* 1184), describes the way in which Architrenius went in search of Nature to find out why he has been made so weak: going through lands embodying Ambition and Gluttony he finds a wife— Moderation.[2] Similar pilgrimages made to the Islands of the Blessed offered scope for theorising about the deliquescent effects of time. Bran was kept, he thought, for a year, but when he returned, he found that his departure had been forgotten, and one of his men turned into 'a heap of ashes, as though he had been in the earth for many hundred years'.

After visiting the city with golden walls (where one day is equivalent to a hundred years on the rest of the earth), other travellers found that church, abbey, city, people, walls, had all vanished. They know nobody and they themselves:

> *Ipsi qui fuerant hodie forma juveniles,*
> *Mane senescentes sunt pelle piloque seniles;*
> *Decrepitos, viles, se miseros vident.*

There is also the story of King Herla who honours his contract with the pygmies by entering a cavern to spend what he thinks are three days, but, in fact, are two hundred years. When he returns some of his retinue turn to dust because they disobey the warning not to dismount before a gift dog has leapt from its keeper.

The penalty of time is paid by all travellers to other worlds. And so the Orphic myth becomes the extravaganza—the story of wanderers outside prescribed limits.[3]

II   WANDERERS OUTSIDE PRESCRIBED LIMITS

The extravagance of the traveller's tale could breed disaffection in a closed society. Like the Shogun, Plato prescribed in his *Laws* (950d)

> First, no man under forty years shall obtain permission to go abroad to whatever place it may be. Second, nobody shall obtain permission in a private capacity; in a public capacity, permission may be granted only to herald's ambassadors, and certain missions of inspection.
>
> . . . And these men after their return will teach the young that the political institutions of other countries are inferior to their own.

One such fictional traveller Raphael Hythloday returned from sailing with Amerigo Vespucci. In the course of his voyage he spent five years on the imaginary island of Utopia, the subtle ambiguity of whose name (no place or a better place), made it one of the Sibylline books of a new technique of social soothsaying. Just as the Archangel Raphael cured Tobit of his blindness, so his secular counterpart Raphael Hythloday tried to open people's eyes to the real causes of social evil by giving them a model of something better.[4]

No subsequent models, from Bensalem (Francis Bacon), Christianopolis (J. V. Andreae), Delectaland (Unitas (pseud.)), Erewhon (Samuel Butler), Freeland (Hertzka), Hesperides (John Palmer), Icaria (Etienne Cabet), Jingalo (Laurence Housman), The New Jerusalem (William Blake), Kennaquhair (Thomas Carlyle), Lilliput (Jonathan Swift), Macaria (Samuel Hartlib), Newtopia (E. Richardson), Oceana (Harington), Perelandra (C. S. Lewis), Quebus (Rabelais), Rampole Island (H. G. Wells), Solente (Fénelon), Thelema (C. R. Ashbee), Upsidonia (Archibald Marshall), Vrylia (Bulwer Lytton), and Weissnichtwo (Thomas Carlyle), for all their inventiveness, have ever circulated so widely.

Nor has the setting—an imaginary island—been improved

upon, for *Robinson Crusoe*, *Gulliver's Travels*, *The Island of Dr. Moreau*, and the *Lord of the Flies* are all so set, and also play on the theme of confidence in man's capacity to master nature or nature's propensity to master man. An island (as Shakespeare showed in *The Tempest*), is a large enough stage on which to display the drama of human beings reacting on each other, insulated from 'outside' and often 'divine' intervention. Much mid-twentieth century science-fiction utilises space islands (planets). Like Utopia, science-fictions are regarded as escapes, blueprints of tomorrow, looks forward, looks backward, allegories, idealisations of contemporary society, quizzical exegeses of Plato, essays in social criticism, overt programmes of reform;[5] all can be read into them, as into More's *Utopia*. Within two and a half centuries it threw up 875 bibliographic items.[6]

With its fifty-four shires, planned county towns, gardens, houses, and streets; its schools teaching everything from astronomy to natural history; its citizens working a six to nine hour day, holding all things in common, its religion of Mithra, its magistrates chosen by universal suffrage, and its ambassadors, priests, and rulers chosen from the young men and its meanest of utensils all of gold, the island of Utopia was obviously an England in which all the customary practices were inverted and idealised. It is also an adumbration of things to come. Delinquents (who had evoked Hythloday's description of Utopia), worked outside their prisons to earn freedom instead of being imprisoned to expiate their crimes. Healthy genetic endowment was ensured by pre-marital examination of couples, fitness by daily exercise, and environmental beauty by prizes to the most successful gardeners. Children were reared by the local authorities after they had acquired the vestiges of autonomy. After visiting it, Hythloday confessed that all other governments seemed to him merely 'a conspiracy of the rich who on pretence of managing the public only pursue their private ends'.

A traveller's tale of Japan probably influenced the construction of another imaginary island—in the North Pacific or the northern part of the South Seas—where Francis Bacon sited Bensalem.[7] (This, with More's *Utopia* and the *Christianopolis* of J. V. Andreae, provides a humanistic paradigm of what society could be, given certain rational assumptions.) Its officials wear green garments covered with blue cloaks, suggesting, in Orphic fashion, eternal spring. Bacon considered the fable was a method commended for science, bringing new light which in its non-fabulous brightness might harm men. In other words, inventions which men were not ready for, could be set forth in fables.[8] To him the 'womb of nature' contained 'many secrets of excellent use, having no affinity or parallelism with anything that is now known'.

Vulgar prophecies, Bacon considered, had done 'much mischief'. Yet, he confessed, three things 'hath given them grace and some credit':

> First, that men mark when they hit, and never mark when they miss; as they do generally of dreams. The second is that probable conjectures, or obscure traditions, many times turn themselves into prophecies; whilst the nature of man, which coveteth divination, thinks it no peril to foretell that which indeed they do but collect. . . The third and last (which is the great one) is that almost all of them, being infinite in number, have been impostures, and by idle and crafty brains were combined and feigned after the event passed.[9]

So his House of Solomon was an institution for altering the future in man's favour. Its 'enginehouses where are prepared engines and instruments for all sorts of motions' included 'some degrees of flying in the air . . . ships and boats for going under water, and brooking of seas . . . and some perpetual motions': hints of what Bacon envisaged society would become if his researching team were to be established. [10] This was, as his continuator Joseph Glanvill wrote, 'Anti-Fanatical Religion and Free Philosophy'.[11]

Similarly, Campanella's sea captain described the *City of the Sun* standing on top of a great hill, girdled by seven enormous walls, on which were engraved all human knowledge. These walls, however, only enclosed the city with knowledge, there was no centre for research and discovery of new knowledge inside— unless one included museums. It took its name from Sol, who is chosen and advised by temple priests operating an astrological institute. These priests scrutinise the heavens for indications of courses of action best open to the citizens, and though they 'write treatises and investigate the science', there seems to be no provision for adding to the knowledge inscribed on the walls.

No one could aspire to the dignity of Sol, unless he knew 'the histories of all nations, their customs, sacrifices, laws and forms of government'.

A man who becomes Sol must know the names of the lawgivers and the inventors in the arts, as also the natural laws and history of the earth and the heavens. Likewise, he must also know all the mechanical arts. (He learns a new one almost every two days, although he does not necessarily become proficient in it in that period of time. However, practice and the study of pictures presently give him proficiency in this matter). In addition he must know physics, mathematics, and astrology. There is not much concern about his knowing languages, since there are numerous interpreters who serve as grammarians in the state. But above all he must understand metaphysics and theology . . . he must also be well read in the Prophets and in astrology. Thus they know long beforehand who will be Sol, but no one is raised to so great a dignity until he is thirty-five years old.[12]

Of his three assistants, Pon (Power), Sin (Wisdom), and Mor (Love), the last named sees to it that men and women are mated to produce the best offspring, and that these offspring are well fed, well clothed, and above all, well educated; the second sees to their instruction in science, the liberal and mechanical arts; and the first to training in the military arts.

Campanella figures as 'companion' to Cyrano de Bergerac in his imaginary voyage to the States and Empires of the Sun. This was the second part of his posthumously published book *L'Autre Monde* (1657). These voyages gave him an opportunity both to depict a Utopia and to air some technological fantasies. These technological fantasies include houses that could be raised and lowered into the ground, tape recorded books, a rocket utilising solar heat, and an early steam monster which 'sweats boiling oil and pisses nitric acid'.[13] For Cyrano had listened to Gassendi, the great French free-thinking mathematician, and had as a friend the equally distinguished French physicist Rohault.

III PROTESTANTISM AND PROJECTION

Only Andreae's Christianopolis comes nearest to Bacon's notion of progress, for in its western quarter:

Everything that the earth contains in her bowels is subjected to the laws and instruments of science. . . . Unless you analyse matter by experiment, unless you improve the deficiencies of knowledge by more capable instruments, you are worthless.[14]

Bowels had another role. For anticipatory fantasies can be, and often are, projections or enlargements of objectionable items in the contemporary picture. Such fantasies make use of the excretory functions, as if the objectionable items were being ejected from the consciousness as faeces are eliminated from the bowels. Thus Protestants identified the Devil with the anus, as Luther's *Table Talk* indicates.

Anality and the reproductive processes figure largely in the works of Rabelais, whose *Pantagruel* and *Gargantua* contain no less than 29 synonyms for coitus, 29 for the male genitals, and 19 for eating.[15] As the mouthpiece of a rising class 'exuberant and conscious of its increasing power and using this weapon to ridicule the shams and absurdities of a decaying society'.[16] Rabelais allows men and women to do not what pleases God, but what pleases them. His Thélème is an inverted monastery. As they lay its foundations, a copper plate is found on which is engraved a prophecy:

> Cheer up your hearts, and hear what I shall say:
> If it be lawful firmly to believe
> That the celestial bodies can us give
> Wisdom to judge of things that are not yet;
> Or if from heaven such wisdom we may get,
> As may with confidence make us discourse
> Of years to come, their destiny and course;
> I to my hearers give to understand,
> That this next winter, though it be at hand,
> Yea and before, there shall appear a race
> Of men, who, loth to sit still in one place,
> Shall boldly go before all people's eyes,
> Suborning men of divers qualities,
> To draw them unto covenants and sides,
> In such a manner, that whate'er betides,
> They'll move you, if you give them ear, no doubt,
> With both your friends and kindred to fall out.
> They'll make a vassal to gain-stand his lord,
> And children their own parents; in a word,
> All reverence shall then be banished,
> No true respect to other shall be had.[17]

Influenced possibly by Rabelais[18] and almost certainly by travellers' tales from China, the first account of an ideal city was written in English by an Englishman: Robert Burton's *The Anatomy of Melancholy* (1621). Written 'to satisfy and please myself', it projected 'a New Atlantis, a poetical commonwealth', in which Burton could 'freely domineer, build cities, make laws, statutes as I list myself'.

Chinese influence on this pioneer operational fantasy is shown in the author's suggestion of public examinations to test the competence of magistrates, lawyers and physicians to practise, and parents intending to beget children. All land and manpower resources were to be exploited to the full.

> I will have [he wrote] no bogs, fens, marshes, vast woods, deserts, heaths, commons, but all enclosed i.e. in use. . . . I will not have a barren acre in my territories, not so much as the tops of mountains; where nature fails, it shall be supplied by art; lakes and rivers shall not be left desolate. All common highways, bridges, banks, corrivations of waters, aquaducts, channels, public works building, etc. out of a common stock, curiously maintained and kept in repair; no depopulations, engrossings, alterations of wood, arable but by consent of some supervisors that shall be appointed for the purpose.[19]

Dress was to correspond to calling. No weapons, monopolies, false weights and measures, and idle folk were to be allowed. Schools of singing, dancing, fencing, grammar, and language were to be provided 'not to be taught by those precepts ordinarily used, but by use, example and conversation, as travellers learn abroad, and nurses teach to children'.

Rabelaisian preoccupations with reproductive processes, and Lutherian identification of the Devil with anality permeates *Mundus Alter et Idem* (1605): Bishop Hall's inversion myth of a traveller—Mercurius—in a moral Antipodes, he finding a bibulocracy, a gynocracy and a moronocracy.[20] In the bibulocracy of Crapulia everyone belches and even the very birds are such heavy feeders that they cannot fly. Devotion to the fork god Trine and his motto 'Frolic fatness here doth dwell: keep leanness out and all goes well', is such that punishment is inflicted by extracting teeth, or by imprisonment in the Temple of Famine. The gynocracy, Shee-Landt, or Womandecoia, is a country where women's tongues wag interminably and 'they hold a continual parliament about their more weighty affairs of state'. The moronocracy—Moronia or Fooliana—has inhibitants rather than inhabitants, who 'abhor company and hate to be interrupted in their airy castle-buildings'. In addition, Mercurius Lavernia visits a country of brigands.[21]

That this should have been printed on one occasion with More's *Utopia* is indicative of the thirst for fantasy now whetted,[22] which, in its intense preoccupation with the bowels, reaches a climacteric in Swift,[23] who considered that:

> The fumes issuing from a Jakes, will furnish as comely and useful a Vapour as incense from an altar.[24]

Yet Swift himself saw the limitations of 'certain foretune-tellers in Northern America, who have a way of reading a Man's Destiny, by peeping in his Breech'.[25] Gulliver explores the universal neuroses of mankind, seeing man smaller (Lilliput) and larger (Brobdingnag) than life, before discovering him to be a Yahoo, lower than the noble horses (Houyhnhnms).[26] These horses:

> looked upon us as a Sort of Animals to whose Share, by what Accident he could not conjecture, some small Pittance of *Reason* had fallen, whereof we made no other Use than by its Assistance to aggravate our *natural* Corruption, and to acquire new ones when Nature had not given us. That, we disarmed our selves of the few Abilities she had bestowed; had been very successful in multiplying our additional wants, and seemed to spend our whole Lives in vain Endeavours to supply them by our own Inventions.[27]

To the Houyhnhnms, Gulliver was 'an exact *Yahoo* in every Part, only of a whiter Colour, less Hairy, and with shorter Claws'.[28] When he saw a reflection of himself in a lake or fountain 'I turned away my face in horror and detestation of myself; and could better endure the Sight of a common Yahoo than my own Person'. Indeed, it was for being a Yahoo—a degenerate anthropoid—that he was banished from Houyhnhnmland.[29] 'Expect no more from man,' Swift wrote to a friend, 'than such an animal is capable of, and you will every day find my description of Yahoos more resembling.'[30]

Certainly the Houyhnhnms made a great impression on later social thinkers, especially William Godwin, who considered Swift's description of their policy exhibited 'more profound insight into the principles of political justice than any preceding or contemporary author'.[31]

IV ANALOGUES WITH THE ANIMAL WORLD

Animal analogues, or exercises in social anthropology, began to multiply.[32] In 1669 the Duchess of Newcastle peopled her society *Blazing World*[33] with ape-men chemists, bear-men experimental philosophers, and frogmen politicians. In the same year George Pine started with four women and some ship's stores to create a community of 1,789 people, in Henry Nevile's *The Isle of Pines* (1667).[34] A new race, the Severambi, who could change the shapes of animals, was first outlined by a Captain Siden, in 1675, as peopling an ideal society set off the Cape of Good Hope. In the same year a Cambridge don, Joshua Barnes, 'one of a singular industry and a most diffuse reading' wanted to write a terato-logical fantasy about a spider and a toad, fleas and a Welshman, but ended up by publishing *Gerania; a new discovery of a little sort of people anciently discoursed of, called Pygmies. With a lively description of their stature, habit, manners, buildings, knowledge and government, being very delightful and profitable* (London 1675). This characteristic production of a scholar who never received the recognition of his fellows may have given Swift hints for Lilliput.

Africa was also the home of another 'new people', the Mezzorar-rians, described by Simon Berington in 1738 as the most indus-trious Race in the Universe.[35] Though deprived of all industrial skills, the 'new men' encountered by Peter Wilkins in Robert Paltock's fantasy, could fly. Like Mark Twain's hero Hank at King Arthur's Court, Paltock's Wilkins is soon industrialising Indian society.[36]

Meanwhile the terms 'New Atlantis' and 'Utopia' had been de-based by constant use. Used by gossips like Mrs. Manley and Mrs. Haywood for their books in 1711 and 1725, they had become inert concepts. Also the unoccupied places in the world were becoming so rare that satirists began to look to the future. Samuel Madden, like Swift, was a graduate of Trinity College, Dublin, but unlike Swift, did not have the courage of his con-victions. So his *Memoirs of the Twentieth Century* (1733) were pub-lished anonymously. Indeed, he published only the first of a pro-jected set of six volumes. According to a MS note in the flyleaf of a copy examined in the Library at Trinity College, Dublin, he also destroyed 899 copies of the 1,000 which were printed. A second, more technological, fantasy—also anonymous—was *The*

Reign of George VI 1900–1925 (1763).[37] In this, corruption still prevails, the Duke of Bedford being the twentieth-century counterpart of the Duke of Newcastle. France is still the bugbear of British foreign policy, but Russia has become the dominant power, controlling Finland, Poland, Scandinavia, and the Crimea, with Prussia controlling Germany, and Italy unified. Britain is laced by a network of water-borne traffic. Rivers that formerly were almost useless were now navigated by large barges, which increased the trade of innumerable towns, and raised new ones in many places. Canals joined rivers, and enabled every part of the kingdom to grow: 'Villages grew into towns and towns became cities.' [38]

But of steam there is no conception. Just as barges are the main carriers on land, so three-decker ships command the seas. The potential of America 'the finest country in the world' was appreciated but grossly under-estimated—'it had never made the least attempt to shake off the authority of Great Britain',[39] and its population was estimated by 1900 to be 11 million souls—one seventh of what it actually became. Even the new capital city of Stanley (near Rutland), which George VI builds and adorns in 1921 with a university—'one of the cheapest seminaries for the education of youth in the world'—is a fantasy in the classical style. It is a measure of his faltering imagination that nothing incongruous strikes the author in the fact that Stanley has forty-three parish churches, whereas the whole country has only thirty-five hospitals.[40]

V MATHEMATICS AND TOMORROW: LUNAR FANTASIES
AND THE ALMANACS

This use of the future as a satiric milieu rather than some imaginary island was influenced by the steady growth of mathematics: 'the crucial discipline in converting human love to a supra-sensual life'.[41] Such mathematisation was developed by the slow building up of information about the heavens in cataloguing and tabling the motions of the stars. Sailors had to know where they were in order to know where they were going. Astronomical techniques, themselves a protest against astrological practices, in turn encouraged habits of prediction. Like auspices in Roman times, such predictions of stellar phenomena were further linked to the

Mohammedan beliefs that the surrounding spheres revolving about the earth were the abode of God.

After the heliocentric theory of Copernicus became generally accepted, one of its great exponents, Kepler, imaginatively anticipated what was on the moon. Rightly, he knew that there was one part of it which the earth never saw. So he wrote *Somnium*, a dream, in which he described Prevolva, the unseen part of the moon and Subvolva, the part which the earth always saw. He depicts it as being inhabited by primeval creatures, mostly fur-covered to withstand the violent extremes of temperature.

The year in which Kepler's *Somnium* was published also saw the publication of a translation of Lucian's story of an imaginary party of sailors accidentally wafted to the moon to participate in a war between the Kings of the Moon and the Sun over the colonisation of Lucifer. The moon troops rode on vultures and fleas, the Sun troops included a formidable army of ants. Lucian's improperly named *True History* also returns the adventurers to earth where they encounter the souls of the bygone philosophers and heroes in the 'Fortunate Islands'. In a second story, Icaromenippus deliberately takes off for the moon from Mount Olympus with wings borrowed from a vulture and an eagle; but his presumption so angered the gods that he was escorted back home and his wings confiscated.

A similar fantasy by an English bishop, *The Man in the Moone*, was posthumously published four years later. The Bishop—John Godwin of Hereford—tells the story of a young Spaniard—Domingo Gonzales—who tames some wild swans and harnesses them to tow him to the moon where he finds a society ahead of anything on earth; a real utopia or society of the future. It made such an impression that three quarters of a century later a play was written about it by Samuel D'Urfey.[42] Speculation about the nature of society on the moon initiated a steady stream of such observations. The creator of that paragon of the man who bent Nature to his will—Robinson Crusoe—also indulged in lunar fantasies with *The Consolidator: or, Memoirs of Sundry Transactions from the World of the Moon*. So did Dean Swift, who wrote an account of Gulliver's visit to the Academy of Lagado where there is an engine for grinding words into books.[43]

Swift also dealt a telling blow at those purveyors of information, the almanac makers, who quarrelled publicly over their forecasts in seventeenth-century England. When Charles I's captain of horse, George Wharton, tried to command the future he was soon involved in a regular war, not of arms, but of almanacs. Such paper wars threw up a new technique, the analysis of variants, applied by William Lilly to Royalist prophecies in *Monarchy or No Monarchy* (1651). Lilly's amanuensis and adopted son, Henry Coley, was, aptly enough, a mathematician and continued his *Merlini Anglici Ephemeris* from 1681 to 1695. For Merlin's name still carried weight. It was adopted by the venomous John Partridge for his Almanac *Merlinus Liberatus* in 1680, in which he quarrelled with another forecaster, George Parker. Partridge's anti-clericalism also provoked Jonathan Swift, who did better than quarrel, he parodied.

His parody, issued under the pseudonym of 'Isaac Bickerstaff' predicted that Partridge himself would die 'upon the 29th of March next, about eleven at night of a raging fever'. So well was the prediction received and later supported by letters from 'Bicker-staff' describing the death, that poor Partridge had the greatest difficulty in proving himself alive. 'Isaac Bickerstaff' became so synonymous with successful prophecy that, when Steele launched *The Tatler* in 1709, he adopted it too. Though Swift never published 'the large and rational defence' of the art of forecasting that he promised, his success stimulated two of the first really satiric tales of the future.[44]

As the clockwork of the universe became more visible and its laws more ascertainable, questions began to arise about the person who wound it up. Leibnitz criticised Newton for giving the impression that the celestial clockwork needed divine attention from time to time, and was himself criticised by Dr. Samuel Clark for positing a system that functioned independently of God or Providence. Leibnitz replied that the pre-established harmony of the universe in no way destroyed Providence, but merely obviated the need for correction.[45]

Newton's concern with the divine maintenance-engineer of the clockwork universe led him to testify:

> The Father is omniscient, and hath all Knowledge originally in His own breast, and communicates Knowledge of future things to Jesus Christ; and none in heaven or earth or under the earth, is worthy to receive Knowledge of future things immediately from the Father but the Lamb. And therefore the testimony of Jesus is the spirit of Prophecy, and Jesus is the Word or Prophet of God.

This, as John Dillenberger has recently said, was:

> one of the last defences of Christianity in a world in which the successors of Newton saw no further need of God. For Newton himself, it was as if the past and present were known and fulfilled in knowledge of the functioning of the mechanical world, but that the future was to be divined from the prophetic tradition, primarily through the teaching of Jesus of Nazareth. In this way, the future was to be known, precisely as the mathematical present was known.[46]

VI PREHENSILE IMAGINATIONS

Since Bishop Wilkins discussed the possibility of human colonies beneath the sea, new societies began to excite an ever widening range of speculation. The coda of his aptly entitled *Mathematicall Magick* (1648) became a creed; and magic, as the alteration of the apparent course of nature by hitherto unsuspected forces, became technology.

A vigorous debate startled the learned world over the possibilities of designing a flying boat buoyed up by four exhausted copper globes and propelled by a sail which was initiated by the Jesuit Francesco de Lana-Terzi in 1670. Most interesting are his own reservations as to the advisability of the enterprise:

> God would not suffer such an invention to take effect, by reason of the disturbance it would cause to the civil government of men. For who sees not that no city can be secure against attack, since our Ship may at any time be placed directly over it, and descending down may discharge Souldiers; that the same would happen to private Houses and Ships on the Sea: for our Ship descending out of the Air . . . may over-set them, kill their men, burn their ships by artificial fireworks and Fire-balls. And this they may do not only to Ships but to great Buildings, Castles, Cities, with such security that they which cast these things down from a height out of Gunshot, cannot on the other side be offended by those from below.[47]

Prehensile minds increasingly grasped the significance and need for certain technological devices. Continuing the vein of fertile suggestion so imaginatively worked by Wilkins, lesser, but no less luminous literati like Richard Owen Cambridge could run to 2,230 lines of heroic couplets in eloquent anticipation of aeroplanes, submarines, and, most important, games. Indeed,

Book IV of his *Scribleriad* (1751) stresses an airborne combat between an Englishman and a German, itself an intimation of technological rivalries to come.[48]

Even the great Dr. Johnson was given to dream allegories. His aptly named (in view of this chapter's title) *Rambler* essays are extravagant extrapolations. Number 105 contains portentions of things to come, like submarines, central heating, long range weather forecasting, all of which except submarines 'Truth' (which has come to earth with 'Justice' to register the demands and pretensions of mankind) refuses to accept.[49] On one side the good use of such forces was perhaps best articulated by Joseph Priestley.

> Thus, whatever was the beginning of this world, the end will be glorious and paradisaical, beyond what our imagi(n)ations can now conceive. Extravagant as some may suppose these views to be, I think I could show them to be fairly suggested by the true theory of human nature, and to arise from the natural course of human affairs. But, for the present, I waive this subject, the contemplation of which always makes me happy.[50]

Whether such forces would offset man's innate depravity has, on the other hand, elicited scepticism from the time of the seventeenth bishop, Joseph Hall, to the days of Aldous Huxley.

But the debate has ranged widely. Indeed these apprehensions, or rather pretentions of things to come, indicate that invention itself may merely be a subconscious response to a need already articulated. Ideas of application seem to have preceded inventions. Even in warning readers against the inevitable, some 'futopias' indirectly put the case for change. Such 'anticipations' by considering the possibility before the actual time it emerges, may well help in the transformation of uncertainty to certainty, like doodles on a scribbling pad precede an actual draft. The great doodler was Priestley's friend, Erasmus Darwin, who saw Priestley's discoveries enabling diving bells to be constructed, which

> roof'ed with spheric glass,
> Ribb'd with strong oak, and barr'd with bolts of brass
> Buoy'd with pure air shall end less tracks pursue,
> And Priestley's hand the vital flow renew—
> Then shall Britannia rule the wealthy realms
> Which Oceans wide insatiate wave o'erwhelms.[51]

The technological model was adopted by political theorists: government itself was regarded as an 'engine', to be improved only after 'trials' of new modifications. So seized of this concept was David Hume that he feared that 'rust may grow to the springs of the most accurate political machine' unless such trials were made. That is why he had no use for the Utopias of Plato or More, but regarded Harington's *Oceana* as a mechanic's blueprint for a working constitution: 'the only valuable model of a commonwealth that has yet been offered to the public'.

Writing in 1752, after he had already made an unhappy attempt thirteen years earlier to 'apply the Experimental Method of Reasoning to Moral Subjects', Hume went on to argue that politics could be reduced to a science since 'consequences almost as general and certain may sometimes be deduced from them as any which the mathematical sciences afford us'.[52]

Not all the eighteenth century philosophers dreamt of heavenly cities. Some indeed saw standing room only, like Robert Wallace, the Minister of New North Street Church, Edinburgh. He pointed out in 1761 that in a perfect state every man and woman would have 412,816,860,416 descendants. The earth would then be too small. For

> under a perfect government the inconveniences of having a family would be so entirely removed, children would be so well taken care of, and everything become so favourable to populousness, that though some sickly seasons or dreadful plagues in particular climates might cut off multitudes, yet, in general, man would increase so prodigiously that the Earth would at last be overstocked and become unable to support its numerous inhabitants.

Wallace saw the population doubling in a third of a century and confounding all hopes of Utopia or a model society.

> Though they should be found consistent with the reigning passions of human nature; though they should spread far and wide; nay, though they should prevail universally, they must at last involve mankind in the deepest perplexity, and in universal confusion.[53]

VII MAKING DESTINY MANIFEST

But it was by no means agreed, even by Priestley's friends, that Britannia would for ever rule the waves. Even, the gentle and virtuous Bishop Berkeley, whose ideas Addison embodied in two hymns, *The Spacious Firmament* and *When All Thy Mercies*, and to whom Pope ascribed 'ev'ry virtue under heav'n', and who was commissioned to attack free thinkers in the *Guardian*, went on record as saying:

> I know it is an old folly to make peevish complaints of the times, and charge the common failures of human nature on a particular age. One may nevertheless venture to affirm that the present hath brought forth new and portentous villainies, not to be paralleled in our own or any other history. We have long been preparing for some great catastrophe . . . our symptoms are so bad that, notwithstanding all the care and vigilance of the legislature, it is to be feared that the final period of our State approaches.

So he planned to use a legacy and some of the revenues from his deanery of Derry to 'plant the Arts and Learning in America'. Some *Verses* on the theme, sent to a friend with the injunction 'shew it to none but of your family, and to allow no copy to be taken of it', bore the title *America or the Muse's Refuge, A Prophecy*. They concluded:

> Westward the Course of Empire takes its Way;
> The four first Acts already past,
> A fifth shall close the Drama with the Day;
> Time's noblest Offspring is the last.

'Time's noblest offspring' certainly imbued all who travelled there with a 'sense of the future'. Thirty years after Berkeley wrote, Andrew Burnaby recorded how he constantly met 'it'. To him 'it' was the conviction that animated the American colonists in the political struggle with Britain. Philip Freneau, the newspapers, Tom Paine: an almost infinite list could be compiled of those who cast what Daniel Webster called intuitive glances into futurity.[54]

Chapter Three

THE DEBATE BEGINS: FROM NOBLE SAVAGE TO LAST MAN

I AMERICA AND THE ROBINSONADES

Robinson Crusoe, or Solitaire, is the simplest of all games. It is also the probability game of man against nature. For Daniel Defoe lived at the same time and in the same town as Abraham de Moivre, the Huguenot émigré, who in his *Doctrine of Chances* (1718) showed how to calculate probabilities of events. Defoe was also a fantast and of all his extravagant fantasies that describing details of a machine discovered in a library in China is most interesting. Called the Consolidator, it was a two cylindered carriage; the cylinders being fed by a certain spirit which produces a flame which 'moves about such springs and wheels as kept the wings in most exact and regular Motion, always ascendant'. His *Memoirs of Sundry Transactions from the World of the Moon* was, like Swift's account of Gulliver's travels, on exploration of contemporary problems and evils.

'Fiction of every kind,' wrote John Lockman, 'is contemptible unless it be of use to mankind and has truth couch'd under it.' He was introducing to an English public his translation of Desfontaines' *Travels of Mr. John Gulliver* (1731): an example of the impact of the Gulliverian satire on the continent. In his voyages John Gulliver visits various islands run by women, physicians, gluttons, ugly men, and people who live for a long time. These secular sermons not only multiplied with the rise of Freemasonry in France but were the subject of debate: the Abbé Desfontaines himself criticising the Chevalier Ramsay's *Voyages de Cyrus* (1727).

Though before Crusoe and Gulliver made the 'philosophic voyage' popular, French scientists like Melchisédec Thévenot[1] had adumbrated its possibilities,[2] and their success stimulated the production of a great many more.[3] So did increasing involvement with America.[4] 'Robinsonades' especially appealed to those who were interested in environmental changes that man might effect and which might affect man. Apart from the welter of arcane republics,[5] noble savages,[6] and utopian Chinese,[7] who fortified, however obliquely, the Deistic debate with the Christians, the simple thematic appeal of the future began to hold the stage.

One who was obsessed by it was L. S. Mercier, whose *L'Homme Sauvage* (1767) was but one of the numerous essays in imaginative reconstruction of the environment. After looking back, Mercier turned to look forward to see what man would make of his environment in *L'an 2440* (Amsterdam, 1770).[8] This, significantly, opened with a quotation from Leibniz: 'the present is pregnant of the future'. Published anonymously, it revealed the fallacy of the primitive instincts when faced with the social consequences of technical progress. For Paris in the year 2440 is set in a world where all nations live in concord and slavery is abolished. Well drained, well lit and replanned, Paris enjoys state-controlled theatres, few books (the few that remain being mainly English, with the exception of those of the Abbé de Saint-Pierre and Fénelon), and a deistic religion which forces agnostics to undergo a course of experimental physics. 'Where can the perfectibility of man stop,' asks Mercier, 'armed with geometry and the mechanical arts and chemistry?'

Translated into English as *Memoirs of the Year 2500* (1772) Mercier's book had quite a vogue in England and America, being republished in 1799 at Richmond and in 1802 at Liverpool.[9] Mercier's interest in applied science persisted, for he called Napoleon's attention to the distress of the engineer N. J. Cugnot and secured the inventor of steam-propelled carriages a pension.[10]

Mercier's friend, the amorist Restif de la Bretonne, followed suit with *L'an Deux-Mille* (1790), a fantasy on a marriage-fête theme when 'all think and produce for the collectivity'. Though a slight affair, this, like other imaginative incursions into republics of fantasy, provided that psychological experience which, as M. Lanson has shown, enabled the French to meet the actuality of revolution with some degree of equanimity.[11]

Restif conjured up his own theory of evolution based on the eternal recurrence of life. Here he anticipated Nietzsche. He also anticipated Samuel Butler in his deliberate inversions, symbolised by his references to the great French scientist Buffon as Nuffob. Most significantly, he anticipated the very modern science fictioneers in envisaging the solar system moving through space.

The passage of time enhanced other significances in his work, so much so that before the nineteenth century expired a period of 'Restifomania' set in, when the mediocre journals concentrated upon him as a typical example of the sexual perversion of shoefetishism.

II OPTIMISM AND THE CALCULUS OF HISTORY

Equanimity is too modest a word for the optimism of those who believed that:

> All that is necessary, to reduce the whole of nature to laws similar to those which Newton discovered with the aid of the calculus, is to have a sufficient number of observations and a mathematics that is complex enough.[12]

So the mathematisation of tomorrow was envisaged by the Marquis of Condorcet. Based on the calculus (to which it is said he gave, as a boy, some ten hours a day of study), and a wide acquaintance with the achievements of men of science, derived from his membership and later secretaryship of the French Academy of Sciences, this mathematisation would ensure accurate planning of the future. 'To tame the future' Condorcet wanted 'a science to foresee the progressions of the human species'. This would be fashioned by applying calculus to history. 'These observations on what man has been and what he is today will later lead to the means of assuring and accelerating the new progressions which human nature still permits him to hope for.' He considered the task of hastening progress to be 'one of his sweetest occupations'.[13]

He had no other. He re-drafted, in eighteenth-century terms, Bacon's scheme as *Fragment sur l'Atlantide*. This envisaged a Wellsian supra-national 'world brain', emancipating men from domination by charlatans, and the inroads of time and nature. Future moral data were to be mathematicised—a theme he had already written up in *Essai sur l'application de l'analyse à la probabilité des décisions rendues à la pluralité des voix* (1785): a foreshadowing of the work of Dr. Gallup.

His belief in the perfectibility of man was sustained even in hiding from the secret police during the French Revolution. 'Nature,' he wrote at the outset of his *Sketch of an Historical Picture of the Progress of the Human Mind*, 'has set no bounds to the improvement of human faculties . . . the perfectibility of man is really indefinite . . . its progress is henceforth independent of any power to arrest it, and has no limit but the duration of the globe on which nature has cast us.'[14]

The need for social divination was to be more vividly advocated by Saint-Simon. 'The highest poetry will be the most powerful predication' he argued, superior in 'generality' and 'universality' to any preceding dogma and embracing all religions of the past by insisting on one social goal, one will, 'the largest principles on which are founded all our views of the future', articulated by *un ordre speculatif*, guiding society to its unitary destination—one world state. This speculative order would provide the priests of a new religion 'greater and more powerful than all the religions of the past'.[15]

Though they never realised this new religion the St. Simonians kindled a school of predictive fantasts. Their chief apostle, Barthélemy Enfantin, outlined the state of industrial society in the year 2240 when a new dynamic force, similar to electricity but better, had been discovered. It created its own industrial problems of reorganisation and, above all, of retraining. Were the people displaced by this new force to be put on public works, or paid for doing nothing, or set to produce objects of no value? Enfantin visualised a form of polytechnic education enabling such people to change jobs without any great difficulty. By this time the southern steppes of Russia had been made arable; while roads and other communications were being built between Caucasia and Georgia and the Russian provinces of Western Asia. The supposed author is given an important section to control, and feels like Napoleon marching on Russia but with exactly the opposite aims. The rest of the supposed author's life is devoted to the development of this section of Georgia, where he finds no conflict between public service and private life. A place in Georgia is named after him and in his old age he is honoured there as the father of the people.[16]

An even more rigorous belief in the possibility of predicting the future was held by the great French mathematician Laplace, who considered that 'an intelligent being who, at a given instant, knew all the forces animating nature and the relative positions of the beings in nature', could, 'if his intelligence were sufficiently capacious to analyse these data, include in a formula the movements of the largest bodies of the universe and those of the smallest atom. Nothing would be uncertain for him: the future as well as the past would be present to his eyes.'[17]

Imaginatively embroidered by personificatory or symbolic fictions, this optimistic vein of prediction reached a climacteric in Charles Fourier. In his future, the passions would be harmonised and poverty abolished. 'Anti-lions' personified the end of the untamed world of nature; 'anti-crocodiles' its shrinkage, and a 'great hen' (which would lay enough eggs to pay off the English National Debt in six months) its increasing wealth. Even the biggest obstacle of all—the salt oceans—would turn into lemonade.

> From the moment that I came to have the two theories of attraction and the unity of the four movements [Fourier wrote], I began to read in the magic book of nature. Its mysteries explained themselves in succession and I thus lifted the veil of thought previously impenetrable. I advanced into a new scientific world . . . till I came to the calculus of the universal destinies or to the determination of the fundamental system which regulates the laws of all the past, present and future movements.[18]

This 'fundamental system' would consist of a series of phalanges of about 1,000 souls, where the three passions, cabalist (intrigue), composite (association), and papillone (vicissitude) would be harmonised. Organised under a world conference, deserts would be conquered, roads built, and forests planted. Armies and police would disappear. Delirious as Fourier's visions might appear, they nevertheless, as Talmon pointed out, 'stood in the same relation to social science . . . as alchemy to chemistry, astrology to astronomy, myth to science, the pre-Socratic speculations to the systems of Plato and Aristotle. We are not covering huge spaces in no time on the backs of anti-lions. We do it in aircraft.'[19]

French fancy played about the prospect of a planned mechanised world. The Daedalian cunning of English technology and the social insights of Robert Owen stimulated a French exile in England to sketch a model society, to which he gave the name of Icaria. 'Discovered' in the conventional fashion by an 'imaginary journey' (by now a hallowed fiction for a look into the future) made by an English peer, Icaria was an early technocracy. One committee of scientists planned the common diet, another devised aptitude tests for vocational selection, yet another the glass covered pavements and the sanitation. If the vision fascinated its author, Etienne Cabet, it intoxicated his fellow countrymen, and on his return a 'movement' got under way to found just such a community. In ten years he enrolled half a million followers, some of whom went to America to establish a community on what they described as 'the most perfect system which modern science can offer to us'. Alas! the name of their model Society was only too apt. Icarus may have been the offspring of Daedalus, but in escaping from Crete he flew so high that the sun melted the wax with which his wings were fastened to his body. So it was with the Icarians. Their escape from France in 1848 to the hot midwest of America was a crashing failure.

The spirit of these secular millenarians reverberates in the fugitive left-wing journals of their successors. Thus *Le Libertaire*—a mid-century New York paper—carried the projection of its editor, the émigré Joseph Déjacque, to the year 2858 when man would, by making rain, and converting the seasons, cultivate the desert and the poles. By that time Déjacque considered that vast cyclideons—or stadia capable of holding half a million people—would be built for ceremonial purposes. Other assembly halls would be in the autonomous communities or humanispheres of five or six thousand people, where government would prevail. The swollen cities of the nineteenth century would, of course, have disappeared, and the only link between the humanispheres would be the book of statistics.[20]

III   THE NOBLE SAVAGE AND THE LAST MAN

Such extravagant declarations of faith in the power of science to unlock the future did not pass unchallenged. Rousseauistic versions of the myth of the noble savage visualised civilisation corrupting away till even the last man and woman refuse to perpetuate their kind. Just such a fantasy, by J-B. François Xavier de Grainville entitled *Le Dernier Homme* (1806)[21] was republished in 1811 for his English patron by young Charles Nodier, who was also thirty years later to write an introduction to a French translation by Elise Voiart of the *Swiss Family Robinson*.

Introduced by Mercier to the Bavarian mystic Dr. Freimuth Sayffert and his translator Nicolas Bonneville, Charles Nodier was entranced. Opium and whoring still further estranged him from reality and soon he was arrested for lampooning Napoleon. Released under surveillance, he married and began to teach, then took a post as secretary to an eccentric Englishman of letters.

Though interested in botany and entomology, Nodier had no head for physical science. Psychologically, he also had difficulties since he was both illegitimate and a victim of Addison's disease. In the early stages of the French Revolution, he came into contact with engineers like Luczot de la Thébaudais at Besançon and went to Paris at the suggestion of another, Pertuisier, who was then studying at the École Polytechnique. But his first experience of scientific work disillusioned him. For in 1801, at the request of the great naturalist Lamarck, he completed a bibliography of entomology, but it was such a failure that he was forced to return to the provinces. Perhaps as a reaction against all this he tumbled into mysticism, illuminism, Rosicrucianism, and the various cult religions that flourished under the Empire. This interest survived after the Restoration and found expression in Nodier's Gothic plays like *Le Vampire* (1820). Indeed the elder Dumas first met him at a performance of that play outlining the future of mankind in rosy terms. But those rosy terms dissolved as Nodier grew older, and by 1830 he was writing a series of satires against scientific progress in the *Revue de Paris*. Later published as *Fantasies du dériseur sensé*, these invested the word 'progressive' with sinister overtones and provided a counterpart to the wilder dreams of the St. Simonians.[22] Since he was a patron of *all* aspiring French writers—Victor Hugo, Alfred de Vigny, and Alfred de Musset were but three of them—Nodier's romantic Gothic flirtation with the non-scientific world was to have strange consequences.

For, as science swept the universe free of spectres, readers turned to Gothic fantasy, the macabre, diabolism, and the occult. Here American materialism, paradoxically enough, strengthened their appeal, for after strange mysterious rappings at a house at Hydesville, New York State in 1847, an 'epidemic of spirits' broke out all over Europe.

The St. Paul of this new religion was Allan Kardec (formerly M. Rivail), whose *Book of the Spirits* (1857) virtually gave this new religion of the other side its creed. Drawn by Kardec's stories, one of Nodier's young friends, Victor Hugo, later turned to spiritualism during his lonely exile in the Channel Islands when he lost his daughter.[23] More surprisingly, the distinguished French astronomer, Camille Flammarion, who had explored, in a work of impeccable scholarship, previous accounts of the real and imaginary worlds,[24] told a most successful tale of the future: *La Fin du Monde* (1893). This was translated into eleven European languages and must have influenced Wells though Wells never once mentioned Flammarion in his writings. Recently it has been argued that Wells may indeed have become a utopian through reading *La Fin du Monde*[25] since similar likenesses can be seen in other of his works like *Anticipations* (Book 2, chapters 1–3), and *In the Days of the Comet*. For, in Flammarion's forecast of future society, electricity supplants labourers in agriculture, provides radio and television, people travel by air machines which land on the flat roofs of houses and even roads are covered. It bears a great likeness to another early Wells story, 'The Star'.[26]

IV   THE DEBATE ABOUT MECHANISATION AND MAN

Vision or nightmare: the dialectic about mechanisation gathered supporters. Here Jules Verne was most percipient when he described Edgar Allen Poe as 'an apostle of materialism' and wrote of him:

> He creates his fantasy *coldly*. . . . I imagine [he wrote in 1864], that this is less due to his temperament than to the exclusively practical culture of the United States; he wrote, thought and dreamed in American, this positivist of a man.[27]

That Verne should castigate Poe for being a 'positivist of a man' was ironic, since Poe himself owed much to the adventures of the French Daedalus, Victorian, as chronicled by Restif de la Bretonne in his *La Découverte australe, par un Homme-Volant* (1787). This was itself an evolutionary fantasy, based on the supposition that there was originally one species, and that the differentiation of the species was due to the different intensities of the sun.[28] Not only did Restif anticipate Blanchard's aerial machine by one or two years, but the name of his voyager, Victorian, may well have influenced Verne's own name for a balloon he designed, under the inspiration of his friend Felix Tournachon: *Victoria*. Though Verne never flew, he wrote *Five Weeks in a Balloon*. In the next eight years he wrote accounts of underground, aerial, and submarine adventures which were to create a new genre.

Verne's underground fantasy *Journey to the Centre of the Earth* (1864) was followed by *From the Earth to the Moon* (1865) and its sequel *Round the Moon* (1870). He struck a note echoed by the English rationalist, Winwood Reade, with his theme of the colonisation of space:

> Mankind will migrate into space, and will cross the airless Saharas which separate planet from planet and sun from sun. The earth will become a Holy Land which will be visited by pilgrims from all quarters of the universe.[29]

The debate is best symbolised by Flaubert. In his unfinished novel, published a year after his death, the two characters from which it is named take turns in predicting the future. Pécuchet, the pessimistic mechanophobe, mourns the way in which the Americanising of the world by science will lead to the deliquescence of morals, ideals, and manners, but Bouvard, optimistic and rebarbative, sees China fusing the two cultures; science creating a new literature and religion, thus enabling man to head for the planets when old earth is exhausted.[30]

American technological strides towards tomorrow—evidenced by Edison's 'imprisonment of the echo' as Villiers de l'Isle Adam[31] describes it—stimulated further sermons on the Pandora's box of science. Villiers himself wrote just such a story—*L'Eve Future* (1886). In this Eden, Lord Ewald—a man who has received all the genetic endowments of nature—is lost when his equally well-endowed fiancée turns out to have a vulgar soul. Science, in the person of Thomas Alva Edison, creates such an absolute double of his fiancée that Lord Ewald believes it is the same person. When this double—Hadaly—and Lord Ewald realise the truth, the double wishes to become human. 'Attribue-moi l'être,' she cries, 'affirme-toi que je suis! renforce-moi de toi-même.'

The incapacity, even of altruistic science, to predict unhappy eventualities, was extended by another group who believed that God had belonged to the human race. Also J. K. Huysmans drew attention in *Là-bas* (1891) to the alleged existence of a band of Satanists or Palladists who, in that belief, worshipped the Devil with inverted rites. Such topsy-turvy Christianity was further publicised by the spectacular ten-year hoax practised by Gabriel Jogan (or Leo Taxil as he called himself), and his associate C. Hacks (known as Bataille) whose *Le Diable au XIXe Siècle* (1893–4) professed to reveal a world network of diabolists working through the Freemasons, and gave an account of his own meeting with the Devil in a Kentucky cave. The agent of this infamous introduction was further revealed as a Miss Diana Vaughan, whose *Mémoires d'une Ex-Palladiste* were serialised in 1895. These 'revelations', including that of her marriage to Asmodeus, were widely believed by Roman Catholics until 19 April 1897 when her chief promoter Taxil publicly described her as a complete invention.

V THE FIRST SCIENTIFIC THEORY OF THE FUTURE: TARDE

The first scientific theory of the future was put forward by Gabriel Tarde. He deplored the habit of looking for a previous to support a subsequent event instead of vice versa and proposed a reverse determinism:

> It seems to me neither more nor less conceivable that the future, *which is not yet*, should influence the present than that the past, *which is no more*, should do so.[32]

As a sociologist, some think the greatest French successor to Comte,[33] Tarde's own *Fragment d'histoire future* (1896) is worth describing.[34] It envisages the establishment of a world confederacy, at peace by the end of the twentieth century after a long period of war, during which the strongest and the best young men were exempted from military service and the weaklings dispatched to the front. A halcyon period follows when great reserves of vigour and activity become available for peacetime service rather than war. The cause of every disease is unravelled and invalids become as rare as double-headed monsters. Greek becomes the universal language spoken by everyone by the middle of the twenty-second century. Work itself becomes voluntary in the international factories and co-operative workshops.

On the site of ancient Babylon a new capital is built:

> An infinite expanse extending as far as the eye could see, to be covered with striking public buildings constructed with magical

speed, with a teeming and throbbing population, with golden harvests beneath a sky of changeless blue, with an iron net-work of railways radiating from the town of Nebuchadnesor to the furthest ends of Europe, Africa and Asia, and crossing the Himalayas, the Caucasus and the Sahara. The stored energy, electrically conveyed, of a hundred Abyssinian waterfalls, and of I do not know how many cyclones, hardly sufficed to transport from the mountains of Armenia the necessary stones, wood and iron for these numerous constructions.

So life gets better and better until the winter of 2409 when it is noticed that the sun seems to be suffering from progressive anaemia, losing its golden crown, fading, in successive summers, from red to orange. As Tarde wrote:

> He might then have been compared to a gold apple in the sky and so during several years he was seen to pass, and all nature with him, through a thousand magnificent or terrible tints—from orange to yellow to green, and from green at length to indigo and pale blue.

Deprived of the sun's heat the seas turned to ice, crystals of nitrogen and oxygen fell from the sky, and thousands are frozen to death beside their braziers.

Civilisation itself freezes up to the borders of Babylon, where those who survive foregather with such remnants of civilisation as they can carry. As Babylon freezes, the survivors under a leader called Miltiades seek salvation underground. There they find warmth, power and light, whilst the earth serves as their food refrigerator. To pass the time they form into groups—or cities— according to their various artistic and intellectual gifts—living in a harmony of mutual admiration. Procreation is limited to males who have accomplished something in one of these functional groups. This is to conserve food, and, for breaking this law twice, offenders are thrown into a sea of petrol.

In their underground burrowings they make contact with another group that had found sanctuary in the womb of the earth: the Chinese. This is a shock, for the Chinese, instead of conserving the artistic treasures of civilisation, and limiting their population, have found how to grow vegetables underground, and supplement these meagre crops by cannibalism. Appalled by such barbarity, the followers of Miltiades block up the galleries to prevent further contact.

But the mischief is done. When the discovery that bread could be made from stone is noised abroad, the population increases, and culture diminishes. Tarde's 'fragment' ends with the suggestion that this brutish element would rise to the surface when the sun reappeared, leaving the wise underground.[35]

VI THE RELIGION OF TOMORROW: RENAN

'Let us die calmly in the communion of mankind and the religion of the future,'[36] wrote Renan two years before his own death. The 'religion of the future' to which he referred is especially manifest in the work of his disciple, Anatole France—'Madame Renan' as he was called. One of his characters says in *The White Stone* (1905):

> It is quite true that the heart fails in the case of many men, when gazing into the abyss of future events. It is, moreover, certain that our all too imperfect knowledge of facts past and gone does not supply us with the elements required to enable us to determine accurately what is to succeed them. However, since the past of human social organisations is in part known to us, the future of those societies, a continuation and consequence of their past, is not wholly beyond our ken.[37]

Going to sleep on 20th September 1903, France's pilgrim of the future wakes up on 28th June 2270: the year 220 of the Federation of Nations. He finds the air full of shadowy countless machines, more populated than the earth, visits an automated bakery housed in a cast-iron building where:

> Hogs tendered themselves spontaneously to the knife which disembowelled them; the flour which escaped from them dropped into troughs where powerful hands of steel kneaded it into dough which flowed into moulds, which when full hastened to put themselves of their own accord into an oven as capacious and deep as a tunnel. Five or six men at most, motionless amid all this motion, supervised the labour of the machinery.
> ' 'Tis an old bakery', said my companion. 'It hardly produces more than eighty thousand loaves a day and its too weak machines employ too many hands. It makes little'.[38]

The flying whales that delivered flour were guided by rays:

> There was no one at the helm, nobody aboard the machine. I could hear in the distance the slight hum of a wasp flying, and then

the thing grew with astounding rapidity. It seemed quite sure of itself, but my ignorance as to what would happen, should it perchance go wrong, caused me to shudder.

Because of his scissored hair, a last relic of tattooing, he was suspected of being a deserter from the United States of Africa, whose 'black provinces' were 'wallowing in a state of barbarism resembling in many aspects the State of France three or four hundred years ago'.

Statistics has stepped into history's shoes: the historians of old related the brilliant deeds of the few. Theirs register all that is produced and consumed.[39] Even the baker is a statistician. Food is synthetic.

> Great intellectuals, surgeons, lady doctors and chemists are allotted aerial machines of 60 h.p., palaces, gardens and immense parks. They are for the greater part individuals, keenly alive to laying hold of the world's goods, and lead a more splendid and more copious existence than the bourgeois of the closed era. The worst of it is that the majority of them are stupid fools who should be recruited for work at the flour mills.

> Money has been replaced by labour vouchers and the value of the products is computed by the length of time their production has taken. Bread, meat, beer, clothes, and aeroplane represent X hours X days of labour. From each of these vouchers, collectivism, or, as it was styled formerly, the State, deducts a certain number of minutes for the purpose of allocating them to unproductive works, metallurgy and alimentary reserves, refuges and private asylums, and so forth.[40]

To the question: 'Are you happy?' the baker, Morin, shook his bearded head and replied:

> It is not in human nature to enjoy perfect happiness. Happiness is not attainable without effort, and every effort brings with it fatigue and suffering. We have made life endurable to all. That is something. But our successors will do better still.[41]

VII VERNAL WORLDS

French speculation about the future was, however, almost exclusively associated with Jules Verne, whose *The Eternal Adam* (1905) set in the indefinite future, describes the discovery in Atlantis by an aged philosopher of a metal cylinder containing the Dead Sea scrolls of a civilisation which had been overwhelmed by a catastrophe. A few survivors had reached Atlantis, which had risen above the sea once more, and had discovered that it, too, had in its turn suffered a similar catastrophe. This dual vision of catastrophe succeeding catastrophe over the ages gives the work a sense of gloom quite absent from his earlier work.

In 1910, with the posthumous publication of *Yesterday and Tomorrow*, readers got a glimpse of other Vernal worlds. *Amiens in the Year 2000 A.D.*—originally read as a paper to the local academy of Arts, Letters and Sciences—is a technocratic paradise where American machines turn fleeces into clothes, pigs into hams, calves into shoes. Music is broadcast over telegraph wires, doctors are paid by results, children are fed by machinery and feminine couture has so far developed that mechanical aids are employed to sustain it.

Yet further forward—*In the Twenty-Ninth Century: The Day of an American Journal in 2889*—Verne visualises Centropolis, the capital of the United States and the World, run by power generated either by solar or geothermal power, whose inhabitants enjoy television and communication with the planets.[42]

By 1926 the copyright of all Verne's stories was secured by the American publisher, Hugo Gernsback, for his new popular magazine *Amazing Stories*. This, and other popular stories based on the potential of science to alter society, rode on a tide long running in the French literary world and as we shall see, in the American world too[43] that we must soon chart. Before doing so, however, we must look at the stream of speculation that had been released in 1859 by the English mathematician J. Clerk Maxwell.

VIII   THE CALCULUS OF PROBABILITIES

For, in the same year, 1859, in which Darwin's *Origin of Species* was published, James Clerk Maxwell applied the calculus of probabilities, not as before to games or public affairs, but to matter in motion.[44] The French feeling for the mathematising of tomorrow was articulated by Laplace,[45] Poisson,[46] Cournot,[47] and Quetelet[48] who all thought it would lead to 'social physics'.

Also in 1859 Victor Hugo's *Légende des Siècles* (1859) culminated in the vision of a perfect universe that would eventuate in the twentieth century by man's conquest of gravity. This evoked shocked comment in England from J. M. Ludlow who exclaimed, 'Such, then, is the deliberate conclusion of the book. Christ's Gospel, according to M. Victor Hugo, is worn out. In its place he presents us with a gospel of—balloons.'[49]

The prospect of aerial navigation also intoxicated Renan's life-long friend, Marcelin Bethelot the French chemist. He envisaged the world becoming, by A.D. 2000, one large garden, with man existing on chemical pills; stock raising, crops and vineyards would disappear. By then aerial travel would have abolished customs unions, trade barriers, wars, and frontiers.[50]

Fourierian springs of optimism had many drinkers. Let us now look at some other springs that offered refreshment at this time.

Chapter Four

THE GOTHIC IMAGINATION

Belief in linear time and the predictable clockwork of the New-
tonian universe was attacked by an engineer who described the
non-material basis of the physical world in terms of the magnetism
that held humans together. He used the analogy of angels and
spirits.[1] Today we would call it 'field theory'. Round this engineer,
Swedenborg, exiled in England, grew a church, one of whose
members, William Blake, wrote in *Jerusalem*:

> I rest not from my great task!
> To open the Eternal Worlds, to open the immortal Eyes
> Of Man inwards into the Worlds of Thought, into Eternity
> Ever expanding in the Bosom of God, the Human Imagination.[2]

Blake also drew on the rich treasury of Orphic myth, sedulously
recovered by Thomas Taylor, whose work also exercised a
powerful influence on contemporaries. Beginning with the
Hymns of Orpheus (1787) and ending with *Works of Plato* (1804),
Taylor's efforts were prodigious.[4] He was a member, with John
Frank Newton and Thomas Love Peacock, of an occult group
which interpreted Plato as an Orphic poet.[5] Blake[6] and Shelley[7]
owed much to him. Taylor's group saw the Orphic myth in terms
of the four ages of man depicted by the Hindu Zodiac. The fall of
man was the result of the Titans' devouring of the body of Dionysius, hence animal food was to be avoided so that man would be
absorbed into a great Community of Nature. Their world being
in the third phase of the Hindu Zodiac, i.e. of Sagittarius, the
hunter (hence animal food and cookery and death), the hope of
mankind lay in the fourth phase, symbolised by Aquarius the

Waterman, who would, in rising from the sea, inaugurate a new golden age of Renovation, or Krishnu.[8]

Taylor influenced Shelley, who rejected the doctrine of linear time, believing that there was a slow increase in human consciousness towards perfection:

> Time is our consciousness of the succession of ideas in our mind. Vivid sensation, of either pain or pleasure, makes the line long, as the common phrase is, because it renders us more acutely conscious of our ideas. If a mind be conscious of a hundred ideas during one minute, by the clock, and of two hundred during another, the latter of these species would actually occupy so much greater extent in the mind as two exceed one in quality.
>
> If, therefore, the human mind, by any future improvement of its sensibility, should become conscious of an infinite number of ideas in a minute, that minute would be eternity. I do not hence infer that the actual space between the birth and death of a man will ever be prolonged; but that his sensibility is perfectible, and that the number of ideas which his mind is capable of receiving is indefinite. . . . Perhaps the perishing ephemeron enjoys a longer life than the tortoise.[9]

Like Condorcet, twenty-year-old Shelley wrote on those 'grand and comprehensive topics' as he called them, the Past, the Present, and the Future. In *Queen Mab*, he foresaw that:

> These deserts of immeasurable sand,
> Whose age-collected fervors scarce allowed
> A bird to live, a blade of grass to spring, . . .
> Now teem with countless rills and shady woods.[10]

The polar regions, the tropics, and the trackless deeps of oceans would become productive:

> All things are void of terror: man has lost
> His terrible prerogative, and stands
> An equal amidst equals: happiness
> And science dawn though late upon the earth;
> Peace cheers the mind, health renovates the frame;
> Disease and pleasure cease to mingle here.

II   THE GOTHIC STANCE

By evoking terror and curiosity by apparently supernatural effects, Shelley's wife, Mary, represents another group that were juggling with time: the Gothic novelists. Significantly the word 'superhuman' was generally introduced into English by one of the leading practitioners of the genre, Mrs. Ann Radcliffe, in her horror story, *The Italian* (1797), a romance of the Inquisition.[11]

Nothing was calculated to evoke more terror than the story of the last man. A novel of that name had been translated from the French in 1806 and sub-titled *Omegarius and Syderia, a romance in futurity*. Byron had flirted with it in *Darkness* (1816):

> The world was void,
> The populous and the powerful was a lump,
> Seasonless, herbless, treeless, manless, lifeless—
> A lump of death—a chaos of hard clay.

Thomas Campbell wrote a poem with that title in 1823:

> The Sun's eye had a sickly glare,
> The earth with age was wan,
> The skeletons of nations were
> Around that lonely man!
> Some had expired in fight—the braids
> Still rusted in their bony hands;
> In plague and famine some!
> Earth's cities had no sound or tread,
> And ships were drifting with the dead
> To shores where all was dumb.

Mary Shelley had particular reasons for dilating upon the last man, since, as Muriel Spark has pointed out,[12] she saw herself, after the death of Shelley and Byron, as the 'last relic of a beloved race'. Both appear in it: Shelley as Adrian and Byron as Raymond. Her story begins in 2073 when Britain is a republic where Lionel Verney, living with the son of the former king, is now known as the Earl of Windsor. Lord Raymond beomes Lord Protector of England and leads a crusade on behalf of Greece against the Turks. Capturing Constantinople, he discovers, too late, that it has been decimated by a plague. This spreads slowly westward populations fleeing before it to England. By 2096 Verney realises that nothing less than emigration will ensure the survival of the human race on earth. Verney and Adrian lead two groups to Paris, but so strong is the plague there that they move on to Switzerland, the party getting smaller all the time. By the time they reach Italy they are four and ultimately only Verney reaches Rome.

The wheel comes full circle when, as the last man, Verney finds himself in Rome—robber and shepherd like its first founder.

Another Gothic fantasy with futurist overtones appeared a year later, when Jane Webb published *The Mummy* (1827). This centres on the resurrection of the Mummy of Cheops and its league with a Roman Catholic priest to secure the election of a queen of England. But the real hero is the scientist, Dr. Entwerfen, 'the fortunate inventor of the immortalising snuff, one single pinch of which cures all diseases by the smell; the discoverer of the capability of caoutchouc being applied to aerial purposes; and the maker of the most compendious and powerful galvanic battery ever yet beheld by mortal'.[13]

Further Gothic fantasies, involving Dr. Entwerfen and his young protégé in a dynastic revolution in Spain, cocoon some shrewd, if bizarre, predictions of social life in England of the year 2126.

Balloons, propelled by mercury vapour, are, with aerial horses and aerial sledges, the common means of locomotion. Since the whole of the country is so completely excavated,[14] to fall upon the surface of the earth was like tumbling on the parchment of an immense drum '. . . only a deep hollow sound'. The post is fired in cannon balls, caught by nets and preceded by hollow whistling balls of wood. Quicker messages were sent by heliograph transmission of light and music.[15] Indeed, 'so many new inventions had been perfected, so many wonderful discoveries made, and so many ingenious contrivances put into execution, that poor nature seemed degraded from her throne, and usurping men stepped up to supply her place.'[16]

Amongst these were moveable houses, equipped with air conditioning, speaking-tubes, steam coffee-machines that roasted, ground, made, poured out, and sweetened coffee in five minutes, 'caloric'—a substitute for fires—and 'malleable glass crockery' made up to fold in pocket-size when not in use.[17]

But what was, from the author's point of view, more important, she envisaged climatic control and steam ploughing—which led one of her reviewers, J. C. Loudon, editor of a horticultural magazine, to seek her out and marry her.

J. C. Loudon was a talented man. He kept a journal in French to familiarise himself with that language and, in spite of the amputation of an arm and a life dogged by sickness, not only edited at one period five journals, but, with the help of his wife Jane—who acted as his amanuensis—laid out the botanical garden at Birmingham, the arboretum at Derby, and numerous cemeteries. Jane Loudon was a good match for him since she busied herself by popularising natural history: her ladies' companion to flower gardens ran to nine editions in thirty years.

The same horticultural enthusiasms also mark Mrs. Mary Griffith's picture of the United States in the twenty-third century. A man entombed by an avalanche thaws out in a world of machines, which 'fill up gullies, dig out the roots of trees, plough down hills, turn water courses . . . (and) have entirely superseded the use of cattle'.[18] These machines also carry out the sowing, reaping, and distribution of corn. Most of the Negroes have emigrated to Liberia.

As a result, women are emancipated. They look after 'all the retail and detail of mercantile operations', they have joint ownership of property in marriage, indeed enjoy equal rights with men. They prohibit war and hard liquor—except for cider and wine—and tobacco. Divorce can be obtained for intemperance. Socialisation, if not socialism, is the key. A great trunk road is built in 1900 from one end of the country to the other, whilst government-operated railways bind the continent. Every college student learns a trade or handicraft and works during his leisure hours.

III   HISTORY AS RETROSPECTIVE PROPHECY

'The English,' complained a Herefordshire rector in 1819, 'have been reproached and derided by foreigners for the ready encouragement that they have ever given to pretensions of this nature (prophecy). And, though they ought not to be exclusively charged with it, the reflexion cast upon them is just.' Writing, not of the wild effusions of his own day—Nixon, Brothers, and Joanna Southcott—but of the numerous manuscript collections of metrical and prosaic prophecies which came down from the monastic libraries, he found that 'their practical influence throughout Wales and England was very extensive'. 'Like the books of the Italic Cumaean Sibyl, they were applied to on grave occasions: they gave sanctions to doubtful claims, or animated revolutionary attempts, and were always considered in a state of progressive accomplishment.'[19]

It is no coincidence that this rector, John Webb, should have been interested in the rise of secular prophecies in England, for history was becoming prophecy in reverse.

> I have not undertaken to see differently from others [wrote De Tocqueville], but to look further; and while they are concerned for tomorrow only, I have wanted to think of the whole future.

By training members of the community to think of their future condition in this world, De Tocqueville believed they would be 'gradually and unconsciously brought nearer to religious convictions'. In other words, he considered that such a concern for the future would replace the expectation that had sustained past ages of faith.[20]

Certainly the obsession with the future prompted an upsurge of materialism in popular religion. As Macaulay, another historian, wrote:

> In England it not infrequently happens that a tinker or coal heaver hears a sermon or falls in with a tract which alarms him about the state of his soul . . . he emerges on from the dark land of gins and snares . . . and ascends the Delectable Mountains, and catches from their summit a distant view of the shining city which is the end of his pilgrimage. Then arises in his mind a natural and surely not a censurable desire to impart to others the thoughts of which his own heart is full, to warn the careless, to comfort those who are troubled in spirit. . . . He harangues on Tower Hill or in Smithfield. A congregation is formed. A licence is obtained. A plain brick building, with a desk and benches, is run up and named Ebenezer or Bethel.[21]

Staffed by a pastorate who, as he said, 'had been to no college' and whose 'commission is the same as that on the Mountain of Ascension was given to the Eleven', these Ebenezers and Bethels had their secular counterpart in the Halls of Science established by the followers of 'that great smooth meditative hare' Robert Owen.

> I am endeavouring to effect today what our common adversary will accomplish tomorrow.—I have but wished to compress within a small compass events which common consent would have assisted to fulfil when extended into futurity.[22]

So pleaded an anti-clerical agitator in John Francis Bray's aptly named *Voyage from Utopia*. A disciple of Owen, Bray described Britain (Brydone), France (Franco), and America (Amrico) as they would be seen by a traveller *from* Utopia, sometimes so starkly that its most recent editor is moved to comment that 'the descriptions of the religious practices of Brydone are reminiscent of the harsh lay-out of a Soviet Union Anti-Religious Museum'.[23] Bray epitomises the change between the theological and secular view of the future that was to be made explicit by Marx and Darwin. For he described theology as a 'horrible caricature of the Incomprehensible but Infinite Good' and urged that it was the paramount duty, as well as the vital interest of all individuals, to transmit to themselves perfect bodies and faculties.[24]

IV   MALTHUS VERSUS MACAULAY AND MARX

The probability of a Gothic future was calculated by the Reverend T. R. Malthus, whose *Essay on the Principles of Population* (1798) foresaw disaster ahead if people multiplied at a geometric ratio and food at only an arithmetic ratio. His conjectural scenario set the tone for high speculation about the future and the past as it affected human beings. Conversely, the confident Whig historian, T. B. Macaulay wrote:

> If we were to prophesy that in the year 1930 a population of fifty millions, better fed, clad, and lodged than the English of our time, will cover these islands, that Sussex and Huntingdonshire will be wealthier than the wealthiest parts of the West Riding of Yorkshire now are, that cultivation rich as that of a flower garden, will be carried up to the very tops of Ben Nevis and Helvellyn, that machines constructed on principles yet undiscovered, will be in every house, that there will be no highways but railroads, no travelling but by steam, that our debt, vast as it seems to us, will appear to our great grandchildren a trifling incumbrance, which might easily be paid off in a year or two, many people would think us insane.[25]

Equally optimistic, Marx and Engels believed that the future could be inductively predicted, if one unravelled the past and present dialectically by considering the interaction of continuous technological improvement upon the class struggle. Marx's old teacher, Feuerbach, had taught him that the world was:

> . . . not to be comprehended as a complex of ready made *things*, but as a complex of *processes*, in which the things apparently stable, no

less than their mind images in our heads, the concepts, go through an uninterrupted change of coming into being and passing away.[26]

As unilinear as the prophets they condemned, Marx and Engels forgot that their dialectical approach was complicated by yet another factor—historico-moral almost—in that the proletariat might, through increased wages, improve its class position and become middle class.[27] Human nature was the non-constant. But for all that they worked, like physicists, by a model.[28]

Corroboration and confirmation of Marx's ideas—as he gloated to Engels—was Charles Darwin's *Origin of Species* (1859). For, by unrolling the canvas of the animal kingdom, to show man evolving over thousands of millions of years from a sub-microscopic pre-cellular viroid to a self-conscious human vertebrate, Darwin set a fashion in genetic speculation that has yet to reach a climax. This, which confessedly owed much to Malthus, was to Marx a most powerful work, since it patiently denied 'supernatural design' in nature. But whereas Marx's disciples hoped that such designing would be the responsibility of the class-conscious leaders of the proletariat, Darwin's disciples looked to an élite based on better breeding: the arrival rather than the survival of the fittest.

Long a utopian dream, eugenics was, in the opinion of Darwin's cousin, Francis Galton, the science of society, the only possible way of preventing the degradation of the nation. Galton wished the state to issue certificates to those qualified to breed, and, to collect further information for the certificates, established a chair in the subject in the University of London. He stated with emphasis that eugenics had 'strong claims to become an orthodox religious tenet of the future'.[29]

V COMING RACES—LYTTON AND MARIE CORELLI

Darwin's theory of the process of species-formation was a development of Malthus' prophecy that the human race was breeding its way to starvation and was, in turn, the begetter of stories about better equipped types of human beings. One famous English novelist, Lord Lytton, who himself had written a Gothic story, 'The Haunted and the Haunters', for *Blackwood's Magazine* in 1859, presented such types for consideration, but, as if realising his presumption, he issued it anonymously.

Long a mystic, Lord Lytton felt that this coming race:

> will have acquired some peculiarities so distinct from our ways, that it could not be fused with us, and certain destructive powers which our science could not enable us to attain to, or cope with.[30]

The peculiarities Lytton suggested would be a form of energy known as Vril, used by a subterranean people. This not only enabled the Vrilya to sustain their subterranean existence by moving mountains, driving machinery and enabling them to fly, but it could be used as a long-range weapon, with physical and psychic effects. Under its influence, sex and class differentials disappear. So do modesty, political life, and psychological problems. Since Vril is also a mood-inhibitor, a tranquilliser, a propaedeutic, and, if necessary, a stimulant, the Vrilyans wore a 'Sphinx-like expression and spent their time in flying acrobatics and, when at home, listening to music'. Every room had 'its mechanical contrivances for melodious sounds, usually tuned down to soft-murmured notes, which seem like sweet whispers from invisible spirits'.

Living in small communities under a Tur or Dictator, the Vrilyans have few disagreements for the disagreer usually emigrates or is comfortably housed in an asylum. Work is done only by children, with their Vril rods.

After escaping from this underground Nirvana the hero—an American—commends its inhabitants as having united and harmonised human problems into one system 'nearly all the objects which the various philosophers of the upper world have placed before human hopes as the ideals of a Utopian future'. But he admits that, for humans at least, the system would not work:

> If you would take a thousand of the best and most philosophical of human beings you could find in London, Paris, Berlin, New York, or even Boston, and place them as citizens in this beatified community, my belief is that, in less than a year they would either die of *ennui* or attempt some revolution by which they would militate against the good of the community, and be burnt into cinders at the request of Tur.[31]

Lytton, himself an early Gothic-type novelist, exercised a great influence over the Gothic prophetess Madame Blavatsky. From his novel *The Last Days of Pompeii* (1834) she took her story of the

Isis Cult in Rome during the first century of the Christian era. From his *Zanoni* (1842) she took further ideas about the occult. 'No author in the world of literature ever gave a more truthful or more poetical description of these beings,' she testified, 'than Sir E. Bulwer-Lytton, the author of *Zanoni.*' Having learned of demons casting prophetic images on the water and of animated statues foreseeing futurity from *The Last Days of Pompeii*, Madame Blavatsky took many references from *The Coming Race*,[32] to buttress her own view that a cycle of 5,000 years of a present dark age was about to end and be succeeded by an age of light. In every century, she wrote in *Isis Unveiled* (1875), a messenger is sent by the adepts from the mountains of Tibet to Western nations. One had appeared in 1875; the next one would appear in 1975. This messenger, she claimed, brought further news of theosophical doctrines that would refute both decadent Christianity and the scientific theories of Darwin, Huxley, and Tyndall. It was, she maintained, a secret wisdom known to Orpheus, Plato, Ptolemy, and the medieval alchemists, and kept alive by the mystical Tibetan brotherhood, with whom she claimed to be in telepathic communication.

Such blends of occultism, religion, and science offered heady stimulus to the public at large as little Minnie Mackay, sister of a former secretary to Bulwer Lytton, found to her profit. Refurbishing a previously rejected piece about 'personal electricity' as *A Romance of Two Worlds* (1886), she found herself a best seller as Marie Corelli. This is the first of many novels. Later she sat for her portrait to a painter whose speciality was painting whilst the subject was in a trance and who had done Madame Blavatsky's portrait too.[33]

VI DARWINISM INVERTED

Whereas Lytton's Vrilyans live in a highly-developed technical society, Butler's Erewhonians do not. Higgs, the creation of an anonymous author first suspected of being Lord Lytton (which may have had something to do with its initial success), but by the fifth edition revealed to be the grandson, namesake, and later biographer of the famous headmaster of Shrewsbury, is arrested for possessing a watch, which is then placed in a museum housing:

> . . . fragments of a great many of our own most advanced inventions;
> but they all seemed to be several hundred years old, and to be placed

where they were, not for instruction, but curiosity . . . all were marred and broken.[34]

The inversion of the title is followed by the inversion of time, for Higgs is visiting a country which has abandoned industrialism four hundred years earlier when a professor of hypothetics in the Colleges of Unreason proved 'that machines were ultimately destined to supplant the race of man, and to become instinct with a vitality as different from, and superior to, that of animals, as animal to vegetable life'. Higgs obtained *The Book of the Machines*, the neo-Darwinian bible of the Erewhonians which divided machines as Darwin had divided animal creation, into 'genera, subgenera, species, varieties, subvarieties and so forth', and the author:

> proved the existence of connecting links between machines that seemed to have very little in common, and showed that many more such links had existed, but had now perished. He pointed out tendencies to reversion, and the presence of rudimentary organs which existed in many machines fully developed and perfectly useless, yet serving to mark descent from an ancestor to whom the function was actually useful.

The Erewhonian author of *The Book of the Machines* feared the 'extraordinary rapidity' with which machines were becoming transformed; 'no class of beings have in any time past made so rapid a movement forward'—and asked:

> Should not that movement be jealously watched, and checked while we can still check it? And is it not necessary for this end to destroy the more advanced of the machines which are in use at present, although it is admitted that they are in themselves harmless?

The danger to the Colleges of Unreason was obvious:

> Have we not engines which can do all manner of sums more quickly and correctly than we can? What prizeman in hypothetics at any of our Colleges of Unreason can compare with some of these machines in their own line? In fact whenever precision is required man flies to the machine at once, as far preferable to himself.

So the decision was taken. Five hundred years before Higgs first arrived in Erewhon the anti-mechanists rose in revolt. A civil war raged for many years reducing the inhabitants by a half, and when the anti-mechanists won they treated their opponents with such severity that all opposition was extirpated.

But not quite. The Professors of Inconsistency and Evasion were too powerful; and insisted that these new principles should not be carried to their logical conclusion. So, instead, the machines were all carefully collected and put into museums where they became a subject of antiquarian study.

The only Erewhonian defender of machines argued that man himself was a machinate animal since machines were part of his physical nature—'extra-corporeal limbs' as it were, or to use the Darwinian image—modified limbs. Thus the handle of the spade is like the knob at the end of the humerus, the shaft is the additional bone, and the oblong iron plate is 'the new form of the hand which enables its possessor to disturb the earth in a way to which his original hand was unequal'.

The defender of the machines did, however, admit that as man became more machinate his powers would be so equalised, and the severity of competition so minimised that people of inferior endowments would transmit their inferiority to their descendants and so cause degeneracy of the race. To prevent this, the defender proposed to classify human beings by their horse-power—or the number of artificial limbs at their command. Respect to the rich (who commanded more horse-power service than the poor), would therefore be justified. But in spite of showing how machines had effected changes in the animal and vegetable kingdom, thereby helping the moral and intellectual development of the species, he did not make a strong enough case. So in the end it was decided to destroy all the machines discovered in the preceding 271 years —a decision which precipitated the civil wars.

Their education, embodied in the Colleges of Unreason, argued that:

> to teach a boy merely the nature of the things which exist in the world round him, and about which he will have to be conversant during his whole life, would be giving him but a narrow and shallow conception of the universe.

So the students were required to give intelligent answers to a 'set of utterly strange and impossible contingencies'. Professors of Inconsistency and Evasion provided the preliminary instruction upon which Hypothetics was based. 'There is hardly any inconsistency so glaring but they soon learn to defend it, or injunction so clear that they cannot find some pretext for disregarding it.' The doyen of the faculty was the Professor of Worldly Wisdom who 'had the reputation of having done more perhaps than any other living man to suppress any kind of originality'. Yet even he was supposed to be rather a radical, being 'President of the Society for the Suppression of Useless Knowledge and for the Complete Obliteration of the Past'.

It was not the satire on Darwin so much as his portrayal of the Established Church as the Musical Banks which made the most immediate impact. His father, Canon Butler, forbade him to visit the house.[35] For with their 'fresh stained-glass windows . . . descriptive of the principal commercial incidents of the bank for many ages', their 'enlarged organs', their 'sinister looking persons in black gowns', their transactions conducted to organ music, and their choirs of men and boys singing in remote parts, seeming 'to have derived their inspirations from the songs of birds and the wailing of the wind, which at last they tried to imitate in melancholy cadences that at times degenerated into a howl', that institutional analogue was apt. The spiritual analogue was even more offensive to believers, since the coins given out by the Musical Banks 'were made of a great variety of metals . . . some of which were hard, while others would bend easily and assume almost any form which their possessor might desire at the moment'. Those dispensing them had 'a cramped expression upon their faces'. This outward and visible sign of the lack of inward and spiritual grace he attributed partly to their education which unfitted them for any other field of employment, and partly to the fact that parents bought the right of presenting the child to the office of cashier whilst he was yet young.

The Erewhonians were on the eve of a great change in their estimate of the Musical Banks:

> Fully ninety per cent of the population of the metropolis looked on these musical banks with something nor far removed from contempt. If this is so, any such startling event as is sure to arise sooner or later, may serve as a nucleus to a new order of things that will be more in harmony with both the heads and hearts of the people.

This startling event was to be provided by the hero himself when he escaped from Erewhon with Arowhena in a balloon.

His departure became the central event in the new religion of Sunchildism, so called because he was credited with ascending into heaven in a chariot drawn by black and white horses. This new religion Butler describes in *Erewhon Revisited* (1901). Its assiduous exegetes were Professors Hanky and Panky and the Musical Banks. Hanky and Panky threatened to kill Higgs if he revealed his true identity and exposed the myth upon which Sunchildism had been founded. They agree to countenance his second departure as an easy way out of the difficulty and, to prevent further excesses, the King starts an aeronautical society.

In a virtual postscript, Higgs' son by Yram, writing to Higgs' other son by Arowhena, reveals that Hank and Panky have been canonised as Saints and that any attempt to dislodge their hold over the country—sustained by Panky's son Pocus—would trigger off a civil war. Scientists and engineers are clamouring for support and the writer—now Prime Minister of Erewhon—urged that the British take them over before someone else did.[36]

Chapter Five

THE OTHER SIDE

I THE SOUTHERN HEMISPHERE

Erewhon owes much to Butler's experience as a sheep-breeder in New Zealand, where he had emigrated after abandoning his intention to take holy orders. His story, like that of Macaulay's famous 'traveller from New Zealand [who] shall, in the midst of a vast solitude, take his stand on a broken arch of London Bridge to sketch the ruins of St. Paul's', appealed to the imagination of Victorians.[1] So did 'the navel of the world', those rock-strewn grasslands and dead volcanic cones with their great stone images that lay twice as far away to the east of New Zealand as Australia lay to the west. And Australia too, with its unpeopled spaces, evoked more speculation on its future. By no means all were prepared to dismiss it as Hilaire Belloc did:

> We had intended you to be
> The next Prime Minister but three:
> The stocks were sold; the Press was squared;
> The Middle Class was quite prepared.
> But as it is! . . . My language fails!
> Go out and govern New South Wales!

For experience of Australia tempered the outlook of several notable Victorians, notably W. S. Jevons and C. H. Pearson. Jevons returned to England in 1859 to acquire a deeper knowledge of statistical method and set himself to compile, whilst reading for a degree, a 'statistical atlas'. He also devoted himself to the construction of a 'reasoning machine' or 'logical abacus' to liberate logic from the metaphysicians. In *The Coal Question: An Inquiry concerning the Progress of the National and the Probable Exhaustion of our Coal Mines* (1865) he forecast that the Victorian dream of material progress would be shattered by the exhaustion of our coal resources, and urged his readers to consider it as a problem of 'almost religious importance'.

Whilst Jevons was exhibiting his reasoning machine in Manchester and Liverpool, C. H. Pearson, a Cambridge history don, was preparing to emigrate to Australia. After eighteen years spent in public affairs, mainly in Victoria, he published *National Life and Character: A Forecast* (1893), in which he envisaged mankind as approaching 'the stationary state', with no countries left to receive immigrants, and more and more dreaded for its barbarity. After a survey of possible developments he concluded

> neither our despondency nor our cheerful expectation can be assumed to correspond with any real forecast of the future. . . . What we mostly trust to, perhaps, is the sentiment expressed by Tennyson, that 'somehow good will be the final goal of ill'.

For Australia provided a theatre for man to be seen in the raw, stripped of the comfortable artifices of civilisation. Both aboriginal and immigrant were object lessons to the political moralist. The immigrant provided Robert Lowe with arguments against democracy, the aboriginal tempted others like the Marquis de Rays to found a phantom paradise at Port Breton.[2] Between the Polynesian triangle and Australia—or rather at the bottom left hand angle—lay New Zealand, already a half-fulfilled prophecy. Here W. D. Hay, an authority on fungi and the Maori, took in 1880 a long look at London, foretelling its 'doom' in 1942.

II SUBMARINE CITIES AND COMMUNES OF NATIONS

Haunted by the Malthusian nightmare, Hay suggested submarine towns, a new form of power ('Basilico-Magnetism'), and a world reorganised into sixty states of the sea, leaving the dry land for 'general purposes'. Climatic control, an 'Oecumenical Parliament' and American leadership, made his *Three Hundred Years Hence* (1881) slightly more realistic than other subterranean fantasies. Aptly, too, it begins with a 'phonographer's preface' as from the History Department of the University of Londinova in the State of Atlantis in the year 2180.

London's future also dominated H. C. M. Watson's self-styled 'Utopia of the future' in which he confesses that he 'refrained from luxuriating in a description of scientific marvels' to concentrate his attention on the horrific nature of Darwinism. Whilst reading Comte, his hero is lured six hundred years ahead by a cuckoo, and finds himself in the year 2400. Westminster Abbey has become a Temple of Humanity on 8th Street, and Oxford Street is 5th Street West. Comte, Darwin, Haeckel, and Mill have not only been canonised but are also patron saints of hotels. Watson's hero stays at the Darwin, discovering that the phonograph had replaced the newspaper, that restaurants are automated, and that the power structure of the world is deployed in great 'communes' of nations.

Slowly, horrific features appear. Children are reared in Baby Farms before entering state schools, Darwin's descendants have been bred back into apes, whilst humans contribute even after death to the common welfare by being boiled down. Indeed, a deprived mother, appealing for the body of the dead child, gives the hero his opportunity to take her to the British Museum where she can read the Bible. By the time she has assimilated its message the hero wakes up. The title of Watson's book, *Erchomenon: or the Republic of Materialism* (1879), shows that it is a sardonic moral tract.

Food and population also dominate Kenneth Folingsby's privately printed *Meda: A Tale of the Future* (1888). He looked still further forward to the year 5575, when after a civil war in 2888 and a union between Great Britain and America in 3334, decreased eating resulted in a new human type with 'great thoughtful faces, great heads and eyes' who move around in an electric harness in a hop, skip, and jump manner.

III ENERGEIATHICS, 'ULTRA-AERIAL' NAVIGATION, AND SEA-FARMING

Others followed.[3] Aware of the pessimism of Darwin's thesis, A. V. W. Bikkers describes Miss Phantasia in *Anno Domini 2071* (1871) as 'like the ingenious author of the Origin of Species' convincing herself that all this makes for greater happiness. He foresaw a standard world-time based on the sun rising over the Aleutian islands. Energeiathics—force holders or energy preservers—would lighten the human lot, which would be further ameliorated by centrally-heated streets and a widespread use of aluminium. The telephone—'a music box of small dimensions' —would provide solace for leisure, and balloons, steered by magnetic rings, would transport everyone in a warless world.

As guides to this new world Miss Phantasia and Roger Bacon explain the geographical changes over the two centuries. London —a city of 12 million inhabitants—occupies most of south-east England and is linked to Paris by a channel bridge. Indeed, a world railway network links all the world towns since states themselves had disappeared. Metals came from mines on the moon and New Zealand was the Britain of the South Pacific.

Another world state is foreshadowed in *Annals of the Twenty-Ninth Century* (1874), a three-volume 'autobiography' of Diogenes Milton, the tenth president of the World Republic. Born in 2776, Diogenes Milton is only thirteen when the Parliament of Man passes a Bill to teach quadrupeds to fly. Later under his leadership the Siberian Council takes up 'ultra-aerial navigation'. The mundo-lunar straits are cleared of satellite rocks to make possible cruises to the moon. Forty-four are made by the year 2820 and soon lunar cities are being built.

Meanwhile on earth great advances are being made in farming the seas, harnessing earthquakes, and converting Vesuvius into a 'caloric work'. Diogenes Milton spurs people on by writing a book, *The Three Aorists*, giving 'the moral of the past', an 'epitome of the characteristics of the present' and 'speculations regarding prognostication of the future'.

Having taken the moon by the horns he abolishes night and introduces interplanetary signalling. Messages are received from Jupiter,' missionaries' come from Mars, and he goes to Venus as president of the Mundo-Lunar Republic. So the expansion continues with the establishment of a Terra-Venusian ecumenical council. The author of this long view ahead was a Scottish physician, Dr. Andrew Blair.

IV   THE TECHNOLOGICAL MOSES

Having examined a number of tales of the future in the British Museum, Edward Maitland observed that they erred in 'regarding physical science as destined to dominate man to such an extent as to destroy the individuality of his character, and mechanise his very affections'. So he set himself to write a story that would show that:

under the reign of Science, Civilisation has come to consist, not in the suppression, but in the development of individual character and genius, to the utmost extent compatible with the securing and convenience of the whole man.[4]

The story concerns the finding of a baby in the basket of a balloon by a party of scientists returning from the then inhabited North Pole. Christened Christmas Carol, he converses with 'angels' whom no one else can see or hear, and becomes, thanks to the discovery of a jewel hoard in his crêche, very rich. He applies his wealth to diverting the Mediterranean into the Sahara, creating a gigantic garden. This fable was Maitland's attempt 'to think out the character of Jesus with a view to elucidating the problem of Christianity'.[5] Called *By and By*, *A Historical Romance of the Future* (1873), this three-volume biography of an imagined technological Moses so enraged the wife of a Shropshire vicar that she 'flung the book to the other end of the room'. 'Then,' she confessed, 'after sitting and thinking for a time I went and picked it up and said "that man shall become a vegetarian".'[6] So began the partnership between Anna Kingsford and Maitland. She was then twenty-seven and he forty-nine. Soon after, she went to Paris to study medicine and returned to work with him as a Theosophist.

One of their friends, the Rev. G. J. Ouseley, also issued his visions, and obligingly appended a bibliography of books that he found helpful in editing them. These ran from the ancient scriptures of India, China, and Egypt, More's *Utopia*, up through Swedenborgian, Mormon, Positivist, and Blavatskyan tracts, to the works of Bulwer Lytton, Frances Power Cobbe, and Samuel Butler. He began with a rhyme:

> In century sixty-nine
> They reconstructed me;
> My volcanoes they abolished
> Subdued my inner fires;
> My mountain ridges too
> They cast into the deep,
> To make Six Zones of Land
> And Continents in Number Twelve
> Twixt these they let the Oceans run
> With Bridges they did join them,
> And sea to sea by rails on land.

This vision appeared to the seeress in the form of a lectern with manuscripts thereon. In the morning she wrote it down. It appeared as *Palingenesia, Or The Earth's New Birth* by Theosopho, Minister of the Holies, and Ellora, a Priestess of the Sanctuary (1884).

V THE BARCHESTER OF 1980; EARLY CLERICAL SCIENCE FICTION

'The denial of the existence of God and of the future state,' wrote the radical historian Goldwin Smith in *Macmillan's Magazine* of February 1878, 'is the dethronement of conscience; and society will pass, to say the least, through a dangerous interval before social science can fill the vacant throne.' He spoke for many thoughtful Englishmen.

Even Anthony Trollope lifted up his eyes from Barchester to envisage the future in 1980 when a group of renegade Englishmen establish a new government on an island off Australia. All citizens of this new government reaching the age of sixty-seven are to be sent to live for a year in comfort in a 'college'. After that they must submit to euthanasia. But just as the first 'case' is being dealt with, a British destroyer sails up, trains its guns on the capital and brings it back to the liberality and freedom of the British Crown. Twenty-three years after *A Fixed Period* (1882) was published the great medical teacher, Sir William Osler, endorsed Trollope's suggestion and evoked a flood of controversy.[7]

Patient Trollopians are really quite puzzled by Trollope's motives for writing this novel. Perhaps it was because it was published in the year of his death. One critic, describing it as a 'failure', confesses that:

> as a study of death it is very puzzling. . . . Generally, Trollope is accustomed to give his own opinion in little asides. . . . But here for once, the ubiquitous personality of the author is excluded by a talkative untrollopian narrator.[8]

Even more percipiently the Rev. W. Tuckwell[9] foresaw that in *The New Utopia, or England in 1985* (1885):

> electricity had superseded the diminishing coalfields and become the sole vehicle of light, heat, motion, force; that in geology the crystallising rocks had been shown to be metamorphic products, early man had been pushed back into the Eocene Age, missing links had been discovered to complete the chain of evolution between the Salpa

and the mammal; that in meteorology the patient comparison of two centuries of collected observations had enabled the two experts to foretell storm and rain and sunshine unerringly for a month to come; that the ease and cheapness with which diamonds could be produced had doubled the power of the microscope; that the chemist was trembling on the verge of the discovery of the plasmic secret, and might succeed at any moment in projecting a living cell on the laboratory table.[10]

Tuckwell held that 'Dreamland is not merely a refuge from the sorrows of a waking world; it is the nebulous haze out of which new worlds are formed'. He urged his readers to remember that 'belief in the world's perfectibility is the logical outcome of belief in the creator's perfection'. 'What is it,' he asked, 'but that Kingdom of God on earth whose establishment was the prime motive and final cause of the teaching of and life of Christ?'[11]

The social reorganisation consequent upon the universal use of electricity he forecast would be shown in decentralised villages, connected by 'carriages passing to and fro by some invisible means of locomotion', houses 'warmed by electrical energy beneath the floor', and in everyone having a small-holding of not more than fifty acres. As Tuckwell saw it, all sects would be merged into one state church, with the parson elected by two-thirds of the population of the parish, and subject to an annual examination in Science, Literature, and Music.

In the wider world, the population of America would return to Ireland to drain its bogs, till its hill tops and 'infuse its towns with manufacturing energy'. The Royal Family would become ordinary citizens at the third generation, and Gibraltar would have been returned to Spain.

But, from our point of view, it is yet more interesting that the occasion of his 'prophecy' was an invitation to address the Birmingham Sunday Lecture Society, a body formed in July 1881 to promote 'the social, moral and intellectual well-being of the Community at Large'.

VI   THE CRYSTAL AGE

Another interpretation of the future as seen through Darwin's eyes was issued by one of Butler's greatest admirers, W. H. Hudson (who 'frequently abused and bantered' his friend and biographer Morley Roberts 'for remaining too critical of much of his biological work').[12] This was *A Crystal Age* (1887), and the author's name did not appear on the title page until the 1906 edition.[13]

It began with a quotation from Darwin:

> judging from the past we may justly infer that no one living species will transmit its unaltered likeness to a distant futurity. . . . We can so far take a prophetic glance into futurity as to foretell that it will be the common and widely spread species . . . which will ultimately prevail. . . . Hence we may look with some confidence to a secure future of great length. And as natural selection works solely by and for the good of each being, all corporeal and mental endowments will tend to progress towards perfection.

And just as Butler drew from his New Zealand experience, so W. H. Hudson drew from his boyhood life on the farms and ranches of Rio de la Plata, when he watched birds and nature with a sensitivity and passion that were to continue for the rest of his life. His book shone all the more brightly for being written in a drab London boarding-house, where Hudson lived in poverty and comparative ill-health from the age of twenty-eight. Evocative of a past that was gone (an earlier book was called *The Purple Land that England Lost* (1885)), *A Crystal Age* tells the story of a modern, and very uncouth, botanist with the unromantic name of Smith who, whilst searching for specimens, is knocked out by a fall of rocks, and finds himself in a strange land, where the vegetarian inhabitants dress like Anglo-Saxons, behave with scrupulous politeness, and listen with incredulity to his account of England. They live by creative work and are amused by his idea that money can buy goods. Revolving round a country mansion, their life and surroundings are so simple, honest, and graceful that Smith's clothes, behaviour, and lack of artistic creativity become an embarrassment to him until he is attuned to them.

Even the horses that plough are as intelligent as he is. His unfortunate love for the girl Yoletta leads first to her seclusion, then to his death, largely because the moral test for mating is too difficult for him.

Hudson's insistence on the past and nature as the foil for exposing the lusts of the modern world is symbolised in *A Crystal Age* by the paramountcy of the Mother of the House, whom the inhabitants regard as God. It is indeed a familial Utopia, where happiness is only achieved through sacrifice of the self and its vulgar methods of expression.

VII   UTOPIA VERSUS RELIGION

Yet the threat to religion presented by the Utopian ideal much exercised Sir Walter Besant. 'We fear not Death and, therefore, need no religion,' say the people in his *Inner House* (1888), where physicising has, through the Great Discovery, abolished death and pain.

> Without the certainty of parting, Religion droops and dies. . . . He who is immortal and commands the secrets of Nature so that he shall neither die, nor grow old, nor become feeble nor fall into any disease, feels no necessity for any religion.

And with religion goes love which cannot live whilst humans undergo no change.

So wanting both Love and Religion, the people revolt in the name of the Great Discovery, 'that to all things earthly there must come an end'. Indeed, the reason for clasping in love is that people are afraid of losing one another.

An epistolary novel, *Caesar's Column*,[14] begins in the year 1988 with the narrator staying in the Hotel Darwin at New York, the whole structure of which 'consists of an infinite series of cunning adjustments for the delight and gratification of the human creature'. Guests propel themselves on electric chairs, the rooms are vast lifts, tables are equipped with 'knobs' that have only to be turned for any kind of food to be automatically produced. Other knobs when turned provide the news of the world on a screen at the end of the table.

Yet with all this there is boredom:

> The truth is that in this vast, over-crowded city, man is a drag—a superfluity—and I think many men and women end their lives out of an overwhelming sense of their own insignificance—in other words, from a mere weariness of feeling that they are nothing, they become nothing. . . . The race has grown in power and loneliness —I fear it has lost its loveableness.

Hence the phenomenon of death-houses: where men select the time and drug by which they wish to die, lie down in their coffins, and pass away to the sound of music. The hero of the story,

Gabriel Weltstein, is in New York to sell wool. Swiss by origin, he farms in Uganda (part of the African federation), and his astonishment at the direction civilisation is taking in America is increased by his encounter with Max, a member of The Brotherhood. For America is a republic in all but name—the aristocracy of the world is Jewish. Cunning rather than intellect rules the world, even though inventions like that of Thomas O'Connor from the University of Oregon are lengthening life, and Professor Henry Myers of California has ascertained that there are 'intelligences' on the world other than those possessed by humans. These observations are laced together by a conventional love story in which Gabriel rescues Estella and returns to Uganda, having seen the tyrant Prince Cabano overthrown.

A similar theosophical background can be seen in the writings of Jack London, who in *The Iron Heel* (1907), foresaw an oligarchy rising out of the ruins of American capitalism, controlling workers by 'savage, screaming, nerve-wracking steam whistles', by slogans, and by hidden persuaders:

> The abjectness of their servitude [he wrote in the form of an imaginary diary of events some three centuries ahead], is incomprehensible to us. There was a magic in words greater than the conjurer's art. So befuddled and chaotic were their minds that the utterance of a single word could negate the generalizations of a lifetime of serious research and thought. Vast populations grew frenzied over such phrases as 'an honest dollar' and 'a full dinner pail.' The coinage of such phrases was considered strokes of genius.

The techniques of the oligarchy—segregation, bestialisation, and dehumanisation—led to a rebellion, but that rebellion only made the oligarchs more secure, with new ethics 'coherent and definite, sharp and severe as steel', perhaps 'the most absurd and unscientific' but 'at the same time the most potent ever possessed by a tyrant class'. The darkness of this picture is, however, lightened by a closing hint that, seven centuries later, an Age of Brotherhood will have arrived.[15]

VIII   NON-LINEAR TIME AND THE PSYCHIC
DIAPHRAGM

Darwin's friend and fellow evolutionist, Alfred Russell Wallace,[16] was as entranced by the subject of non-linear time as were mediums like Daniel Douglas Home. Confirmed in his beliefs by the inquiries of Sir William Crookes, he helped form the British National Association of Spiritualists in 1873 and a London Spiritualist Alliance in 1884. More important, the Society for Psychical Research was established in 1882 under whose auspices F. W. H. Myers put forward the concept of the 'psychic diaphragm' separating the supraliminal and subliminal self. This Myers did so successfully that William James suggested that the unconscious should be known as 'Myers' Problem'.

Myers' theory of the future was to question whether the words 'past' and 'future' were 'really more than words'. He asked whether the present idea of the two as 'a stream of consequences' could not be regarded as 'only an ocean of coexistences',[17] and argued that it might be possible to extend artificially the period of past, present, and future. In much the same way Bertrand Russell suggested 'a complex of compresence': a moment in which past, present, and future are all apprehended together. Precognition involves admitting, as a subsequent member of the Society suggested, that the future already exists: 'In precognition the present perception or awareness is merely of contemporary images referable in thought to the future.' It also involves the abandonment of the linear conception of time and the acceptance of several dimensions of it:

> whatever its uses may be as a mathematical conception, time is not in reality a unilinear irreversible series of events flowing in one direction only, from the past to the future, but it must be regarded as being rather a *totum simul* in which past, present and future coexist, though they appear, to normal consciousness, to be successive phases in a temporal flow.[18]

This revival of interest in the mind was accelerated by the loss of faith involved in accepting Darwinism.[19] 'Mr. Sludge the Medium' was more than a figment of Browning's imagination. The 'subliminal self' of F. W. H. Myers and the 'collective spiritual reservoir' of William James were aspects of an interest perhaps best exemplified by Frances Power Cobbe. 'I have found no woman writer since Descartes (that excludes Santa Teresa), who put on record her interest in the unconscious mind earlier than the intelligent Miss Frances Power Cobbe,' wrote Lancelot Law Whyte.[20] Whyte drew attention to an article she wrote in *Macmillan's Magazine* for November 1870 on 'Unconscious Cerebration'. Two years later she published *Darwinism in Morals* (1872); then under the title of Martin Nostradamus she published *The Age of science; a newspaper of the 20th century (1877)*: an ironic forecast of future events.

The worlds of psychic travel opened up by the Society for Psychic Research were used by novelists. Henry James used one of the incidents reported to it as the basis for *The Turn of the Screw* in *The Two Magics* (1898), whilst M. P. Shiel, another expatriate author, quarried several fantasies from its proceedings, notably *The Purple Cloud* (1901), where Miss Wilson 'could travel in every direction and easily in all directions, North and South, up and down, in the past, the present and the future'. One of her forays into the future—some fifteen to thirty years hence—reveals the devastation of the world by waves of cyanide gas emanating from the South Pacific. It kills everyone except the 'hero', aptly called Adam, who is at the North Pole. He returns to burn and ravage the deserted cities of the world in an orgy of fire, fearing that he will find someone alive. He does—a woman in a cellar in Constantinople.

Equipped with a 'psychophone' by a space creature on a moon of Jupiter, another of Shiel's heroes, the scientist Dr. Warwick, returns to earth to organise the young men against the old. Calling up his space allies on this psychophone to help him, he destroys the air fleet of the old men in a universal tempest. Hence its title, *The Young Men are Coming*.

Shiel, a former medical student turned mathematician, was the son of a Methodist minister and was haunted by a dark, if secular, apocalypse. His novel, *The Yellow Danger* (1898) falls into the category of novels about a future war that formed the nightmare reading of late Victorians. It describes the descent of a Sino-Japanese horde on Europe and the measures, ranging from torpedoes to cholera, dispatched by the English against it. In his next novel, *The Lord of the Sea* (1901), Jews supplant the Chinese as the menace. Their commercial acumen buys up England, but thanks to hero Hogarth's luck in finding a diamond, they are ultimately repatriated to Palestine.

Tapping the fears of his generation, Shiel's next novels of a future war were *The Yellow Wave* (1905) and *The Dragon* (1913). In the latter an 'overman' delivers Britain from yet another invasion by a blinding ray.

In 1928 Shiel wrote 'The Future Day' (reprinted in *The Invisible Voices* (1935)), a story of airborne cities set in the year 2073. By now he was infected with lunar fancies, as another story in the collection, 'The Place of Pain', deals with indescribable horrors discovered on the moon by accident.

In retrospect Shiel confessed:

> We know the Gospel, the tidings of Great Joy, that we are related to snakes, that there is a principle of Progress in Being, leading on to lives that will one day be wiser, finer, more wildly delighted than ever entered our little hearts to fancy. . . . No archangel appeared to the mother of him who proclaimed this Revelation to say 'You shall bear a son and shall call his name Charles', yet *he* was the Messiah. . . . What is amusing is that priests, professional experts in the Gospels, did to him what they did to those who announced that the stars are suns—reviled, denied him.[21]

IX SECULAR ESCHATOLOGIES AND THE POSITIVIST CHURCH

One of Darwin's disciples who came to fiction after serving as an exegete of evolution was Grant Allen. He told a story of the birth of a club-footed child to a delicate mother. The rulers of the community thinking 'first and foremost of the progressive evolution of universal humanity' order that the child must be executed. This is done on Darwin, 20th December. The mother dies.[22] Allen also used the tale of the future to pillory the present. In *The British Barbarians* (1895), Bertram Ingledew, a scientist from the twenty-fifth century, finds himself in the respectable suburb of Brockenhurst, England, in much the same position as an anthropologist among savage tribes or Voltaire's *Micromégas* among the earthlings. The taboos of class, work, property, and sex are embodied by Montieth and, by stealing his wife, Ingledew undermines them. Grant Allen used to lecture in a positivist 'Bethel', if one may so describe the positivist centre at Newton Hall in London. Here Darwin's piano was installed to make music for the congregation. Within two years of its foundation, Newton Hall became such a success that the *Pall Mall Gazette* of the 29th November 1883, featured it as number two in a series on 'Centres of Spiritual Activity'. Number one was St. Paul's Cathedral. As well as listening to Grant Allen, the positivist congregation were entertained by others who spoke of a Utopian future, a new heaven and a new earth 'with reverence'. Frederic Harrison, their leader, confessed, 'we have never dreamed of witnessing in our age any such Apocalypse, and assuredly we have never presumed to attempt any crude model of a society which after ages will have to work out in reality'.

As befitted its name, Newton Hall made a gallant attempt to cultivate reverence for statistics. As Frederic Harrison wrote:

> The whole Company of Jesus and the Roman propaganda could not screw anything celestial out of the elements of geometry and conic sections; and in teaching mathematics they are forced to put theology, the Creeds, and the Bible aside. But when the Positivist lecturer treats the first book of Euclid or conic sections, he is inspired with memories of some of the critical epochs in the history of humanity; he recalls with reverence the names of Pythagoras and Archimedes; he points out the places they hold in the sacred calendar of humanity. . . . When the Positivist is teaching mathematics, he knows that he is teaching *religion*.[23]

Deserting the arid pages of the *Secular Review*, G. C. G. Jones published, under the name of George Griffith, a number of futurist romances. One of them tells of an aerial stronghold in Africa—Aëria—from which a crusade to establish world justice is launched. In the struggle between Franco-Russian and Anglo-German power blocs, England is only saved by the Aërians and the Americans. The Czar is driven off the English shore and ultimately off his own. Here the first book—*The Angel of the Revolution* (1893) ends and its sequel *Olga Romanoff* (1894), takes up the story to the twenty-first century. In this the Aërians, thanks to their aeroplanes and vril, are able to renounce their control of the world, now connected by monorails and possessing cheap power from atomised carbon and petroleum. Communication has been established with Mars. Indeed everything looks peaceful until a descendant of the last Czar (from whom the book takes its name), kidnaps the son of the President of Aëria, obtains the secret of Aërian strength and builds an invasion fleet at Mount Terror near the South Pole. She is well on her way to overthrowing world government when the earth is burnt to a cinder by a comet. Everyone is killed except the Aërians who have taken refuge under a granite mountain, from which they emerge to repopulate the world.

Griffith, today unknown, unwittingly set the pace of much of the science-fiction in the century to come.[24]

X   THE EUGENIC CREED: GALTON'S *Kantsaywhere*

'Men of the present day are, to those we might hope to bring into existence, what the pariah dogs of the streets of an Eastern town are to our own highly-bred varieties.' Francis Galton's call for 'supermen', though made in numerous scientific memoirs and books, would not, he realised, be effective unless he could embody it in a striking parable or fable. Such a parable he finally wrote six months before his death, only to have it rejected by a publisher, whereupon he gave orders for its destruction.[25]

From pieces which survive, however, the main outlines of the story are clear: *Extracts from the Journals of the late Professor I. Donaghue* concern experiences in the eugenic state of Kantsaywhere. The professor discovers that 'everybody is classed by everybody else according to their estimate or knowledge of his person and faculties' for they 'think more of the race than the individual'. 'Their creed, or rather I should say their superstition—for it has not yet crystallised into a dogmatic creed—is that living beings, and pre-eminently mankind, are the only executive agents of whom we have any certain knowledge. They look upon life at large as probably a huge organisation in which every separate living thing plays an unconscious part, much as the separate cells do in a living person.'

So everyone is subjected to a thorough examination for a P.G. degree (passed for genetics) before being allowed to marry. Those who fail came under a Bureau 'charged with looking after the un-classed parents and their offspring, and much was done to make the lot of the unclassed as pleasant as might be, as long as they propagated no children. If they did so kindness was changed into sharp severity.' For the very inferior, 'Labour Colonies' were established where they were 'segregated under conditions that are not onerous, except that they must work hard and live in celibacy'.[26]

Galton believed that Eugenics had 'strong claims to become an orthodox religious tenet of the future, for Eugenics co-operates with the workings of nature by ensuring that humanity shall be represented by the fittest races. What Nature does blandly, slowly and ruthlessly, man may do providently, quickly and kindly.'[27]

But he held out no 'expectations of a near golden age'.

After listening to him in 1904 Bernard Shaw said 'there is no reasonable excuse for refusing to face the fact that nothing but a eugenic religion can save our civilisation from the fate which has overtaken all previous civilisations'.[28]

XI THE OTHER SIDE OF THE MIRROR

'When we travel by electricity—if I may adventure to develop your theory,' said Lewis Carroll in *Sylvie and Bruno* (1889) to his travelling companion, 'we shall have leaflets instead of booklets and the murder and the wedding will come on the same page.'

'A development worthy of Darwin!' his companion exclaimed enthusiastically. 'Only *you* reverse his theory. Instead of developing a mouse into an elephant, you would develop an elephant into a mouse!'[29]

To 'develop' an elephant into a flea a professor in the story has a megaloscope which 'minimfies' elephants to fleas and maximises fleas into flying horses.

Carroll was obsessed with the ways in which things turn into something else—as the verses of the mad gardener in *Sylvie and Bruno* show—but not so much organically as symbolically. He hovered on the borders of surrealism, devoting much of his time to photography, the theory of games and mirror images.[30] All come together in the mazy world of wonderland, and all are illuminated by his earlier heroine, Alice, who, when she has finished her journey in wonderland, cries, 'You're nothing but a pack of cards'.[31] The pilgrim's progress of this little girl through the crazy illogicalities of the adult world where live animals, people, and symbols are manipulated through fields of place and time, like chessmen, became from its first printing in 1865 'a regular and inescapable part of our everyday lives', and translated into forty-seven languages.[32] As a later book, *Sylvie and Bruno* is a sociological tract rather than a children's story.

Sylvie's life-work is to eliminate the old Adam from her brother Bruno's makeup. So she arranges the letters E. V. I. L. on a board and asks him what it spells. 'Why it's LIVE backwards,' he exclaims.

'How *did* you manage to see that?' she says.

'I just twiddled my eyes,' said Bruno, 'and then I saw it directly.'

Carroll had been twiddling his eyes for thirty years or more, flashing a mirror to the young to show them what their adults were up to. (Indeed he seemed to lose interest in his little friends when they grew up.)

His most likeable character is the ridiculous White Knight in *Through the Looking Glass and What Alice Found There* (1872), whose sinistral inventions won't fit a dextral world, yet is the only character with the wit or courtesy to show Alice the way out of the wood when she is lost.

According to Professor Empson (like Carroll a mathematician and poet) 'The White Knight stands for the Victorian scientist who was felt to have invented a new kind of Roman virtue; (who) . . . without sensuality, without self seeking, without claiming any but a fragment of knowledge . . . goes on labouring at his absurd but fruitful conceptions.'[33]

Lewis Carroll tapped the lode of non-Aristotelian speculation that in the mind of Alfred Korzybski was to provide a technique for coping with the advance of science. He also foreshadows Norbert Weiner's warning that cybernetics poses the same moral problems as theology once did. Other twentieth-century Carrollingians, besides these two, were A. S. Eddington and Albert Einstein.[34]

This can be abundantly illustrated, especially from *Through the Looking Glass and What Alice Found There* (1872),

> 'I wonder if all the things move along with us,' thought poor puzzled Alice. And the Queen seemed to guess her thought for she cried 'Faster! Don't try to talk!'
>
> Alice runs till she is exhausted and stops to lean against a tree which is the very one they started from and exclaims, 'In *our* country . . . you'd generally get to somewhere else—if you ran very fast for a long time as we've been doing.'
>
> 'A slow sort of country!' said the Queen.
>
> 'Now, *here*, you see, it takes all the running you can do, to keep in the same place. If you want to get somewhere else you must run twice as fast as that!'[35]

The Queen's appeal for a quickening of imagination has given rise to what has been called the 'runcible' stream in speculation about science and the world. Brian Aldiss, himself a distinguished modern exponent of the genre now known as science fiction, contends that it 'owes a greater debt to Lewis Carroll than to H. G. Wells'. He identifies the conversation between Alice and the Unicorn as a prototype of future confrontations between humans and aliens.

'I always thought (says Alice) Unicorns were fabulous monsters too! I never saw one alive before.'

'Well, now that we *have* seen each other,' said the Unicorn, 'if you believe in me, I'll believe in you. Is that a bargain?'[36]

XII THE LAST TERRESTRIAL TERMINUS: AFRICA

The fearful wonderlands opened up by Darwin and Galton were doubly relevant, for the primeval jungle of Africa was acquiring an economic importance at the same time as ideas of natural selection and genetic endowment were stirring popular imagination. So when a writer offered an escape route from the unpleasant necessity of thinking out their implications, he scored an enormous success. With the story of Tarzan, an orphan born of English parents, marooned in Africa and reared by an ape foster mother, Edgar Rice Burroughs struck the right note, more especially since he caused Tarzan to fall in love with an American girl. A town in California was, indeed, named Tarzania in his honour.

As an exploiter of ideas brought to the surface of popular consciousness, Edgar Rice Burroughs had no equal. The significance of so-called 'canals' on Mars (first announced by Schiaparelli in 1894) had already been explored by Garnett P. Serviss in *Edison's Conquest of Mars* (1898), a hymn to the emergent technocracy, and Mark Wicks' *To Mars via the Moon* (1911), a deliberate attempt to popularise the work of the astronomer Percival Lowell, who considered Mars to be inhabited and predicted the existence of Planet X (discovered in 1930 and named Pluto). Indeed, one commentator has discovered a tendency among American writers to regard Martians as in the vanguard of terrestrial evolution.[37] But to Edgar Rice Burroughs, Mars was an even bigger playground than Africa, and in some ten novels, beginning with *Under the Moon of Mars* (1912), he romped, disclosing a canvas of tomorrow that reached a climax in the trilogy *The Moon Maid* (1923), *The Moon Men* (1926), and the *Red Hawk* (1926): a bloody story of four centuries up to 2430 in which the earth is invaded by Orthis with his Kalkares. Burroughs' preoccupation with war is significant. For he was an advocate of non-intervention in the First World War, reinforcing his beliefs with a story of the world in 2137: 'Beyond Thirty' which envisaged the First World War lasting till 1972, leaving Europe isolated from America and others by the 30th degree of longitude. One man, Jefferson Turck, breaks the barrier and finds Europe at war with China and Ethiopia whilst Britain is split by the tribal warfare of the royal family.[38] *The Moon Men* (1926) envisaged the world of 2050 united around America and England.[39]

His astonishing success, however, was due to his provision of imaginative comestibles for the American appetite for 'futuribles': an appetite that had grown with feeding on the unfolding 'vista of ages'. An indication as to how it had been whetted comes from Missouri as early as 1880, when William McClung Paxton, a Missouri lawyer, was moved to hymn:

> . . . the bright glories this land
> In the next hundred years shall possess
> When genius and science, with industry's hand,
> This country and people shall bless

His Darwinian (the adjective refers to Erasmus rather than Charles) predictive rhapsody envisaged colour photography, artificial weather, and new sources of power and transport when:

> . . . a motor, much stronger than steam, had appeared,
> Yet cheap, economic and mild

enabling the United States to support a billion people, among whom:

> . . . men, on light wings, in the atmosphere sported
> Or walked, as they pleased, on the ground.
> With the new motive power, one man could do more
> Than fifty, without it, could do.[39]

But this vein of speculation marks a new tack on which we must now turn.

Chapter Six

BELLAMY AND THE MECHANICAL MILLENARIANS

I THE AMERICAN HUNGER FOR FUTURIBLES: BOSTON A.D. 2000

So sharp was the American appetite for pictures of the future that the editor of the *New York Herald* asked Jules Verne in 1885 for an imaginative account of life in the United States in a thousand years' time.[1] This editor, Gordon Bennett, was an enterprising man. Fifteen years earlier he had sent Stanley to find Livingstone, regarded Paris as much his home as New York, and established the Gordon Bennett trophies for yacht, car, and aeroplane racing. Verne caught him up in his story as Francis Bennett, editor of the *Earth Herald*: Francis has more power than his supposititious ancestor Gordon, since he can direct scientists to do what he pleases —from controlling the weather to revolving the moon. Large-scale engineering schemes like melting the polar icecap, transporting cities, and investigating atomic structure are explored.

Verne's shrewd impression of the shape of things to come is reflected in his forecast that Britain would be an American, Indian, or Russian colony. Moreover, Bennett copes with the Chinese population-explosion by imposing the death penalty on all who break the laws governing birth control. For solar and isothermal electricity have abolished the need for servile labour in agriculture and commerce. Television—by wire, and undersea transport tubes —facilitate centralisation. Hence the name of the capital of the U.S.A.—Centropolis—which is virtually the capital of the world.[2]

However flattering Verne's picture of the United States in the world economy of the future might be, it was sufficiently barbed to warrant Gordon Bennett's not publishing it.[3]

Perhaps it was also too remote. The approaching millennium,

as opposed to that coming afterwards, was an easier task and the person who visualised it was Edward Bellamy:

> Suddenly, one day, in looking at his own children, and reflecting that he could not place them beyond the chance of want by any industry or forecast or providence; and that the status meant the same impossibility for others which it meant for him.[4]

Bellamy was inspired to read widely on economics and government and to write *Looking Backward 2000–1887* (1888). Like Verne, the notion of a universally socialised state possessed him, but unlike Verne, he brought back the time originally set for its consummation from A.D. 3000 to A.D. 2000.[5]

Whether its specifically millenarian setting in the Boston of A.D. 2000 or its exultant assumption that, by that time a technological apocalypse would have renovated society was responsible, certainly no Utopian novel had such an immediate and striking appeal. This eulogy of mechanical energy-slaves reached more readers than the previously most successful American novel—also a sentimental picture of a human energy-slave—*Uncle Tom's Cabin*.[6] Imitated, continued, reviled, and refuted in well over sixty further books,[7] *Looking Backward* was adopted by a religious sect—the Theosophists;[8] became the manifesto of a political party—the Nationalist Party of America:[9] and virtually made peering into the future a respectable literary activity, to be differentiated from calculating the numbers of the beast.[10]

The story is based on a simple Rip-van-Winkle formula. Julian West, normally a tense and sleepless person, is given a sedative in the Boston of 1887, and is excavated from a cellar a hundred and thirteen years later in a state of immaculate preservation. When he reappears above ground he finds a new social order in full swing:

> The nation was organised as the one great business corporation in which all other corporations were absorbed; it became the one capitalist in the place of all other capitalists, the sole employer, the final monopoly in which all previous and lesser monopolies were swallowed up, a monopoly in the profits and economies of which all citizens shared. The Epoch of Trusts had ended in the Great Trust.[11]

Bellamy described his story as:

> . . . a fairy tale of social felicity. There was no thought of contriving a house which practical men might live in, but merely of hanging in

mid-air, far out of the reach of the sordid and material world of the present, a cloud-palace for an ideal humanity.[12]

But according to another source he had:

the definite purpose of trying to reason out a method of economic organisation by which the republic might guarantee the livelihood and material welfare of its citizens on a basis of equality corresponding to and supplanting their political equality.[13]

Certainly 'social felicity' was insured: 'the nation guarantees' observed the hero, Julian West, 'the nurture, education and comfortable maintenance of every citizen from the cradle to the grave'.[14] All between the ages of twenty-one and forty-five were compulsory members of the Industrial Army, which deployed them in assignments for which their physical and mental endowments best suited them and which were most profitable to the nation and most satisfactory to themselves. Hours of labour were varied in inverse ratio to the attractiveness of the assignment. Wages were not in money but in credit-cards, issued annually and representing an equal share of the national wealth. The credit-card was used for purchases at the government stores and items bought were set off against it.

These credit-cards were also issued to all those over forty-five who had served their time in the Industrial Army. Everyone had the same since 'all men who do their best do the same'.[15] Nor could they be exchanged, for all surplus credit reverted to its source, the Government, at the end of the year.

The awakened Julian West makes a living by lecturing on his own day and age for the citizens, and by doing so, as well as in his softer interludes with Edith Leete—whose family were very kind to him—he can indicate just how much things have changed since he was put to sleep. The new Boston is part of a new world-state. War is abolished, labour is organised and retirement obligatory at forty-five. Technological marvels abound from the radio to a pneumatic shopping delivery system. The state provides free education up to the age of twenty-one, houses, parks, and every amenity, prints books and fosters matrimony. Julian West indicates clearly that progress to the new Boston of A.D. 2000, where all were happy consuming members of a vast industrial army, working, living, and loving to piped music, was being held up by the monopolists subsidising socialist agitators to wave the red flag and so frighten people away from demanding that the means of production be nationalised.

Bellamy predicted that the final consolidation of industry and ensuing nationalisation would take place in the early 1900s. By the year 2000 human 'beasts of prey' would have been transformed by the environmental revolution, and the abolition of hoardable dollars. Competition for money would disappear, but for merit would increase, hence colleges would be thronged. Hours of labour would vary with the collective desire: a teacher might work eight hours a day to a miner's two.

II THE DEBATE: WILLIAM MORRIS'S LONDON A.D. 2012

This 'cockneyfied paradise' of 'industrious professional middle-class men of today purified from their crime of complicity with the monopolist' and becoming 'independent instead of being, as they now are, parasitical'[16] shocked William Morris.

He wished to emphasise the relations of man to man rather than man to machinery and within six months had begun to publish *Chapters from a Utopian Romance* emphasising this by its significant subtitle: *An epoch of rest*. For it was the restlessness of America that Morris saw as dangerous. His sleeper wakes from a sleep after travelling in 'that vapour bath of hurried and discontented humanity, a carriage of the underground railway', and finds himself in Hammersmith of the year A.D. 2012, on a new Thames-side:

> The soap-works with their smoke-vomiting chimneys were gone; the engineers' works gone; the lead works gone; and no sound of rivetting or hammering came down the west wind from Thorny-crofts.[17]

The great clearing of houses had taken place in 1955; the 'beastly monuments to fools and knaves' had been cleared from West-minster Abbey, and the Houses of Parliament had become 'a sort of subsidiary market and storage place for manure'. Idleness had been overcome. After the great battle of Trafalgar Square in 1952, factories had become banded-workshops—places where people collect who want to work together. Work itself had become localised since 'power was now available at the places where they lived'. People lived till they were ninety, and one veteran of 105 lived in the British Museum. This veteran, Old Hammond, tells the story of what had happened. Manchester had disappeared, so had most great towns: 'we discourage centralisation all we can, and we have long ago dropped the pretension to be the market of the world'. This, together with gardens, woods and public eating-houses, was made possible by 'the great change in the use of mechanical force'.[18]

But above all the industrial pace maker, America, which Bellamy had so idealised, had undergone a radical change:

> The Northern parts of America—that part of it, above all, which was once the United States—are now and will be for a long while a great resource to us. For these lands, and, I say, especially the northern parts of America, suffered so terribly from the full force of the last days of civilisation, and became such horrible places to live in, that they are now very backward in all that makes life pleasant. Indeed, one may say that for nearly a hundred years the people of the northern parts of America have been engaged in gradually making a dwelling-place out of a stinking heap; and there is still a great deal to do, especially as the country is so big.[19]

These changes, especially in England, had only been brought about by civil war. For when the upper and middle classes were convinced that the Communism which lay ahead would be un-endurable, they 'set on foot a counter revolution':

> Bands of young men, like the marauders in the great strike . . . armed themselves and drilled, and began on any opportunity or pretence to skirmish with the people in the streets. The Government neither helped them nor put them down, but stood by, hoping that something might come of it. These 'Friends of Order', as they were called, had some successes at first, and grew bolder. . . .
>
> A sort of irregular war was carried on with varied success all over the country; and at last the Government, which had at first pretended to ignore the struggle, or treat it as mere rioting, definitely declared for the 'Friends of Order'.
>
> It was too late. The end, it was seen clearly, must be either absolute slavery for all but the privileged, or a system of life founded on equality and Communism.[20]

Needless to say the latter alternative prevailed.

When it did, the commune, ward, or parish became the basic unit of management, working through the Mote. It was in opposition to 'the so-called science of the nineteenth century' which was 'in the main an appendage to the commercial system; nay not seldom an appendage to the police of that system'. It was medieval in form since to the medieval spirit 'heaven and the life of the next world was such a reality, that it became to them a part of the life upon the earth'.[21]

The message of the vision, conveyed by the eyes of Ellen, the girl for whom Morris's dreamer feels great affection, was:

> Go back again, now you have seen us, and your outward eyes have learned that in spite of all the infallible maxims of your day there is yet a time of rest in store for the world, when mastery has changed into fellowship—but not before.[22]

Morris really looked backward—to the golden days of King Arthur—and the focus of his vision of an ideal society, obscurely limned in an early sketch for an Arthurian epic, was a theme that captured others, too, from Tennyson to Swinburne, Lawrence Binyon, Arthur Symons, Thomas Hardy, T. S. Eliot (*The Waste Land* owes something to Miss Jessie Weston's theories of the Origins of the Grail), and John Masefield. Nor can we omit, of course, Charles Williams, whom we shall meet again.[23]

In turn, Morris influenced W. D. Howells, who perhaps because he lacked what Henry James described as 'a really *grasping* imagination',[24] regarded Tolstoy as 'precisely the human being' with whom he found himself 'in greatest intimacy'.[25]

Two years in the Boston of 1889 to 1891, and intensive discussion with groups of like-minded men and women led Howells to sketch a Morrisian commonwealth based on manual labour and craftsmanship in *A Traveller from Altruria* (1894). The traveller, Aristides Homos, is the guest of the novelist at a summer hotel, where a banker, a professor, a minister, a manufacturer, and various women inadvertently explain American as compared to Altrurian practice.

Aristides marries and carries his bride back to Altruria, and their letters form the sequel—*Through the Eye of the Needle* (1907). In a public lecture on Altruria, he explains how 'The Accumulation' (capitalism), had been voted out of power and 'Neighbourliness' (Altrurism) took its place.

Howells' sympathy for Bellamy was qualified. He confessed to not being attracted by 'the material character of the happiness which West's story promises men when they shall begin to do justice and to share equally in the fruits of the toil which operates life . . . I should have preferred,' he told his readers in the *Atlantic Monthly*, 'if I had been the chooser, to have the millennium much simpler, much more independent of modern invention.' Like Bellamy, Howells involuntarily stimulated a social movement, in this case, the short-lived Utopian community of Altruria which took shape in 1894 under Edward B. Payne in California. Payne also had other Utopian connections. He was a friend and associate of Edward Everett Hale, perhaps better known as the first man to write a story about an earth satellite—'the Brick Moon'. [26]

III   THE ANTI-ARTHURIAN CONNECTICUT YANKEE

King Arthur's world (or its American variant Altruria), was mercilessly caricatured by Mark Twain. Reading *Looking Backward* on the train on 5th March 1889, he found it 'a fascinating book' and a month later described it as 'the latest and best of all the Bibles' and its author as a 'man who has made the accepted heaven paltry by inventing a better one on earth'.[27] Bellamy later responded to Mark Twain's invitation to visit him at Hartford on 9th July 1890.

By that time Twain had published *A Connecticut Yankee At King Arthur's Court* (1889). In this a 'Yankee of Yankees' who 'had learned to make everything: guns, revolvers, cannon, boilers, engines, all sorts of labor-saving machinery . . . anything a body wanted—anything in the world, it didn't make any difference what; and if there wasn't any quick new-fangled way to make a thing, I could invent one—and do it as easy as rolling off a log,'[28] found himself transported from the America of 1879 to the Britain of 528 o.s. Finding himself 'a giant among pygmies, a master intelligence among intellectual moles', he soon outwits Merlin (personifying magic and superstition), by science and forethought. He acquires a realistic but unromantic name that 'fell casually from the lips of a blacksmith'—Sir Boss—and gets to work converting Camelot into Hartford, Connecticut:

In various quiet nooks and corners I had the beginnings of all sorts of industries under way—nuclei of future vast factories, the iron and steel missionaries of my future civilisation. In these were gathered together the brightest young minds I could find, and I kept agents out raking the country for more, all the time. I was training a crowd of ignorant folk into experts—experts in every sort of handwork and scientific calling. These nurseries of mine went smoothly and privately along undisturbed in their obscure country retreats, for nobody was allowed to come into their precincts without a special permit—for I was afraid of the Church.[29]

For the Church indeed he had no high opinion. She:

had converted a nation of men to a nation of worms. . . . She was wise, subtle, and knew more than one way to skin a cat or a nation; she invented 'divine right of things' and propped it all around, brick by brick, with the Beatitudes—wrenching them from their good purpose to make them fortify an evil one.[30]

For he was in competition. His 'Man-Factory' under Clarence (Amyas le Paulet), was 'turning, groping and grubbing automata into *men*'[31] and gave no admission to 'chattel of the church, nor bondslave of pope or bishop'.[32] So he concentrated on boys, before they could be corrupted. He was able to gloat: 'My boys are experts in all sorts of things, from the stoning up of a well to the constructing of a mathematical instrument.'[33] The Round Table is employed for 'business purposes'. Schools, mines, factories, the telegraph and telephone indicate that 'slavery was dead and gone' and 'the march of civilisation was begun'. The church steps in and places Britain under an interdict. Hank and his ally Clarence, with some fifty-two boys, are confined to a cave and have to fight for their lives with guns, dynamite, and electric fences. The fences kill so many that the stench of the corpses asphyxiates them. Hank is hypnotised by Merlin in disguise and sleeps on till the nineteenth century, when he can give his diary to Mark Twain. If Twain's hero 'Sir Boss' could claim that he had 'exposed the nineteenth to the inspection of the sixth', Mark Twain himself could claim to have exposed the considerably vestigial elements of the sixth for the inspection of nineteenth-century Britain. That is why the illustrations for the book were drawn from 'life' by Daniel Carter Beard, who brought out the allegory that 'the reader might have missed'.

Its tragic ending saves *A Connecticut Yankee* from being a trivial book and places it, as Kenneth Lynn remarks, 'not with the shallow prophecies of Bellamy and Howells, but alongside *The*

Education of Henry Adams'.[34] Like Henry Adams, Twain was really a prophet. He scribbled in his notebook:

> For a play: America in 1985. The Pope here & an Inquisition. The age of darkness back again. Pope is temporal despot *too*. A fitted aristocracy & primogeniture. Europe is *republican* & full of science & invention—none allowed here.[35]

IV THE MANIPULATION OF JULIAN WEST, THE CRYSTAL BUTTON SOCIETIES, AND SOCIOLAND

For the religious nature of Bellamy's millenium was obvious to others than Twain. Howells observed that Bellamy had 'revived throughout Christendom the faith in a millenium', while the foundress of the Theosophists described *Looking Backward* as 'admirably representing the Theosophical idea of what should be the first great step towards the full realisation of universal brotherhood'. So Theosophists rallied to the Nationalist Clubs which sprang up in the wake of Bellamy's book in Boston, New York, Chicago, and California. But when the 'Nationalist Clubs' became political the Theosophists abandoned them.[36]

A regular theo- (or rather socio-) logical debate erupted around the significance of Julian West, the 'prophet' of mechanisation. His adventures thirty-seven years on[37] were described by Ernst Müller. His 'son' was the central figure of yet another prophecy by the learned and imaginative American rabbi Solomon Schindler,[38] whilst his successor's lectures at Shawmut College, a Professor Won Lung Li—are the vehicle for A. D. Vinton's *Looking Further Backward* (1890).

One of Bellamy's critics was Richard C. Michaelis (1839–1909), the editor of the Chicago *Freie Presse*, an organ of German social-democrats, who published *Looking Forward* and *Looking Further Forward* in the same year (1890). The latter evoked a vigorous pro-Bellamy reply by Ludwig A. Geissler in the form of a sequel to *Looking Backward* entitled *Looking Beyond* (1891). The possibility of establishing Bellamy's industrial army, together with industrial cities and industrial army-homes, was canvassed by F. S. Giles who outlined some preliminary steps in *The Industrial Army* (1896). He had previously given his view of the future in *Shadows Before: or a century onward* (1894). An equally bitter attack on the very concept of an industrial army came from the Anglophile philologist David Hilton Wheeler whose essay on *Our Industrial Utopia and its Unhappy Citizens* (1895), sounded a note to become all too familiar in the century to follow.

Just such another secular religion—the Crystal Button societies —based on the teachings of John Costor that every man should be true to himself and others—is outlined in Chauncey Thomas's *The Crystal Button* (1891). The Costorians initiate a convention of a council of all nations in A.D. 3500 at Carrefour, a great city 'located on the isthmus midway between the two Americas'. An international police force, a court of arbitration for each division of the world and a Grand Council of all Nations followed. A new chronology begins. 1392 years later (i.e. in the forty-ninth century of the Christian era), this civilisation is visited by a Bostonian— Paul Prognosis—on a ten-year leave of mental absence from his native city. He finds that legislative assemblies, elections, parties, and politics have also disappeared and in their place is a humane administration known as 'The Government of Settled Forms'. Various departments of government work in conjunction with the Congress of Nations. This Congress established a universal unit of valuation 'based on the world's surplus of food-products as accurately reported each decade, proportionate to the world's population at the same date'. Based on such surplus food-products, certificates (like Bellamy's 'credit-cards') circulate throughout the world. Universal government annuities and insurance remove the evils consequent on economic dependence. All this is necessary, for, as Paul Prognosis is to learn, the population is 'vast beyond the imagination of the nineteenth century' and now covers 'nearly every other habitable portion of the globe'.

Described in the preface as 'a fitting companion piece to Mr. Edward Bellamy's *Looking Backward*', *The Crystal Button* literally describes a push-button society. Paul's best friend is Professor Prosper of the City of Tone who informs him that transport is publicly owned, criminals are hospitalised for 'moral illness, and that the white crystal button symbolises the secret spring of society'.[39]

This prefiguration of a smoothly running administrative world was even more immediately envisaged by King C. Gillette, inventor of the safety razor, who proposed that population and production should be concentrated round the vast power resources of Niagara Falls. Large apartment blocks with central kitchens were to house equally large labour battalions. Gillette offered a million dollars to Theodore Roosevelt if he would serve as president of his 'World Corporation', as he registered it in Arizona. Roosevelt refused.[40]

Conversely the unsuccessful inventor of sewing machines (especially of the principle of the continuous feed, the vertical needle, and the horizontal table), John Bachelder (1817–1906), came forward with a gloomy picture of the year *2050 A.D.: Electrical Developments at Atlantis By a Former Resident of the Hub* (1890).

A similar belief in potential environmental change led Albert Chavannes, a Tennessee builder and timber factor, to construct an imaginary commonwealth in Africa, to be established in 1950. This commonwealth has, oddly enough, a capital city called Spencer. Its 50,000 inhabitants (as described by Samuel Balcom, the equally imaginary visitor who reports on it in the year 1950), are furnished, free of cost, with all the bread they wish to consume, all the gas they can burn, and water they can drink. Hospitals and asylums, schools, parks, laundries, and clubs are free; the aged and needy are pensioned, while 'all methods through which one class of people can live at the expense of the other' have been eliminated. As his guide informs him with a twinkle in his eye, 'all governments are somewhat Socialist, some a little more, others a little less. We are a little more.' *What Samuel Balcom saw in Socioland* is the subtitle of Albert Chavannes' *The Future Commonwealth* (1892),[41] an amplified supplement: *In Brighter Climes, or Life in Socioland* (1897).

V   THE GROUNDSWELL OF FANTASY

Bellamy's work strengthened the growing tradition of American popular-science writing.[42] It was thanks to Jefferson's biographer, George Tucker—the first professor of moral philosophy at his own non-sectarian University of Virginia—that these predictive fantasies multiplied. Tucker's *A Voyage to the Moon* (1827), is made possible by the metal lunarium, which, by offsetting gravity, enables Joseph Atterley to make an airship to visit the Glonglins, who had internal combustion engines operated by powder; the Morosotians who wore outrageous clothing, and the Okalbians who enjoyed birth control.

His pupil, Edgar Allan Poe, envisaged the moon as the site of a temple of Daphnis by the year 2848. Pundita is in a balloon over an ocean, worried because it is going at only 100 miles an hour whereas most of them can go at 150. Railway travel is at twice that speed on rails fifty feet apart. America is an empire of which New York is a pleasure island.[43]

Just as Poe may have owed something to Professor Tucker, so Bellamy may have owed something to Professor John Macnie who, under the pseudonym of Ismar Thiusen, published *The Diothas; or A Far Look Ahead* in 1883. Bellamy's biographer mentions the 'tradition' at the University of North Dakota that the two of them 'had gone over the themes' before *The Diothas* was published.[44]

But Macnie looks much further forward than any of them—to the ninety-sixth century, when Manhattan had become a warehouse, the world was a federal republic, controlling its own climate, utilising its sewage, making synthetic food, communicating by telephone, reckoning on a duodecimal system, and enjoying a system of universal education that was interrupted at seventeen for eight years of labour service. All honeymoons were to be spent at the University.

Though Macnie expressly disavows 'the communistic ideas now so attractive to many', he nevertheless foresees the state exercising rights of vocational guidance, insurance, and controlling inherited wealth.

Four years later—and a few years before Bellamy—Anna Bowman Dodd took up the theme in *The Republic of the Future* (1887) where everything is done by machinery since food is in pellets; children were reared by the state, and women were so free that they had invaded even the foreign service so that foreign statesmen were willing 'to concede anything rather than . . . continue negotiations with them'. Furniture was relegated to museums; 'erotic' sentiment had decayed, and leisure produced such boredom that the arts had languished.[45]

Far more sophisticated is the world of 2000 in J. J. Astor's *A Journey in Other Worlds* (1894). Energy abounds. It is captured in the hollow masts of electric ships, or by solar mirrors that enable Africa to support a larger white population than America. Electricity is broadcast, and trains are moved by powerful magnets every fifty miles. Aluminium aeroplanes, electric cars, water spiders (like modern hovercraft), make travel a commonplace; metals are obtained by tapping the core of the earth with freezing drills controlled by electronic eyes. Rainmaking is a science. But above all, tidal dynamos provide the power to drain and fill the Arctic Oceans to vary the weight of the Pole.

Tiring of life in this supermachine world, the chief engineer of the Terrestrial Axis Straightening Company, Col. Bearwarden with his friends Dr. Cartland and Ayrault the scientist, make up their minds to light out on a voyage to Jupiter. There they find themselves behind the times, meeting mastodons, dinosaurs, and pterodactyls. Then they visit Saturn where they are ahead of time and a spirit allows one of the travellers to see his own funeral.

Astor could see that such forward projection was itself a necessary ingredient in education:

> The protracted struggle between science and the classics appears to be drawing to a close, with victory about to perch on the banner of science, as a perusal of almost any university or college catalogue shows. Since the classics have been thoroughly and painfully threshed out, and it seems impossible that anything new can be unearthed,' Astor suggested, 'how much more interesting it would be if . . . instead of reiterating our past achievements, the magazines and literature of the period should devote their consideration to what we do *not* know.' [46]

Authors seemed to follow his advice. Frank R. Stockton (1834–1902), laid the scene of *The Great Stone of Sardis* (1898) in the year 1947 when Roger Clews and his scientifically-minded fiancée Margaret Raleigh, working from his laboratory in Sardis, New Jersey, invent a submarine that navigates under the icefloes to discover and chart the North Pole, as well as discovering that the centre of the earth is a huge diamond. It has been suggested that Sardis was modelled on Edison's laboratory at Menlo Park.[47]

Bellamy's own socialism, more explicit after the publication of his *Equality* (1897), evoked yet more books. George A Sanders' *Reality: or, Law and Order vs Anarchy and Socialism* (1898), made a strong case against him. Bradford Peck, a publicist for the Co-operative Association of America, has in *The World of a Department Store* (1900), his hero Percy Brantford falling asleep in 1899 to awake on 7th April 1925 to find that over the intervening quarter of a century 'The Co-operative city of Maine' had been built.[48]

VI THE APOTHEOSIS OF THE MACHINE

How reflexive this habit of mind was becoming amongst academic scientists can be seen from the writings of Simon Newcomb (1835–1909). Like Macnie, a professor of mathematics, Newcomb indulged himself in an operational fantasy of the future. Having taught mathematics to the U.S. Navy for thirty-six years, he signalised the advent of the new century by envisaging life in 1941. His hero, significantly enough, a physicist, Professor Campbell, discovers 'etherine' an anti-gravitational device, a 'thermic' engine, and a cheap recovery technique for aluminium. These enable him to build a fleet of aeroplanes and submarines manned by his own pupils. They sink the world's navies, disarm the world's troops, and ensure universal peace under the physicist who is accorded the title of the book *His Wisdom the Defender*.

Nor was this confined to academic scientists.[49] In his shrewd and comprehensive appraisal of what he calls the 'economic novelists' in America, Walter Fuller Taylor observed that:

They put on record—indeed, with virtual unanimity they put on *favorable* record—the coming of the Machine. Seldom if ever do they make the Machines *per se* the object of critical attack. American fiction offers nothing comparable to Samuel Butler's ingenious questioning of the Machine process itself, nothing comparable to Ruskin's bitter hostility toward the factory system entire, and little that parallels William Morris's deep concern over the preservation of the values of craftsmanship. In America, in the course of the conquest of immense distances . . . the usefulness of the machine was a thing difficult indeed to call in question; and, whether because of a tacit understanding of that difficulty, or because of some other causative factor, American novelists practically never did so. Instead, they mostly agreed with Mark Twain in welcoming the Machine, seeing in mechanical power, properly controlled, simply a means of realizing the old democratic dream of universal material well-being.[50]

But as Twain might have reminded him, the Mad Philosopher 'merely builds prognostications, not prophecies . . . builds them out of history and statistics, using the facts of the past to forecast the probabilities of the future'.[51]

And these facts of the past were, at this very time, being used to forecast the probabilities of the future. As the historian Brooks Adams wrote to his brother Henry on 18th November 1901:

> In theory you believe as I do that men are automatic, that we cannot do otherwise than we do—that there is no advance and in practice you are always worrying for an American Eutopia. You complain because we don't find something new under the Sun. Dear man—we are only repeating Babylon. We are going over the same ground only faster. Were you to discover Eutopia, nature would stop. There can be no American system. It's a contradiction to every philosophical principle. We are having our little day just now. Let us thank God and enjoy it. Those who follow will pay. We may shine through.[52]

VII THE FRENCH ATTACK ON SOULLESS MECHANISM

Bellamy's expression of American belief in the industrial Americanisation of Europe provoked sharp protests from the French utopist disciple of Paul Verlaine: Gustave le Rouge.[53] With Gustave Guitton he wrote a two-volume story of an Edison-type American engineer called Ned Hattison, who with a food king, William Boltyn, plans the scientific destruction of Europe. On the other hand, a French group of scientists led by Professor Golbert of the Academy of Sciences and Olivier Coronal, an inventor, is anxious to strengthen the comity of nations by an undersea railway. This is destroyed by the American millionaires. Their own secret arsenal of iron men and frightful weapons, and its inventor, Ned Hattison, are in turn destroyed by Olivier Coronal. Undeterred, the American financiers resort to psychological warfare and launch squads of mind-readers who leech ideas from European scientists and project them telekinetically to the U.S.A. But here too they are foiled by Professor Golbert and his friends. *La Conspiration des milliardaires* (1899) was one of Le Rouge's many utopist science-fiction stories. Others were the four-volume *Princess of the Airs* (1902) a Robinsonade centring round passengers of an 'aero scaphe' shipwrecked in Asia, *Le sous-marin 'Jules Verne'* (1903) and *Le prisonnier de la planète Mars*

(1908–9). The obviously Wellsian atmosphere of the last mentioned, together with the superhuman quality of his later heroes like Doctor Cornélius, Doctor Mohr, or the millionaire detective Todd Marvel, lead us naturally to the growth in Europe of the concept of a 'superman', as opposed to Bellamy's 'Super-System'. Doctor Cornélius also posed the conflict between good science (represented by the naturalist Prosper Bondonnat) and bad science (represented by the surgeon Cornélius Kramm), the former, helped by an eccentric English peer, the latter by malignant Germans like Fritz Kramm and Baruch Jorgell. 'Good' science has a utopian Breton setting; bad science, international hideouts in the Aleutians.[54]

Chapter Seven

SUPERMAN AND THE SYSTEM

I KINETIC UTOPIANISM

'I class with George Griffith as a purveyor of world "*pseudo-scientific* extravaganzas",' complained H. G. Wells to Arnold Bennett in 1902.[1] But, he added confidently, 'There's a quality in the worst of my so-called pseudo-scientific (imbecile adjective) stuff that the American does not master which differentiates it from Jules Verne, e.g. just as Swift is differentiated from fantasia —isn't there? There is something other than either story writing or artistic merit which has emerged through the series of my books, something one might regard as a new system of ideas.'

This 'new system of ideas' Wells considered was to be found 'in *Anticipations* especially chapter 15 and it's in my Royal Institution Lecture, and it's also in *The First Men in the Moon* and *The Invisible Man* and Chaffery's chapter in *Love and Mr. L.*'

The 'new system' was operational or, as Wells called it, kinetic utopianism and it owed as much to Nietzsche as to Darwin. The process of evolution, argued Nietzsche, would, if left to itself, only lead to the 'last man', a complacent, conformist, uncreative hedonist. From such a fate mankind could be rescued by overmen. Overmen overcame themselves and, therefore, led others. Only frustration of this will to become perfect (i.e. a superman), led to the base desire to seek power over others. Nietzsche challenged Christianity not in Butlerian terms, but as ministering to weakness. It was 'the revolt of failures'; the antithesis to the *Ubermensch*, or drive to achieve a higher and more powerful state of being. To perfect himself, recreate himself, become an 'overman', man had to acquire God-like qualities. This will to power (like the *élan vital* of Bergson or the *libido* of Jung), had to establish values around Reason and Eros.

91

Nietzsche saw contemporary man on the broken icefloes of the middle ages and forecast that the twentieth century would be the classic age of war, ending with the emergence of overman, served by a slave class. To avoid the inertia of China and the cash-nexus (a Carlylean overtone), of America, Europe would unite.[2]

'Remain faithful to the earth, and do not believe those who speak to you of other worldly hopes,' he cried in the prologue to *Thus Spoke Zarathustra* (1883–4). A messiah, not so much of a religion as an anti-religion,[3] he gave to the world what he thought was a fifth gospel in the long unfinished series of allegorical images. It begins with Zarathustra—the Iranian name of a Persian prophet whom the Greeks knew as Zoroaster—going up into a mountain and staying for ten years. Emerging to the market place he finds a tightrope-walker (mankind), walking on a rope, from which he is knocked off by a fool (a nineteenth-century intellectual), and killed. The fool then advises Zarathustra to leave town. This he does, dragging with him the corpse, which he stows in a tree.

Zarathustra now decides to appeal only to the few select. In the third part of the allegory, he surveys the city (symbolising society), and presages it must be destroyed by fire. Then, he assembles men possessing elements of supermen in his cave to tell them 'we do not in the least wish for the Kingdom of Heaven. We have become men. Therefore it is the Kingdom of Earth we wish for.'[4]

Nietzsche's views became a bible to those depressed by scientific advance, by the elevation of mediocrity, and by the democratic doctrine of progress. They were summed up in another work four years later, entitled *Götzen-Dämmerung* (The Twilight of the Idols), with its characteristic subtitle *Wie man mit dem Hammer philosophiert* (How one Philosophises with a Hammer).

English ears, attuned to Thomas Carlyle's conviction that 'All history, is an imprisoned Epic, nay, an imprisoned Psalm or Prophecy',[5] and his apostrophe 'Millennium of Anarchies;—abridge it, spend your heart's blood upon abridging it, ye Heroic Wise that are to come',[6] received Nietzsche's prophetic message loud and clear. So did German ones.

II THE GERMAN FANTASTS: LASSWITZ TO WALTHER RATHENAU

That religion could no longer motivate social improvement was the constant refrain of Kurt Lasswitz, pupil and biographer of the physicist-psychologist Georg Fechner. Kurt Lasswitz saw that it had been replaced by the power of man over nature, 'the conviction of the possibility of theoretically understanding and technically controlling nature. Modern man attained maturity with the growth of the natural sciences.' He also regarded an ideal future state as a chiliastic vestige, and revolution as an inadequate substitute for the exercise of reason and hard work. Only technological progress could 'idealise' society by lightening the burden of maintaining life and diffusing ethics and aesthetics to ever-widening circles. From *Bilder aus der Zukunft* (1878) to *Sternendau: Die Planze vom Neptusmond* (1909), Lasswitz published a number of optimistic fantasies of the future. One of the stories in *Bilder aus der Zukunft* is set in the year 2371 and visualises the city standing on pillars with farms beneath and gardens above; a Poet (Magnet) and a Scientist (Oxygen) quarrel over a girl player of the 'perfume piano' which exudes odours to correspond with its music. Against Oxygen's view that ultimately all the arts will be abolished, Magnet believes that the elemental forces of the will will prevail. Their quarrel leads to the death of the pianist and the escape of the scientist to the planets.

Another story in the same book is set in the year 3877 when moods and feelings can be transmitted by a psycho-kinetic motor. Another scientist also in love with a musician finds that a mathematical formula prevents their union. The villain, Atom, looks to a time when various attributes will be discharged by various types of human beings.

Auf zwei Planeten (1897) visualises the Martians visiting the earth in space ships, bringing news of their world, where solar energy, moving roads, natural parks and artificial foods, the cinema and radio are common and everyone has to read live newspapers of opposing views. To the Martians the earth appears to be 'several hundred thousand years back' in history, still drawing its energy from the plant kingdom, and they consider it their 'solemn duty to bring to humans the blessings of our culture'—an anticipatory echo of German aspirations to come.

Journalists caught the cue. The fifty-year-old editor of *Die Gesellschaft*, Michael Georg Conrad, wrote a thirtieth-century frolic, *Inder purpurnen Finsternis: Roman-Improvisation aus dem dreissigsten Jahrhundert* (1895), where the population live underground and are fed by pellets (Surros).[7] This shows two societies, Teuta (the ultimate in automation, with no 'nature', based on mechanics plus mysticism), and Nordica (a Rousseau-type idyll). The real hero is Grege, a Nietzschean superman in conflict with Teuta. Grege, as being concerned in, rather than observing, society, is here an innovation. Though 'free-enterprise' Nordica is preferred to 'socialist' Teuta, Grege turns to the girl Hala, a seer and dancer (a mixture of dark and light), as representing the true way, and rejects Nordica because man has reached happiness there 'too early'. The author is interested in the superman potential of man, seeing Nietzsche as the answer to the threat of automation.

Extrapolations were the subject of Carl Grunert's *Im Irdischen Jenseits* (1908) and Martin Atlas's *Die Befreiung* (1910). The latter tells of a simple power State, Peron, in the middle of the ocean whose inhabitants enjoy unlimited inanimate power enabling them to enjoy radio (Fial), cinemas (Pial), telekenesis (Kial), and unlimited powers of reproducing anything (Rial). Peron becomes a world power under a President with the motto *Scientia redemptor mundi*. This redemption is accompanied by complete democracy, thanks to being able to appreciate, through Kial, each others' opinions on every question. Equality of the sexes, eugenics and birth control together with availability of new inventions, wipe out sexual and social inequalities. Even racial differences are removed by blanching Negroes and Asiatics.

'Der Weltseele wollen wir näher sein,' exclaimed Paul Scheerbart as he opposed that cosmic feeling which foresees the future in *Na Prost!* (1898), *Die Wilde Jagd* (1901), *Kometentanz* (1903), and *Perpetuum Mobile* (1910). For him Nietzsche was 'The God of Journalists' whose futuristic forays were objectionable. More perceptive evaluations of these mechanistic tomorrows came from scientists. Bernhard Kellerman, product of the Munich *technische Hochschule*, wrote an anti-mechanistic fantasy *Der Tunnel* (1913), showing its collapse at the virtual moment of achievement and the killing of thousands. Kellerman shows man changed by the machine without losing the reader's sympathy. His experiencing subject, MacAllan, is a new type of man who sacrifices all that the bourgeois world holds dear for his technical project, and suffers the loss of his sensitive, art-loving wife, and the madness of his friend, a famous architect. He makes a 'realpolitikal' marriage with a financier's daughter. The author, by showing that the technical achievement will be superseded, indicates that he has no love of technological achievement for its own sake.

The great electrical manufacturer and statesman Walther Rathenau in *Von Kommenden Dingen* (1917) explored more clearly misgivings articulated by Oswald Spengler in *Der Mensch und die Technik* (1931). Other dark intimations, like Georg Kaiser's *Gas I* (1918) and *Gas II* (1920), and the more futuristic Theo von Harton's *Metropolis* (1926) lead up to Alfred Döblin's *Giganten* (1932), the only German example of 'kinetic Utopia'. This presents a panorama of the biological *evolution* of man at the centre, rather than a picture of self-contained society. It covers three centuries of third-millennial, machine-centred world, whose technology has become arcane owing to the strength of the opponents of machine-culture. Political and psychological unrest leads to a war with the primitive Easterners and indecisive world-war. This historical section of the novel deals with control of man by man, the relationship of technological man to nature, and concludes that man cannot escape nature because of his own nature. Technology won't help of itself: adventure is the driving force of history.

The second part deals with the subsequent de-icing of Greenland, through volcanic energy transported from Iceland. As a result it becomes menacingly over-luxuriant in flora and fauna. Volunteers expose themselves to volcanic rays, become giants, but keep the menace at bay. The scientists do the same to themselves, becoming giants—individuals above society—and get less and less human, finally growing into earth. The conquerors of Greenland return, form a new society with the opponents of machine-culture, and insist on the importance of the law.[8]

III H. G. WELLS AND THE KERYGMA OF SCIENCE

But the most assiduous architect of 'kinetic utopias' was H. G. Wells for whom the projection of evolution was a constant occupation. His *The Time Machine* (1895)—a virtual rewriting of *The Chronic Argonauts*—offered a Darwinian–Marxist picture of the year A.D. 802701: Marxist in that the pleasant relaxed society of the Eloi was communistic; Darwinian in that the species had been considerably modified by the environment. Another Marxist touch, too, appears in the Morlocks, a dark, hard-working, machine-making underground race, so like Victorian north of England mining classes, on whom the playful Eloi apparently depend. 'Apparently' is important, for Wells, as if to show Marx wrong, reveals that the Eloi are merely cattle on which the Morlocks feed. But Darwin has the last word when both Eloi and Morlocks disappear before a race of giant crabs. These crabs, in turn, disappear after the year A.D. 3,000,000, leaving the planet to livid green liverworts, lichens, and ice, and ultimately to total darkness.[9]

From now on Wells exploited every literary device of the Utopians, the extravagantic and the fantastic. He took the classic Utopian situation, shipwreck on an island, to examine the bestiality of man in *Island of Dr. Moreau* (1896). Here, on a seven-square-mile Pacific island, Dr. Moreau, a former London vivisector, has made some sixty or so Beast Men and Women. These caricatures of humanity have one friend in Moreau's drunken assistant, Montgomery. But Montgomery can't prevent Moreau being savaged and killed by a puma he is trying to transform, nor can he prevent being murdered himself. For the Beast Men revert as soon as they taste blood. The narrator, a young naturalist called Edward Prendick, who was shipwrecked on the island, finds himself fighting for life against them and using both whip and gun before he eventually escapes.

'I could not persuade myself,' he concluded after returning to civilisation, 'that the men and women I met were not also another, partially human, Beast People, animals half wrought into the outward image of human souls, and that they would presently begin to revert, to show first this bestial mark and then that.' Even the preacher in the chapel seemed to 'gabber Big Thinks even as the Ape Man had done'.

Wells was the Gulliver of Space. His aptly-timed and aptly-titled *The First Men in the Moon* (1901), virtually inaugurated science-fiction, since Dr. Cavor, thanks to his discovery of a new propellant, reaches the moon, and finds the Selenite race of specialists. Each is a perfect unit in a world machine: aristocracy with big heads: administrators (responsible for a certain cubic content of the moon's bulk), experts (who were trained to perform certain operations), and the erudite (the repositories of all knowledge). Since the heads of the last had to serve as libraries and records, 'much as the honey ants of Texas store honey in their distended abdomen', these erudite ones 'were led about by little watchers and attendants; some of them being altogether too great for loco-motion' and were 'carried about from place to place in a sort of sedan tub, wabbling jellies of knowledge'.[10]

Cavor describes the making of these specialists:

> I came upon a number of young Selenites confined in jars from which only the fore-limbs protruded, who were being compressed to become machine-minders of a special sort. The extended 'hand' in this highly developed system of technical education is stimulated by irritants and nourished by injection, while the rest of the body is starved.

and reflects:

> That wretched looking hand-tentacle sticking out of its jar seemed to have a sort of limp appeal for lost possibilities; it haunts me still, although, of course, it is really in the end a far more humane pro-ceeding than our earthly method of leaving children to grow into human beings and then making machines of them.[11]

The Grand Lunar disliked what Cavor told him of earth men; their aggressiveness and proclivities for war. So when Cavor admitted that upon himself alone hung the possibility of further men reaching the moon, that was enough. Cavor disappeared for ever.

Remembering how Cavor met his end on the moon, a later fictional space traveller, Dr. Ransom in C. S. Lewis's *Out of the Silent Planet* (1938), felt 'shy'.[12] Well he might, for whereas Cavor was in a scientific Utopia, Dr. Ransom was in a Heaven above, peopled by eldils (angels) and rational animals.

Wells betrays the sources of his inspiration in the arguments of Willie with his mother's lodger-curate in *In the Days of the Comet* (1906):

> I used the names of Karl Marx and Engels as biblical exegetes with no little effect. I was moved to denounce Christianity as the ethic of slaves, and declare myself a disciple of a German writer of no little vogue in those days named Nietzsche.[13]

Willie's letters to his girl-friend Nettie 'broke out towards theology, sociology and the cosmos'. His mind 'ran persistently' one evening 'upon revolutions after the last French pattern' and he 'sat on a Committee of Safety and tried backsliders'. Arguments with his friend Parland about the relative merits of science and socialism led him to believe that they were 'an impossible opposition'. Jilted, his premeditated murder of the faithless Nettie was arrested by a great cosmic Advent—the brushing of the earth by a comet. Thereafter everything changed; not only for Willie but for the whole earth:

> The former revivals spent themselves; but the Great Revival did not spend itself, but grew to be, for the majority of Christendom at least, the permanent expression of the Change. For many it has taken the shape of an outright declaration that this was the Second Advent —it is not for me to discuss the validity of the suggestion, for nearly all it has amounted to an enduring broadening of the issues of life. . . .

That 'broadening' was the Great Change, when the world began anew, following the 'green vapours' exhaled by the comet. Willie reminisces:

> As I look back into the past, I see a vast exultant dust of house-breaking and removal rise up into the clear air that followed the hour of the green vapours, I live again the Year of Tents, the Year of Scaffolding, and like the triumph of a new theme in a piece of music—the great cities of our new days arise. Come Cuerlyon and Armedon, the twin cities of lower England, with the winding summer city of Thames between . . . I see the great cities America has planned and made; the Golden City, with ever ripening fruit along its broad warm ways, and the bell-glad City of a Thousand Spires. I see again as I have seen, the city of the theatres and meeting-places, the City of the Sunlight Bright, and the new city that is still called Utah; and dominated by its observatory dome and the plain dignified lines of the university façade upon the cliff, Martenabar, the great white winter city of the Upland Snows.

With new cities came new books. The old 'dropsy of the nation's mind' was burnt:

> 'It seemed to me,' said Willie, 'that when we gathered those books and papers together, . . . we gathered warped and crippled ideas and contagious base suggestions, the formulae of dull tolerances and

stupid impatiences, the mean defensive ingenuities of sluggish habits of thinking and timid indolent evasions. There was more than a touch of malignant satisfaction for me in helping to gather it all together.'

There was much of Macaulay's Ebenezers and Bethels about the city itself:

> He put down his hand, and quite noiselessly the great window widened down to us, and the splendid nearer prospect of that dreamland city was before me. There for one clear moment I saw it; its galleries and open spaces, its trees of golden fruit and crystal waters, its music and rejoicing, love and beauty . . . ceaselessly flowing through its varied and intricate streets.[15]

This quasi-religious appeal of Wells was sensed by his contemporaries. Bernard Shaw said he 'effected a conversion and a conviction of sin comparable to the most sensational feats of General Booth or Gypsy Smith'. As a result, Clara in Shaw's *Pygmalion* (1912), found that Wellsians were:

> People she had thought deeply religious, and had tried to conciliate on that tack with disastrous results.

But when she began to talk about Wells they 'suddenly took an interest in her, and revealed a hostility to conventional religion which she has never conceived possible except amongst the most desperate characters'.[16] After meeting Wells, she talked of nothing for 'weeks and weeks afterwards'.

Like the pulpit orators of Macaulay's time, Wells began to preach rather than write. His lay sermon (or his 'thirty nine articles'[17] as the *New York Herald* percipiently called it), was given to the world as *Anticipations of the Reaction of Mechanical and Scientific Progress upon Human Life and Thought* (1902). In this he envisaged an élite consisting of scientists, engineers, and physicians 'controlling and restricting very greatly the . . . non-functional masses'. He tried to convert the Fabians to the idea of scientifically classifying the temperament of all citizens to determine their function in society and putting them under a ruling élite of scientists—the 'Samurai'—composed of those who had proved themselves by a series of difficult examinations. 'To talk a little of the upper slopes of the mountain we think we are climbing would but the trees let us see it.' He wrote *A Modern Utopia* (1905) ostensibly telling a mere story of personal adventures among Utopian philosophies, but he was realistic enough to acknowledge that the Thing in Being would not be silenced by the miraculous aggregation of the *Samurai*:

> Things do not happen like that [he confessed], God is not simple, God is not theatrical, the summons comes to each man in its due time for him, with an infinite subtlety and variety. . . . First here, then there, single men and then groups of men will fall into line—not indeed with my poor faulty hesitating suggestions, but with a great and comprehensive plan wrought out by many minds and in many tongues.[18]

Yet at the same time he believed quite firmly that:

> An inductive knowledge of a great number of things in the future is becoming a human possibility. I believe that the time is drawing near when it will be possible to suggest a systematic exploration of the future. . . . So far no first class mind has ever focussed itself upon these issues. . . . I think we are inclined to underrate our chances of certainty in the future, just as I think we are inclined to be too credulous about the historical past.[19]

It was with this in view that he was later to undertake his own survey of world history:

> I believe that the deliberate direction of historical study and of economic and social study towards the future, and an increasing reference, a deliberate and courageous reference, to the future in moral and religious discussion would be enormously stimulating and enormously profitable to our intellectual life . . . such an enterprise is now a serious and profitable undertaking.[20]

Indeed, he considered:

> It is our ignorance of the future and our persuasion that that ignorance is abolutely incurable that alone gives the past its enormous predominance in our thoughts.

That future, however, lay in the hands of the scientists:

> As a matter of fact prophecy has always been inseparably connected with the idea of scientific research. . . . Until a scientific theory yields confident forecasts you know it is unsound and tentative.[21]

Or, as he was to say later:

> A Utopia is the first sketch plan of a prepared replacement or change in human institutions . . . a vision of the being required. . . . Every Utopia is a treason to the thing that is . . . a slight to the people who are.[22]

He took his stand beside the great Utopists of the past whose 'essential value', he wrote, lay in their 'power to resist the causation of the past, and to evade, initiate, endeavour and overcome'.[23] This is why he left novel-writing to turn to sociological tracts: 'cet horrible cafouille que l'on appèle sociologie'.[24]

IV RESTRICTIVE CLAUSES IN THE TECHNOCRATS' WARRANTS

Far from supplying open warrants for technocrats to take over society, Wells drafted a number of restrictive clauses designed to bring the reader to a full realisation of the implication of his fables. Thus the inhuman control of function in the lunar society endorsed by Dr. Cavor in *The First Men in the Moon* shows that all vestiges of amorality and ethics have been dissolved in selenite rationality. So, too, the super-state of the year 3002 with its flying machines, television, public address systems, and roofed-in cities in *When the Sleeper Wakes* (1899) is based on a deluded and controlled population, as Ostrog, its controller, frankly acknowledges:

> You feel moved against our pleasure cities . . . the excretory organs of the State, attractive places that year after year draw all that is weak and vicious, all that is lascivious and lazy, all the easy rogueries of the world, to a graceful destruction. They go there, they have their time, they die childless, and mankind is the better. . . . Suppose that these swarming yelping fools . . . get the upper hand of us, what then? They will only fall to other masters. . . . Let them revolt, let them win, and Kill me and my like. Others will arise— other masters. The end will be the same.[25]

The type of these restrictive clauses blurred after 1901. This was due, suggests his son, to the combined influence of the Fabians and of William James. For James's principle of operative truth whereby 'ideas (which are themselves but parts of our experience), become true just in so far as they help us to get into satisfactory relations with other parts of our experience', and that 'true ideas are those we can assimilate, validate, corroborate and verify' lead inexorably to the view that the true is only the expedient.[26]

Wells tried to persuade himself and others that nature could be improved, but he felt there were restrictive clauses in his sermons. He wrote them in bold type, and they were often emphasised by those who felt it incumbent upon them to circumscribe the freedom which he accorded to the human spirit. These critics, amongst whom were G. K. Chesterton, Rudyard Kipling, and E. M. Forster, were responsible for 'Wellsian' becoming a quasi-pejorative adjective.

V THE 'GOSPEL OF SHAVIANITY'

If the adjective 'Wellsian' carried overtones of the grandiose, 'Shavian' epitomised pith and point. To Bernard Shaw, Wells's fellow-Fabian, the Superman was 'as old as Prometheus', so he has the Devil prophesy in *Man and Superman* (1901–3), that:

> The 20th century will run after this newest of the old crazes when it gets tired of the world, the flesh, and your humble servant.[27]

Shaw's own evolutionary panorama was an imprisoned epic play: *Back to Methuselah* (1920). It began with Adam and Eve and leaping from the contemporary scene it projects three tableaux of tomorrow—one in the year 2170, the next in the year 3000, and the last in the year 31920. Each tableau is an imprisoned prophecy of the next.

The first begins with the President of the British Isles facing, with the help of a Chinese chief secretary and a Negress Minister of Health, the problems posed by mankind's longevity—the life span now being three hundred years. The wise archbishop of York, 'with more than a century and a half of fully adult experience' reminds him:

> The thinking, organising, calculating, directing work is done by yellow brains, brown brains and black brains, just as it was done in my early days (he was born in the Victorian era), by Jewish brains, Scottish brains, Italian brains, German brains. The only white men who still do serious work are those who . . . have no capacity for enjoyment, and no social gift to make them welcome outside their offices. . . . We are letting all the power slip into the hands of the coloured people. In another hundred years we will be simply their household pets.[28]

When the President discovers that he, too, may have to live for three hundred years, his relations with his Negress Minister of Health have to remain 'purely telephonic, gramophonic, photographic and . . . platonic' because if he visits her at Fishguard (she can't stand the cold of the East Coast), he might find himself catching rheumatism through being parachuted into the bay, and as he says, 'I will not face an eternity of rheumatism for any woman that was ever born.'

His Chinese secretary Confucius congratulates him on becoming President:

'you are no longer what you call a sportsman: you are a sensible coward, almost a grown-up man'.

The second view is of the year A.D. 3000. By this time there is a patron saint of discretion—Sir John Falstaff—to whom the Irish have erected a statue. The statue, now regarded as an oracle, is visited by Joseph Popham Bolge Bluebin Barlow, O.M., Chairman of the All-British Synthetic Egg and Vegetable Cheese Trust in Baghdad, accompanying his son-in-law the prime minister Mr. Badger Bluebin, his daughter and grand-daughter and the Emperor of Turania (a reincarnation of Napoleon travelling incognito as General Aufsteig). But the Irish, who by now had acquired the art of living for three hundred years, regard them as freaks and imprison Joseph Barlow behind an electric fence. To them his O.M. was a 'name for certain wild creatures, descendants of the aboriginal inhabitants of the island'—the O'Mulligans. The rest of the visitors are marshalled by an Irishman with a kind of 'walkie-talkie'—like a tuning fork. But Joseph Barlow is told the story of how the scientists were brought under control after the general massacre of men of science that took place in the twenty-first century of the pseudo-Christian era, when all their laboratories were demolished and their apparatus destroyed. He hears how:

When Science crept back, it had been taught its place. The mere collectors of anatomical or chemical facts were not supposed to know more about science than the collectors of used postage stamps about international trade or literature. The scientific terrorist who was afraid to use a spoon or a tumbler until he had dipt it in some poisonous acid to kill the microbes, was no longer given titles, pensions and monstrous powers over the bodies of other people: he was sent to an asylum, and treated there until his recovery. But all that is an old story: the extension of life to three hundred years has pro-vided the human race with capable leaders, and made short work of such childish stuff.[29]

The story moves him so much that he has no heart to return to Baghdad and dies.

To die like Joseph Barlow when you wanted to was indeed a privilege as became evident in the third phase of gerontopia—'as far as thought can reach'—the year A.D. 31920. Since the life span is now eight hundred years, a new method of gestation, taking two years, has come about. Normal processes of growth that once took twenty years, now take fifteen months, and the subsequent span of fifty years, now takes four years. No one dies of decay. A man and woman are made by Pygmalion in his laboratory, but having such passions as jealousy, they die quickly.

> There was a time [says a she-ancient to the newly-born], when children were given the world to play with because they promised to improve it. They did not improve it; and they would have wrecked it had their power been as great as that which you will wield when you are no longer a child. Until then your young companions will instruct you in whatever is necessary. You are not forbidden to speak to the ancients; but you had better not do so, as most of them have long ago exhausted all the interest there is in observing children and conversing with them.[30]

Having forgotten 'how to speak; how to read; even how to think' the ancients so discourage the young that they begin to lament the shortness of their real life and one of them exclaims:

> I made up my mind on that subject long ago. When I am three years and fifty weeks old, I shall have my fatal accident. And it will not be an accident.

VI NIETZSCHEAN APOCALYPTICS

Such Nietzschean apocalyptics, however, were explored yet further by Hermann Hesse, Franz Werfel, and Ernst Jünger. Set in 'Kastalien', Hesse's *Das Glasperlenspiel* (1943) postulates a different historical development from the 1920s on, with certain groups concerned with spiritual rather than journalistic values. These groups develop the 'Glasperlenspiel', a private game in the face of a socialist-mechanistic educational and cultural system.

The game of glass pearls is a compound of science and art and he who has mastered it will have achieved serenity, that 'Ruhe über den Wirbeln'. They play and juggle with the total content and values of our civilisation, searching for God whom they see as the force which unifies all these disparate elements. These Glasperlenspieler become the meritocrats, the philosopher–scientists, the thinkers whose work is translated into educational action by the next layer of highly educated intellectual technocrats. But harmony between 'world' and 'spirit' is easily broken, particularly where it is institutionalised. Knecht (the hero) tried to combine 'living reality' and the spirit; and goes through an internal conflict as to whether the pure thinker has political responsibility. He comes to the conclusion that his values are higher than politics. Therefore Glasperlenspiel is not used to conquer reality. The conclusion is that the schoolmaster is the true contact between intellect and reality since he passes on values.

In *Der Stern der Ungeborenen* (1946), the author, Franz Werfel, is called via a séance, to the 'astromental age'. A change in solar intensity enables people to live to 200 in such bodily perfection that external technology is unnecessary. In this brave new world there are four estates: the church, politicians, workers, and chronosophs (to whom learning is a way of life). Werfel's presence acts as a catalyst for the revolt of a fifth estate: the jungle-living primitives. Against them, politicians (as they are too indecisive), and the chronosophs (as they are too rarified) fail. Only the Church can help. In other words, social reality, however perfect, is not enough.

Lastly, we come to Ernst Jünger, whose two novels *Heliopolis* (1949) and *Gläserne Bienen* (1957) go beyond Utopia. In the first de Geer, the non-conformist in the Utopian society, the man who has reached the summit and sees no way on, the wanderer through Utopia, knowing all Utopias, seeks a new Utopia. He is commandant of the Prokonsul's military academy, finds himself at the hub of a conflict between Prokonsul (an aristocrat) and the popular hero Landvogt (a bailiff). Failure leads to a messenger from the Regent (God the father figure), bearing an invitation to join Regent's order in the other world. The Prokonsul and Landvogt stand for the army and the people, but also for the human and the technical. Three partial solutions to the basic conflict lie in the attitudes of the 'Parsen' (Jew-equivalents), who turn inward into the spiritual regions; the 'Mauretanier' (Nazi-equivalents), the technicians of power at the expense of human feeling; the 'Besten' (intellectual) élite of outward-looking, seeking approximations to the kingdom of the Regent on earth.

In the second novel Jünger's hero, Richard, can also see no way out. He is trying to get a job with Zapparoni's (the Utopia), set in an allegorical, quasi-real world. Waiting in Zapparoni's garden for interview, he sees glass bees collecting honey more rationally than real ones. He admires the mechanism, but realises how absurd it is to have *mechanical* bees. He concludes that old human perfection and new technical perfection are irreconcilable—one or the other must be sacrificed. Richard himself is an 'old human', but we are left with the knowledge that a new human, reconciled to and a part of the technical world, is at hand.[31]

VII THE NOVEL AS THE HOLE IN THE WALL: D. H. LAWRENCE'S *Rainbow*

It was while twenty-seven-year-old D. H. Lawrence was visiting his old professor at Nottingham about a teaching post at a German university that he met, and eloped with, the professor's wife, Frieda Weekley Richthofen. They went to Munich. Lawrence loved Germany: he had reviewed two German anthologies by English academics in the *English Review* (X 373–4, 374–6). Its editor 'was of the opinion that Lawrence was a well-read German scholar who had absorbed Nietzsche, Marx, and Wagner as his daily breakfast'.[32]

Certainly he rejoiced that his generation was 'waking from the dream of demolition'. Because 'faith and belief were getting potbound, and the temple was more a place to barter sacrifices, therefore faith and belief and the Temple must be broken'. The breakers were Nietzsche and Hardy and Flaubert. 'And behold, out of the ruins leaps the whole sky.'[33]

He protested that:

> The Moses of Science and the Aaron of Idealism have got the whole bunch of us here on top of Pisgah. It's a tight squeeze, and we'll be falling very, very foul of one another in five minutes unless some of us climb down. But before leaving our eminence let us have a look round, and get our bearings.
>
> They say that way lies the New Jerusalem of universal love: and over there the happy valley of indulgent Pragmatism: and there,

quite near, is the chirpy land of the Vitalists: and in those dark groves the home of successful Analysis, surnamed Psycho: and over those blue hills the Supermen are prancing about, though you can't see them. And there is Besantheim, and there is Eddyhowe, and there, on that queer little tableland, is Wilsonia, and just round the corner is Rabindranathopolis. . . .

But Lord, I can't see anything. Help me, heaven, to a telescope, for I see blank nothing.[34]

But what he did see was that:

We have made a mistake, laying down love like the permanent way of a great emotional transport system. There we are, however, running on wheels on the lines of our love. And of course we have only two directions, forwards and backwards. Onward, Christian soldiers, towards the great terminus where bottles of sterilized milk for the babies are delivered at the bedroom windows by noiseless aeroplanes each morn, where the science of dentistry is so perfect that teeth are planted in a man's mouth without him knowing it, where twilight sleep is so delicious that every woman longs for her next confinement, and where nobody ever has to do anything except turn a handle now and then in a spirit of universal love. . . . That is the forward direction of the English-speaking race. The Germans unwisely backed their engine. We have a city of light. But instead of lying ahead it lies direct behind us. So reverse engines. Reverse engines, and away, away to our city, where the sterilized milk is delivered by noiseless aeroplanes, at the very precise minute when our great doctors of the Fatherland have diagnosed that it is good for you: where the teeth are not only so painlessly planted that they grow like living rock, but where their composition is such that the friction of eating stimulates the cells of the jaw-bone and develops the superman strength of will which makes us gods: and where not only is twilight sleep serene, but into the sleeper are inculcated the most useful and instructive dreams, calculated to perfect the character of the young citizen at this crucial period, and to enlighten permanently the mind of the happy mother, with regard to her new duties towards her child and towards our great Fatherland . . .

Here you see we are, on the railway, with New Jerusalem ahead and New Jerusalem away behind us. But of course it was very wrong of the Germans to reverse their engines, and cause one long collision all along the line. Why should we go their way to the New Jerusalem, when of course they might so easily have kept on going our way. And now there's wreckage all along the line! But clear the way is our motto—or make the Germans clear it. Because get on we will.[35]

Though Lawrence never wrote about the future, his prophetic quality is paramount. One critic considers *The Rainbow* to be 'the only English novel to record with a prophetic awareness of consequences the social revolution whereby Western man lost his sense of community.' It taught that: 'There is no help any longer except in the individual and his capacity for a passional life.'

'Always in Lawrence,' writes another, 'there is the ulterior view of the future'.[36] In *Fantasia of the Unconscious* Lawrence urges:

> We've got to rip the old veil of a vision across, and find what the heart really believes in, after all: and what the heart really wants, for the next future. And we've got to put it down in terms of belief and knowledge. And then go forward again, to the fulfilment of life and art.

For Lawrence was insistent that 'you've got to find a new impulse for things in mankind, and it's really fatal to find it through abstraction', and suggested that the novel world 'break a way through like a hole in the wall', enabling the 'sheep' to filter through the gap and find a new world outside. Though Lawrence powerfully endorsed the novel as an operational medium for making a hole in the wall he confined his own efforts to secularised versions of Christianity, and advocating a return to the breast and the womb. Of Dionysian, Nietzschean, and Theosophic elements all compounded, he detested mechanisation which he said was wearing down the common man, and suggested:

> I would like him to give me back the responsibility for general affairs, a responsibility which he can't acquit, and which saps his life. I would like him to give me back the responsibility for thought, for direction . . . I would undertake my share of the responsibility if he gave me his belief.

In *Fantasia of the Unconscious* he gave a blue-print for an age to be:

> All schools will shortly be converted either into public workshops or into gymnasia. . . . Active training in primitive modes of fighting and gymnastics will be compulsory for all boys over ten years of age. . . . The great mass of humanity should never learn to read and to write—never. First and foremost establish a rule over them, a proud, harsh manly rule.

VIII YEATS AND THE DISSOCIATION OF MYTH AND
FACT

A similar trend towards a 'proud harsh manly rule' can be detected
in W. B. Yeats, to whom man was the active shaper of the historical
process. This process alternated endlessly between Dionysian (or
anarchic) and Apollonian (or severely disciplined) civilisations.
Each was the opposite to what it succeeded:

> When a civilisation ends, task having led to task until everybody
> was bored, the whole turns bottom upwards, Nietzsche's 'trans-
> valuation of values'. As we approach the phoenix nest the old classes,
> with their power of co-ordinating events, evaporate, the mere multi-
> tude is everywhere with its empty photographic eyes. Yet we who
> have hated the age are joyous and happy.[37]

Out of Nietzsche (whom he first read in 1903), supplemented by
readings of Blake, Swedenborg and Boehme, Yeats evolved his
own outlook best expressed in 1920:

> Turning and turning in the widening gyre
> The falcon cannot hear the falconer;
> Things fall apart; the centre cannot hold;
> Mere anarchy is loosed upon the world,
> The blood-dimmed tide is loosed, and everywhere
> The ceremony of innocence is drowned;
> The best lack all conviction, while the worst
> Are full of passionate intensity.
>
> Surely some revelation is at hand;
> Surely the Second Coming is at hand.
> The Second Coming! Hardly are those words out
> When a vast image out of Spiritus Mundi
> Troubles my sight: somewhere in sands of the desert
> A shape with lion body and the head of a man,
> A gaze blank and pitiless as the sun,
> Is moving its slow thighs, while all about it
> Reel shadows of the indignant desert birds.
> The darkness drops again; but now I know
> That twenty centuries of stony sleep
> Were vexed to nightmare by a rocking cradle,
> And what rough beast, its hour come round at last,
> Slouches towards Bethlehem to be born?

Five years later, Yeats had issued, privately, *A Vision*, which begins with Owen Aherne, a Neo-Thomist, telling of his recent meeting with Michael Robartes, an occultist, of Robartes' adventures in the Orient, about their mutual religious differences and their friendship with the poet himself. Following this come four essays: 'What the Caliph Partly Learned', 'What the Caliph Refused to Learn', 'Dove and the Swan', and 'The Gates of Pluto'.

In the third of these Yeats applies and develops universal history in the light of the Nietzschean cycles seen through his own models of the *Great Wheel*, lunar phases and interpenetrating gyres or whirling spirals, which alternately contract and expand. 'Dove and the Swan' concerns the cycle of two thousand years in which the period from 1927 to 1965 represents phases twenty-three, twenty-four, and twenty-five of the Larger Wheel.

Yeats believed that myth and fact had fallen apart: and for that reason man is calling up myth 'which now but gropes its way out of the mind's dark, but will shortly pursue and terrify'. Phase twenty-four will be followed first by a kind of passive obedience, and after by decadence. He wrote:

> I foresee a time when . . . a ceaseless activity will be required of all; and where rights are swallowed up in duties, and solitude is difficult, creation except among avowedly archaistic and unpopular groups will grow impossible. Phase 25 may arise, as the code wears out from repetition, to give new motives for obedience. . . . Then with the last gyre must come a desire to be ruled or rather, seeing that desire is all but dead, an adoration of force spiritual or physical, and society as mechanical force be complete at last.

This would, he prophesied, be confirmed in phases twenty-six to twenty-eight covering the years 1965 to 2000, when 'anarchic violence with no sanction in general principles' (symbolised by the widening turning inwards of the gyres), and when 'false leaders will appear and an expansion will take place'.[38] It is remarkable that while Yeats was writing this in Galway, Spengler's *Decline of the West* was published in Germany. Yeats confessed, 'I had never heard his name and yet the epochs are the same, the dates are the same, the theory is the same.'[39]

Yeats spoke of rewriting for the seventh time that part that deals with the future, yet not till 1937, a year and a half before his death, was a corrected version published.[40] In this he expanded the

introduction as 'Stories of Michael Robartes and his Friends'.
Robartes prophesies the coming of war and advocates a world-
wide revolution to destroy our civilisation:

> Love war because of its horror, that belief may be changed, civi-
> lisation renewed. We desire belief and lack it. Belief comes from
> shock and is not desired. When a kindred discovers through appara-
> tion and horror that the perfect cannot perish nor even the imperfect
> long be interrupted, who can withstand that kindred? Belief is re-
> newed continually in the ordeal of death.[41]

Chapter Eight

THE DISENCHANTED MECHANOPHOBES

I MINISCULE MEDIEVALISM: CHESTERTON

As a direct reply to 'prophets like Mr. H. G. Wells and others who thought that science would take charge of the future' G. K. Chesterton wrote *The Napoleon of Notting Hill* (1904). By 1984, when his novel begins, people having come to believe 'in a thing called Evolution' had lost faith in revolutions. Democracy was dead, for though the king was elected, he was elected only from someone in the official class. The choice of King Auberon Quin (like Chesterton a medievalist joker) inaugurates his appeal for the revival of the ancient rights, customs, and ceremonials of the ancient boroughs in London. His appeal is taken seriously by the Lord High Provost of Notting Hill, who refuses to allow one of his streets to become part of an arterial road. Notting Hill—or Nothing Ill as King Auberon would have it—was an ideal Chestertonian principate of wayward fancy. To its romantic provost, Adam Wayne, its mean streets possessed 'the ultimate and ancient sentiment that went out to Athens or Jerusalem'. Like Chesterton, Adam Wayne:

> knew that real patriotism tends to sing about sorrows and forlorn hopes much more than about victory. He knew that in proper names themselves is half the poetry of all national poems. Above all he knew the supreme psychological fact about patriotism . . . that the patriot never under any circumstances boats of the largeness of his country, but always, and of necessity, boasts of the smallness of it.[1]

In this miniscule world Chesterton found the deepest significance. When the small force of Notting Hill defeats the massed armies of Kensington literally by turning out the lights, it acquired a twenty years' hegemony of London. And when it was finally defeated in the great Battle of Kensington and the King confesses to Provost Adam Wayne that the medieval revival was a joke, Adam Wayne replies in the true voice of Chesterton:

> When dark and dreary days come, you and I are necessary, the pure fanatic, the pure satirist. We have between us remedied a great wrong. We have lifted the modern cities into that poetry which everyone who knows mankind knows to be immeasurably more commonplace than commonplace.[2]

Chesterton's other fantasies had a gaiety of their own: following *The Napoleon of Notting Hill* (1904), *The Flying Inn* (1914), and *The Return of Don Quixote* (1927) were in the very best tradition of realistic (as opposed to nominalist) political fantasy. For Chesterton disagreed that 'causation of the past' could be evaded.

> 'Progress,' he remarked, 'is simply a comparative of which we have not settled the superlative. . . . It is not merely true that the age which has settled least what is progress is this "progressive" age. It is, moreover, true that the people who have settled least what is progress are the most "progressive" people in it.'[3]

Especially did he deplore Wells's habits of beginning, not with the human soul, but 'with some such thing as protoplasm'. Nor did he warm to Wells's jettisoning of 'original sin':

> The weakness of all Utopias is this, that they take the greatest difficulty of man (i.e. original sin) and assume it to be overcome, and then give an elaborate account of the overcoming of the smaller ones. They first assume that no man will want more than his share, and then are very ingenious in explaining whether his share will be delivered by motor car or balloon.[4]

Of the New Jerusalem Chesterton confessed that he:

> was always running out of my architectural study with plans for a new turret only to find it sitting up there in the sunlight. . . . For me, in the ancient and partly in the modern Sense, God answered the prayer, 'Prevent us, O Lord, in all our doings'. . . . My own conception of Utopia was only answered in the New Jerusalem.[5]

Chesterton wanted to write of an imaginary voyage centred round an English yachtsman who slightly miscalculated his course and discovered England under the impression that it was a new island in the South Seas.

'Romance' to G. K. Chesterton had 'the mystery and ancient meaning of Rome': When he tried to be ten minutes in advance of the truth he found himself eighteen hundred years behind it.[6]

II DISENCHANTMENT WITH POLITICS: KIPLING

Setting his sights further forward than Chesterton to attack the debilitating effects of a scientific mandarinate operating on a world scale, Kipling described the activities of the Aerial Board of Control,[7] which under the motto of 'Transportation is Civilisation' allowed mankind 'to do as it pleases as long as it did not interfere with traffic and all that it implies'. Mankind becomes so 'tolerant, humorous and lazy' by the year 2056 that even the Board's Official Reporter was asking: 'Isn't it almost time that our Planet took some interest in the proceedings of the Aerial Board of Control?'[8] Though rich (farming was carried out by remote control), long-lived (everyone could reasonably expect to be a centenarian), and underpopulated (only four and a half hundred millions were alive), there were some who wanted to turn the clock back a hundred years to the days of the Crowd and the Plague. This dissentient group was in Northern Illinois and caused the mayor such trouble that he appealed to the Aerial Board of Control to take over. The ease with which it did so is described in *As Easy as A.B.C.* (1912): It was easy in that scientific coercive instruments enabled them to bind (by electrical lasso loops), blind (by disorienting lights), and strike dumb (by ultrasonic rays).

The dissentients against whom such coercive instruments were employed were known as Serviles:

> 'They *will* talk,' said the Mayor, 'and when people take to talking as a business anything may arrive. . . . So from talking in houses and on the streets our Serviles go to calling a meeting. . . . There's nothing to prevent anyone calling meetings except that it's against human nature to stand in a crowd, besides being bad for the health. . . . There were as many as a thousand in the market place, touching each other.'

They talked about how badly things were managed in the city and the Mayor confessed:

> . . . that pleased us . . . because we hoped to catch one or two good men for City work. You know how rare executive capacity is. Even

if we didn't it's—it's refreshing to find anyone interested enough in
our job to damn our eyes. You don't know what it means to work
year in, year out, without a spark of difference with a living soul.[9]

The grim irony of the prosperous planet now emerges. Nobody
wants to do anything except mind his own business:

> 'You *can't* do anything,' complains the Mayor, 'with folk who
> can go where they please, and don't want anything on God's earth
> except their own way. There isn't a kick or a kicker left on the
> Planet.'

Except, of course, the Serviles.
The official recorder of the Board of Control reported one of
them demanding:

> . . . that every matter of daily life, including most of the physical
> functions, should be submitted for decision . . . to anybody who
> happened to be passing by or residing within a certain radius, and
> that everybody should forthwith abandon his concerns to settle the
> matter, first by crowd-making, next by talking to the crowds made,
> and lastly by describing crosses on bits of paper.[10]

To this the inhabitants reacted by asking the Board to take
over, crying:

> We've finished with Crowds! We aren't going back to the Old
> Days! Take us over! Take the Serviles away! Administer direct or
> we'll Kill 'em! Down with the People!

So the A.B.C. take over, and remove the Serviles with their family
for exhibition at Earls Court as an entertainment, an old world in
miniature, something to get under the 'world's iridium-plated
hide'. The impresario speaks to them by long-distance phone and
the Serviles 'thanked him and demanded (we could hear his
chuckle of delight), time to discuss and to vote on the matter. The
vote, solemnly managed by counting heads . . . was favourable'.
Delighted, he arranged for them to perform in a series of old-
world plays and asks 'where *do* you suppose they picked up all
their misery from, on this sweet earth?'
The Serviles, reaching London, weep.

III   THE MACHINE STOPS

Another acknowledged 'reaction to one of the earlier heavens of H. G. Wells' was E. M. Forster's *The Machine Stops*.[11] Here the population of the world lives underground like bees in a hive. 'With a face as white as fungus' Kuno's mother crouches in her hexagonal room near the centre of the earth, so 'busy' that she can only spare five minutes to talk to her son on the video-phone. She listens with horror to his desire both to see her face-to-face, and to visit the surface of the earth; construing it as blasphemy against the Machine—the vast apparatus that keeps their underground world supplied with food, air and continuous music. Her own room supplies all her needs:

> There were buttons to call for food, for music, for clothing. There was the hot-bath button, by pressure of which a basin of (imitation) marble rose out of the floor, filled to the brim with a warm deodorised liquid. There was the cold-bath button. There was the button that produced literature. And there were of course the buttons by which she communicated with her friends. The room, though it contained nothing, was in touch with all that she cared for in the world.

The only survival from the 'age of litter' was one book—The Book of the Machine—which, if she was hot or cold or dyspeptic or at a loss for a word, told her which button to press.

Yet at her son's entreaty she goes to visit him. Clutching the Book of the Machine she makes her way through the lifts to the surface of the earth where she catches an airship to the Northern Hemisphere, and by vestibule, lift, tubular railway, platform, and sliding door—she reaches her son's room. He tells her that he has found a way to the surface without an Egression permit, and without following the official vomitories, by discovering the ventilation shafts. But he does not enjoy his freedom for long. For white worms pursue him, bind his legs and drag him back to his room.

For his refusal to abide by the dictates of the Machine—for being 'non-mechanical'—he is refused a permit to be a father as not being a type which the machine wished to hand on. Believing that man is the measure of all things, he built up his strength by exercise, by climbing through the old ventilation shaft to discover the hills of Wessex. 'Happy the man, happy the woman,' he said, 'who awakes the hills of Wessex.'

> Cannot you see, cannot all you lecturers see [he asks his mother], that it is we that are dying, and that down here the only thing that really lives is the Machine? We created the Machine to do our will, but we cannot make it do our will now. It has robbed us of the sense of space and of the sense of touch, it has blurred every human relation and narrowed down love to a carnal act, it has paralysed our bodies and our wills, and now it compels us to worship it.[12]

Sadly he admits:

> I have no remedy—or, at least, only one—to tell men again and again that I have seen the hills of Wessex as Alfred saw them when he overthrew the Danes.

But his mother thinks he's mad.

In the years after Kuno's venture to the surface two developments take place: respirators (used for visiting the surface) are abolished and religion is introduced. The Machine was worshipped, not only as a unity but in its particular parts:

> one believer would be chiefly impressed by the blue optic plates, through which he saw other believers; another by the mending apparatus, which sinful Kuno had compared to worms; another by the lifts, another by the Book. And each would pray to this or to that, and ask it to intercede for him with the Machine as a whole.

Kuno's conviction that the Machine was stopping was silenced by his mother and by her friends. First the beds fail to appear, then the music is interrupted, then the bath water begins to stink, then the poetry machine emits defective rhymes. But so deepseated is the habit of acquiescence that, unchallenged, things go from bad to worse. The light fails, and only with the cessation of the Machine's hum do the people panic, rushing out of their cells to do what Kuno did—to reach the upper air.

Kuno comes for his mother, to help her in the stampede. As they swirl in the stream of fugitives they weep for 'the sin against the body . . . the centuries of wrong against the muscles and the nerves, and those five portals by which we can alone apprehend—glazing it over with talk of evolution until the body was white pap'.[13] But before they could recapture life 'as it was in Wessex when Alfred overthrew the Danes', an airship crashes into the vomitorium and kills them. 'Humanity,' says Kuno before he dies, 'has learnt its lesson.'[14]

IV TALIESIN REDISCOVERED

A friend of E. M. Forster's tutor, Goldsworthy Lowes Dickinson, and associated with him in promoting a 'League of Nations' in 1915,[15] was C. R. Ashbee, an architect with schemes for re-designing towns on Morrisian principles. Two years after visiting America, where Morris's ideas had taken root on the prairie, Ashbee had issued his *Building of Thelema* (1910).

In America, like others before him, Ashbee had seen the way in which such ideas had been (in the words of Frank Lloyd Wright) 'steadily confusing, as well as in some respects revealing, our opportunities'.[16] Just as Morris looked back from A.D. 2000, Frank Lloyd Wright looked back from A.D. 3000:

> Suppose [he asked] historians or antiquarians were to seek significance of what *we* were in the veins of us, the veins that remained, what would they find? That we were a jackdaw people with a monkey psychology given over to the vice of devices, looking to devices for salvation.[17]

Frank Lloyd Wright's own answer was *The Disappearing City* (1932), where the kilowatt hour was exploited as Morris would have wished in Broadacre City. Broadacre City embodied Wright's belief that though it was necessary 'to dream of the future' people had to 'realise that the future is now and here. It is imperative to go to work with it, no longer foolishly trying to stand against it.'[18] Wright phased (some think fazed) town and country in Usonia—the name was taken from Samuel Butler—where each citizen was to live on an acre of ground, with universities and museums near-by but commuting to a factory some miles away.

Symbolically Wright names his design centre Taliesin, since:

> Taliesin, a Druid, was a member of King Arthur's Round Table. He sang the glories of fine art—I guess he was the only Britisher who every did—so I chose Taliesin for a name because it means 'shining brow'.[19]

Taliesin was, in its creator's words, 'a little research station on the way toward reality'.[20]

Taliesin (the spelling was his own), was the theme which occupied Charles Williams, the English interpreter of that 'spy of God', Kierkegaard, whom he persuaded the Oxford University Press, his employers, to publish. Williams delivered the first public lecture on Kierkegaard in England.[21] Three years later in 1938, he produced *Taliesin Through Logres* and *He Came Down from Heaven*, both existentialist manifestoes, enunciating the principles of co-inherence and exchange, on which King Arthur and his table ordered their visible life. For their life co-inhered with the spiritual, the Grail communicated the spiritual to the fleshly and helped unify them. Supernatural co-inherence ceased when the Round Table broke down. Exchange involved giving up our grip on ourselves, and our conception of ourselves and accepting other people, love, facts. In co-inherence, substitution, and exchange, the new order, Camelot, comes with Galahad,—the capacity for Christ in every man.[22]

Charles Williams used the Arthurian legend that Milton had considered and rejected, and in the words of one modern critic 'had enough contact with the occult and with various modern forms of theosophy to grasp that those who tried to brush aside the proper distinction between Matter and Spirit all too often only succeed in presenting spirit as a very, very thin kind of matter.[23]

V   PLEAS FOR EXISTENTIAL LIVING: W. H. AUDEN AND REX WARNER

Williams' influence was profound and embraced amongst others W. H. Auden and Rex Warner. 'Preserve me from the Shape of Things to Be,' wrote Auden in *Letters from Iceland* (1937). He now rejected 'Utopia, free of all complexes' and the 'Withered State'. In *Journey to a War* (1938), he drew an apocalyptic moral: that our own machine age was the third great disappointment—the first being Greece and Rome, the second the middle ages. For the refrain of the machine age was:

> Leave Truth to the police and us; we know the Good
> We build the Perfect City time shall never alter . . .

From now on Auden was to warn his readers against escaping into the future or the past and press the need for existential living. 'For us like any other fugitive' was a prelude to Auden's return to Christianity.[24] His experiences in Spain, the shock of Nazidom, and the influence of Charles Williams were all responsible. 'Trust in God and take short views' was his motto—as it had been of Sydney Smith before him.[25] His Christmas Oratorio *For the Time Being* points out:

> That the Dream of a Perfect State or No State at all,
> To which we fly for refuge, is a part of our punishment.[26]

'New Year Letter' in *The Age of Anxiety* (1947) sees the future of

> Tidy utopias of eternal spring
> Vitamins, visas for dogs

The implications of such tidy utopias were explored by his Oxford friend Rex Warner in *The Wild Goose Chase* (1937). Selecting the wild goose as 'a symbol of our Saviour' because of its fierce indifference to bye-laws and 'quiet flying, unearthly song, neck like thunder and lightning and your mysterious barbaric love', Warner tells the story of how it was sought by three brothers: the masculine motorised Rudolf, the elegant and intelligent, mechanised David, and the honest pedestrian George—naturalist and ornithologist.

George is in tune with the natural order of things. His favourite books are Shakespeare, Karl Marx, *Tom Jones*, and Isaiah. Like the Saviour, he meets on his pilgrimage a companion who later betrayed him. Crossing the frontier in search of the wild goose he finds that the countryfolk are being tyrannised and duped by an alien city folk, and bled of their crops in exchange for blue beads and cigarettes. But this tyranny is a new one. For though the laughing policemen's truncheons are made of straw, their crystal helmets, ornamented, were 'vehicles for the most potent electrical forces'. 'And mark you this,' George is warned by the veteran agitator Pushkov:

> These policemen are among the minor government officials. Subordinate to them are secret service agents of all kinds, and above them men of science, politicians, and ministers of religion capable of exerting terrific power. . . . Every agricultural instrument is magnetised and can be controlled from the town. Every child born in the country, has, by order of the medical authorities, an owl tattooed on its belly. In every household there are spies. Not far away there are prisons where some people have been tickled to death.[27]

The centre of this tyranny is the Convent, all of whose inhabitants have been surgically treated so that they can fulfil the functions of both sexes. Both Rudolf and David end up there, but George refuses the operation and discovers that the Wild Goose is stuffed.

His role is to knock the stuffing out of the wild goose and out of tyranny. In refereeing a football match where the results are determined beforehand, he attempts to enforce free play, but the team predestined to lose gets shot. Penetrating further, he finds that the convent is ruled by an invisible machine-mind operating behind a rubber curtain, just as the city itself is sealed off from both sky and the surrounding country by concrete roofs and walls.

Escaping from it to the country, George helps lead a revolution of the farmers and the miners. Together they overthrow the technarchy of electricity and science. In the battle he meets his elder brother Rudolf, now blinded and also betrayed. As his victorious army penetrates the vast concrete of the Convent where all the psychological stratagems against the liberating armies were conceived and launched, George discovers a mathematician 'with a wasted body thrown like a cloth over a chair' babbling 'God must be a great mathematician'.

> In neighbouring cells were discovered other men and women, all equally obsessed with some science or art which they exercised in its purity, all equally unable to give any account of their activities. There was a poet who had invented a new language, but could neither pronounce a syllable of it nor attach any meaning to any of its words. There was an artist who spent his time rapidly arranging fir cones on the floor of his cell, and sweeping them together again with his hand when he was for an instant satisfied with their arrangement. A critic had discovered what literature ought to be; but he was unable to write. A philosopher had explained the world of sense; but he was blind and deaf, had lost his sense of touch, and had been, he informed them, since childhood unable to distinguish one odour from another.[28]

George ordered them to be exposed to fresh air in the country. Why then did George's two elder brothers surrender to the religion of the stuffed wild goose? David gave the answer:

> I entered it as though it was Paradise. The system of Government, the courses of study, the conventions of morality seemed to me just those ones which I had imagined to be ideal. It was like visiting a

house and finding it to be a house of which one has dreamed; and it is only recently that I have discovered that my dream was not a dream, or was too much so, that reality is not and never can be made of dreams. There is always included in the real some indefinable substance that cannot be pictured in the mind.[29]

VI THE WORLD OF MUSTAPHA MOND

Rex Warner's convent is reminiscent of an earlier technarchic horror, the thirty-four-storey London hatchery in Aldous Huxley's *Brave New World* (1932) where Alphas and Betas of the Brave New World of the year A.F. (After Ford) 632 were discriminatingly bred together with Gammas, Deltas, and Epsilons by the Bokanovsky process for assignment to their proper place in the social and economic hierarchy. 'Round pegs in square holes tend to have dangerous thoughts about the social system and to infect others with their discontents.'

Here the 'causation of the past' that Wells urged should be 'evaded' was simply ignored since History was bunk. So said 'Our Ford—or Our Freud, as, for some inscrutable reason, he chose to call himself when he spoke of psychological matters.'[30] With education replaced by hypnopaedia (sleep learning) and conditioning, natural feeling by pregnancy-substitutes and promiscuity, and even force itself for the 'slower but infinitely surer methods of ectogenesis, and Neo-Pavlovian conditioning', the state was all comprehending. Through the interstices, however, one dissident had managed to emerge—the despised and despising Bernard Marx. Just as his name is a symbolic fusion of the two religions, so he makes a pilgrimage back to nature—to the reservation—with the girl Lenina. Himself an artificially bred Alpha plus—although one where the predictive techniques of the Central London Hatchery went astray—he finds a young man in the settlement, where the Lawrentian ethic holds sway, who enables him to discover that simple human love exists outside the rigid breeding targets of the *Brave New World*. This is John the Savage, son of the Director of the Central London Hatchery and a Beta Plus Girl whom he had been forced to abandon. Securing for John and his mother a permit to leave the reservation, Bernard Marx brings him to London, where, confronted with them, the Director of Hatcheries and Conditioning resigns. John finds 'civilised infantility too easy'. He despises the hypnopaedic machines in the dormitories and the malthusian drill in the classrooms of co-educational Eton. He refuses to sleep with Lenina, or to go to the 'frolics'. He prefers to stay at home and read Romeo and Juliet, rather than attend a party, organised by the Arch-Community-Songster of Canterbury. Later he reads to another latent rebel against the planned uniformity of the Brave New World—Helmholtz Watson—a lecturer in the College of Emotional Engineering. After his mother's death, the Savage initiates a riot, and with Bernard Marx is taken to meet the Mustapha Mond.

This confrontation of the old primeval decencies by the amorality of the Fordian world enables us to learn the story of its evolution. The experiment began when Cyprus was colonised in A.F. 473 with a batch of twenty-two thousand alphas. The results were disastrous. Civil war broke out in six years and after nineteen out of the twenty-two thousand were killed, the remainder petitioned the World Controller to restore the previous government.

A second experiment, this time of a four-hour day for the lower castes of Iceland, was tried with equally disastrous results. As a result, Mustapha Mond remarked, they decided that:

> Every change is a menace to stability. . . . Every discovery in pure science is potentially subversive; even science must be treated as a possible enemy. . . . Science is dangerous; we have to keep it most carefully chained and muzzled.[31]

So science in the brave new world was:

> just a cookery book, with an orthodox theory of cooking that nobody's allowed to question, and a list of recipes that mustn't be added to except by special permission from the head cook. 'And,' said Mustapha Mond, 'I'm the head cook now.'

By banishing Bernard Marx and Helmholtz Watson to an island, Mustapha Mond gives them the chance of meeting 'the most interesting set of men and women to be found anywhere in the world. All the people who for one reason or another have got too self-consciously individual to fit into community life. All the people who are not satisfied with orthodoxy, who've got independent ideas of their own. Every one, in a word, who's any one.'

As for the Savage, Mustapha Mond showed him, locked in a safe, the Bible, the *Imitation of Christ*, and *The Varieties of Religious*

Experience—'God in the safe and Ford on the shelves.' For as he
said:

> God isn't compatible with machinery and scientific medicine and
> universal happiness. You must make your choice. Our civilisation
> has chosen machinery and medicine and happiness. That's why I
> have to keep these books locked up in the safe. They're smut.

Realising that in his pueblo he had been excluded from com-
munal life and that in London he could not escape from it, the
Savage takes himself off to a hermitage where, still pursued by the
Brave New Worlders, he hangs himself.

Fifteen years later, Huxley remarked:

> . . . at the time the book was written, this idea, that human beings
> are given free will in order to choose between insanity on the one
> hand and lunacy on the other, was one that I found amusing and
> regarded as quite possibly true.

He went on:

> If I were now to rewrite the book, I would offer the savage a third
> alternative. Between the Utopian and primitive horns of his dilemma
> would be the possibility of sanity—a possibility already actualised,
> to some extent, in a community of exiles and refugees from the Brave
> New World living within the borders of the Reservation. In this
> community economics would be decentralist and Henry-Georgian,
> politics Kropotkin and co-operative. Science and technology would
> be used as though, like the Sabbath, they had been made for man,
> not (as at present and still more so in the Brave New World), as
> though man were to be adapted and enslaved to them. Religion
> would be the conscious and intelligent pursuit of man's Final End,
> and intuitive knowledge of the immanent Tao or Logos, the tran-
> scendent Godhead or Brahman. And the prevailing philosophy of
> life would be a kind of Higher Utilitarianism, in which the Greatest
> Happiness principle would be secondary to the Final End principle—
> the first question to be asked and answered in every contingency of
> life being 'How will this thought or action contribute to, or interfere
> with, the achievement, by me and the greatest number of other
> individuals, of man's Final End?[32]

'The end to be achieved,' Huxley wrote, 'is not regarded as
existing in some utopian future period, beginning say in the
twenty-second century or perhaps even a little earlier . . . the end
exists in "heaven".' Heaven, in the terms of what he called 'the

perennial philosophy' was not a 'posthumous condition of indefinite personal survival', but a delivery 'here and now' from egocentrism, a state of 'non-attachment and selflessness'. He cited William Law and the Chandodya Upanishad as examples of what he meant.[33]

The sharpening of Huxley's vision of the future is reflected in the more determinable date at which he decided to unfold it: 20th February 2108, when, as a result of universal and final destruction following the Third World War, society has descended to the baboon stage. The 'narrator', as in the case of Bernard Marx, is also symbolically named William Tallis: Tallis (Tallith) being the shawl donned by orthodox Jews when starting to pray. So too is the title—*Ape and Essence*—of the book, which describes a theocratic dictatorship in California. Its ruler, the Arch-Vicar, presides over a Community whose members rob graves to strip corpses of their clothing, and, because of the spread of radiation—induced mutations, worship Belial. Asked by Dr. Alfred Poole of the New Zealand Re-Discovery Expedition why they should worship something that was destroying them, the Arch-Vicar replies: 'Why do you throw food to a growling tiger? To buy yourself a breathing space.'[34]

VII   THE TRANSVALUATION OF CORAL ISLAND

'The Blowfly in every individual's Heart' for whom Aldous Huxley's Bishop of Hollywood rescues books appears again in William Golding. This classic transvaluation of childhood, *Lord of the Flies* (1954), tells the story of a party of British schoolboys wrecked on an island after the outbreak of a nuclear war. Their leaders bear the same name as Ballantyne's heroes Ralph, Jack, and Peterkin with the exception that Peterkin is renamed Simon. The island on which they are wrecked is a boat-shaped island,[35] the ship being an archetypal symbol of salvation to the early Christians. They react against Ralph (commonsense) and Piggy (intelligence) by not keeping the beacon lit (their only way of establishing contact with the adult world). By subsequently failing to preserve latrine discipline and forgetting their responsibilities to others—a child dies in a thoughtlessly lighted forest fire—they become savages.[36] Ironically the leading savage, Jack, is a headchorister who can sing C sharp.

He whets the blood lust of his choir by first hunting a pig. From this they graduate to murder the Christlike Simon who only wishes to explain to them that 'the Beast'—whom Jack, the Ripper of pig's guts, had tried to propitiate by offering a pig's head on a stick—is really only a dead parachutist. This dead parachutist symbolises History—'an ugly emblem of war and decay that broods over the paradise and provides the only objective equivalent for the beast the boys imagine'[37]—whilst flies that gather round the propitiation, the pig's head, symbolise the advent of Beelzebub—the Lord of the Flies—into this incipent boys' Eden.

For seeing behind the Lord of the Flies the tragic figure of the dead parachutist, Simon is killed like a pig, whilst Piggy, the embodiment of commonsense, is hurled dramatically to his death on the rocks, leaving Ralph, alone, deserted and hunted, to be chased out of his forest refuge by the now blood-hungry young savages. Panting, at the end of his tether on the beach, Ralph finds himself looking up into the green shade, not of the forest whence he had just escaped, but of a peaked naval cap. That this green shade should be surmounted by 'a crown, an anchor, and gold foliage' adds the final touch of irony. For we know that when he is asked: 'What have you been doing? Having a war or something?'[38] his rescuers are only grown-up versions of his tormentors.

VIII   RETRACING OUR STEPS: ROBERT GRAVES

'We must retrace our steps or perish' was the conviction of another mechanophobic fantasy—*Seven Days in New Crete* (1949). There are no machines in New Crete, except a water wheel and a lathe. Travelling is done on foot. Warriors are greased before their battles and even the battles are ritual affairs with padded quarter-staffs. Books are telescoped for simplicity's sake—Tseliot had swallowed up Yeats and Rupert Brooke. Even the manufacture of paper is abolished. This latter is surprising for the author was Robert Graves who had hitherto been calling on the old world to redress the balance of the present. As one of the most learned as well as versatile men of letters of his day, Graves gives his view of the post-Christian era.

Following the transfer of the papacy from Rome to San Francisco and its subsequent abolition at the World Council of Churches at Pittsburg, a devastating war between The Roman

(Europe and America) and Orthodox (Eastern Europe and the Far East), results in a third of the world being made uninhabitable by radioactive rain. Following an era of neo-communism, Logicalism holds sway 'hinged on international science . . . a gloomy and anti-poetic age'. So great becomes the sense of futility in this age of 'ice-cold logic' that outbreaks of Colabromania break out. It takes the form of a hallucination of being whipped round like tops by a white-faced, hawk-nosed woman. In an incredibly quick time the hallucination carries off the Logicians, leaving the way open for the Sophocrats to assume power.

The Sophocrats form an Anthropological Council which is charged:

> . . . to decide under what social conditions mankind, viewed dispassionately as livestock, though with due allowance made for certain ineradicable artistic, literary and religious impulses, lived in the greatest concord and health, and at the same time, how to clear away the detritus of the two previous epochs and safeguard the dwindling natural resources of the world.

They decide that a new religion is needed, but that it must be rooted in primitive not over-civilised soil. Having examined some seventy utopias, from Plato's *Timaeus* to Huxley's *Brave New World* 'and various works of the twenty-first to the twenty-fourth centuries', a member of the council, ben-Yeshu in *A Critique of Utopias*, comes to the conclusion that 'we must retrace our steps or perish'.

He recommends that in various undevastated parts of the world 'anthropological enclaves' should be established representing successive stages of civilisation. These were to be sealed off from the world for three generations and continuously observed by the Anthropological Council with a view to finding 'when and why the freight train of civilisation leapt the rails'.

Once started, those 'enclaves' become, after three generations, so over-populated, that their inhabitants are invited to send colonists to the island of Crete, where vegetables like tomatoes, potatoes, tobacco, and soya—hitherto withheld from them—were made available. Soon all the members of the Anthropological Council have agreed that 'if mankind were to survive at all, the goddess must be re-instated in power', and that they had 'collected sufficient archaeological data to be able to restore her worship in convincing detail'. The goddess, consulted by painting pictures in quince-huts, symbolises Love as opposed to the Father God of the late Christian era whose sole business was war.

Wenn-Thomas (Graves' experiencing hero), discovers how civilised the New Cretans are without 'science' which is merely for clubmen's toys. 'Would I ever get accustomed to the fairytale ways of New Crete?' he asks himself. 'Such fantastic ingenuousness of faith!' His answer was clear enough.

The enclaves are moved to New Crete, now regarded as 'the seed-bed of a Gold Age'. So popular does it become that immigration has virtually to be forbidden. Divided into Kingdoms, each with five estates corresponding to the fingers of a hand—the thumbs (captains), the forefinger (recorders), the third finger (the commons or middle estate), the fourth finger (the servants), and the fifth finger (the magicians)—New Crete so impresses Wenn-Thomas that he declares that if he 'had to choose between New Cretan half-wittedness and American whole-wittedness', he would 'choose the former and avoid stomach ulcers'.[39]

Aware that traditional myths were 'wearing thin' Graves tried to reinterpret, in the light of Frazer's *Golden Bough*, those drawn from the Biblical and classical sources. Aptly enough he began with the 'Song of Taliesin' going on to Greece and then to Ireland. It became, as *The White Goddess* (1948), a plea for the revival of goddess worship and the abandonment of perverse intellectuality. Speaking at the Massachusetts Institute of Technology in 1963 he complained:

> In ancient Greece, the Goddess Athene ruled every art and natural science until ousted by the upstart God Apollo. Apollo was the first to patronize unnatural science—science as an intellectual perversion, science for the sake of science.

Graves saw that:

> the future of thought does not lie in the cosmical nonsense-region of electronic computers, but in the Paradisal region of what he will not be ashamed to call 'magic'. He must obey Deborah's summons to the palm-tree, follow her irrational instructions, trust her implicitly, and allow full weight to the scientifically imponderable.[40]

Chapter Nine

VIRGILS OF THE DYNAMO

Meeting an Adams, said William James, the American philosopher, was 'like meeting the augurs behind the altar and none of
them smiling'.[1] The mantic gloom of the fourth generation of
that remarkable Bostonian brahminhood of Henry and his brother
Brooks was visible when Henry came home from Europe in 1893
and his brother Brooks asked him to read the draft of what was to
become *The Degradation of the Democratic Dogma* (1896). After
doing so he warned Brooks: 'the gold-bugs will never forgive
you. You are monkeying with a dynamo.'[2]

The dynamo was a favourite symbol of disturbance for Henry
Adams, who wrote:

It has brought me so near the end that I hardly care to wait for
the last scenes. There are things in it which run close to the day of
judgment. It is a new century, and what we used to call electricity is
its God. I can already see that the scientific theories and laws of our
generation will, to the next, appear as antiquated as the Ptolemaic
system, and that the fellow who gets to 1930 will wish he hadn't.
The curious mustiness of decay is already over our youth, and all the
period from 1840 to 1870. The period from 1870 to 1900 is closed.
I see that much in the machine-gallery of the Champ de Mars. The
period from 1900 to 1930 is in full swing, and, gee-whacky! how it is
going! It will break its damned neck long before it gets through, if it
tries to keep up the speed. You are free to deride my sentimentality
if you like, but I assure you that I,—a monk of St. Dominic, absorbed
in the Beatitudes of the Virgin Mother—go down to the Champ de
Mars and sit by the hour over the great dynamos, watching them run
as noiselessly and as smoothly as the planets, and asking them—with
infinite courtesy—where in Hell they are going. They are marvellous.
The Gods are not in it.[3]

For Adams unconsciously continued the French debate about tomorrow. A passage in his copy of Michelet's *History of France* reveals his preoccupation:

> It was the universal belief of the middle ages, that the thousandth year from Nativity would be the end of the world. In like manner, before Christianity, the Etrusci had fixed ten centuries as the term of their empire; and the prediction had been fulfilled. Christianity, a wayfarer of this earth, a quest, exiled from heaven, readily adopted a similar belief.[4]

That preoccupation sharpened when he read Renan, who like him, regretted failing to acquire a scientific education in his youth, and who, also like him, could dramatise personal events with conscious art. Renan's *Prière sur l'Acropole* is like Adams's prayer to the Virgin at Chartres. For it was at the Paris Exhibition of 1900 that Adams conceived of that great watershed in time separating the age of the Virgin from that of the Dynamo. The Dynamo was to be for him the symbol of the apocalyptic power of science. For him as for Renan, science would enable history to generalise.

And generalise Adams did. Applying the second law of thermodynamics to history he saw the year 1921 as a time when man's power of thought would reach the 'limits of its possibilities', though, as a kind of mental insurance, he thought the terminus might be extended to 2025. His autobiography, privately printed in 1907, and reprinted with an introduction by James Truslow Adams in 1931, was to become one of the most influential personal documentaries of the twentieth century.

The dynamo became a central image of the Futurist movement. The men of the two-thousandth century would, said E. F. T. Marinetti in *Le Futurisme* (1912), be 'extremely revivified, shaken and tamed by new electrical energies'. He foresaw them enjoying 'a life of power between walls of iron and crystal', with 'furniture of steel, twenty times lighter and cheaper than ours . . . free at last from the examples of fragility and softness offered by wood and fabrics with their rural ornaments. . . . Heat, humidity and ventilation regulated by a brief pass of the hand, they feel the fullness and solidity of their own will. . . .'

Or as another futurist wrote:

> We need Utopians of genius, a new Jules Verne; not to sketch on broad perspective an easily grasped technical utopia, but the very

existence of future men whose basic laws of being respond to instinctive simplicity as well as the complicated relationships of life.[5]

Perhaps the rise of the cinema helped, for its potential, as exhibited in *The Testament of Dr. Caligari*, seemed to excite the Futurists and Expressionists. Their influence is perhaps better seen in the futuristic ballet in Elmer Rice's *The Subway* (1929), where scientists discover the most characteristic artefacts of Western civilisation to be false teeth and a pair of five-cent earrings. One of Rice's other heroes is told by his boss in *The Adding Machine* (1923):

> You're a failure Zero, a failure. A waste product . . . the raw material of slums and . . . the ready prey of the first jingo or demagogue or political adventurer who takes the trouble to play upon your ignorance and credulity and provincialism.[6]

At Ridgefield, Connecticut, Eugene O'Neill was inspired to write *Dynamo* (1929) to 'dig at the roots of the sadness of today'. This celebrated 'the death of an old God and the failure of science and materialism to give any satisfying new one for the surviving primitive religious instinct to find a meaning for living, and to comfort its fears of death with'. A Nietzschean long after he ceased to be a socialist, O'Neill, from laborious construing of *Also Sprach Zarathustra* whilst at Harvard, to his zealous missionary work at the Provincetown experimental theatre, retained his admiration for Nietzsche, even attending rehearsals with a copy of the *Birth of Tragedy* in his pocket.[7]

II TECHNOCRACY: GERNSBACK AND BRADBURY

Such small experimental groups as the Provincetown players were forming elsewhere amongst the apostles of 'efficiency engineering' like Gantt and C. G. Barth, who tried to form an organisation called 'The New Machine'. Another such was 'Technical Alliance' of electrical engineers, economists, and others who, like Henry Adams, had a thermodynamic mystique. This began in 1919 to discuss the re-shaping of the North American Republic around the dynamo. This later took shape as Technocracy Inc. which argued that if sufficient energy employing devices to replace labour were installed and 'energy certificates' were to replace money, 'labour' would be abolished. A-historical, they believed that all previous 'social wisdom' was invalidated by technological progress. 'Technology,' wrote the founder, Howard Scott, 'has no ancestors in the social history of man. It creates its own.'[8]

Extending its long-range vision after being incorporated in 1932 as Technocracy Inc., it attracted Hugo Gernsback, who, as early as 1909, had founded the first magazine to be devoted to radio: *Modern Electrics* in which he had, in 1911, published a story about the year 2660 called 'Ralph 124c+'. This contains, amongst other remarkable anticipations, a description of radar. Helped by T. O'Connor Sloane, another electrical engineer, Gernsback built up the Experimenter Publishing Company which was swept away in the Stock Market crash of 1929. He promptly organised the Stellar Publishing Corporation which issued, amongst other journals, *Science Wonder Stories* and in which he first used the name 'science fiction'.[9]

To publicise its ideas Gernsback issued the *Technocracy Review* in 1933, but the apparent adoption of its ideas by the New Deal seems to have caused his enthusiasm to wane, for the review ceased after the second issue.[10] Six years after Gernsback broke off his flirtation, a nineteen-year-old young man in Los Angeles took it up and, in a duplicated magazine of his own, *Futuria Fantasia*, indicated that technocracy combined 'all the hopes and dreams of science-fiction. We've been dreaming about it for years —now, in a short time, it may become a reality.'[11]

He was, as we shall see later, to change his mind. His name was Ray Bradbury. But let us return to Hugo Gernsback.

One of the sectarian offshoots of Technocracy—a recent historian calls it 'the most direct derivative'[12] was the Utopian Society 'which accepted its technological imperative but organised itself in secret fraternal groups'. By the summer of 1934 it had a membership of half a million, serviced by a paper of its own: *Utopia News*. In that year too Gernsback formed his Science Fiction League, probably based on the society of wireless amateurs he had organised a quarter of a century earlier.[13] This banded together readers and writers of science-fiction to exchange magazines, books, and views. In the early nineteen-thirties, the Scienceers of New York had put out a magazine, *The Planet*, edited by Allen Glasser, and their example was followed wherever the genre found a public. Publishers opened readers' columns. Coalescing as a world science-fiction convention just before the

Second World War, they found their Bishop Sprat in Sam Moskowitz, whose history of the movement (in 1954) and the genre (1957) added further impetus to the debates about tomorrow. Both magazines[14] and fan clubs[15] also took root in England before the war.

By providing 'feedback' from readers, collectors, and addicts—these fan clubs were utterly modern. They can also be seen as an extension of groups like the Order of the Golden Dawn in which, at the beginning of the century, W. B. Yeats used to discuss Rosicrucianism with A. E. Waite, its historian, and Arthur Machen the fantast.[16]

Like Hermetics, these groups discussed the mechanical analogues of telepathy, ecstatically contemplating new universes, sharing messages, exchanging collectors' items, or compiling bibliographies—virtually a major activity.[17] Authors also worked in groups. One of the best known was the Milwaukee Fictioneers, who included Ralph Milne Farley (pseudonym of Senator Hoar), Raymond A. Palmer, later an Editor of *Amazing Stories* and Stanley G. Weinbaum.

A Futurian Literary Society, amongst whom were Frederick Pohl, Cyril Kornbluth, and Donald Wollheim, was a mutual-aid society of authors. Pohl himself was able to aid others when in 1940 he became an editor. Today (1966) his journals include *If* and *Worlds of Tomorrow*. So, too, the Science Fiction Association in Britain, through its roneoed journal *Novae Terrae*, had amongst its members John Christopher (C. S. Youd), William F. Temple, and Arthur C. Clarke. *Novae Terrae* was, after the Second World War, to emerge as *New Worlds*.[18]

Indeed no genre has been so conscious of its reading public. One editor instituted a survey in 1949 in America and found that four out of five readers were under thirty-five and that over 66 per cent were directly concerned with science and engineering as administrators, researchers, or technicians.[19] A similar distribution was revealed by an English survey in 1954. This estimated that the proportion of readers with secondary or higher education was 'very substantial and far higher than the proportion which these bear to the population as a whole'.[20] A reputable English political observer considered that this reflected the new popular faith that 'though there are many things modern technology cannot do now, there is no reason to suppose they cannot be done in the future and many reasons to suppose that they can'.[21]

In 1964 one English science-fiction magazine found that its readership was composed mainly of young technicians in the mid-twenties, who tended to purchase an average of four paperbacks a month.[22]

III   THE DETECTIVE STORY AS PARADISE REGAINED

These magazines reaped readers and authors from detective stories, where similar groups of fans (like the notable Baker Street irregulars), had been forming. This is not surprising as stories of the future, like the great exemplar of detectives, Edgar Allen Poe's Dupin, use the same techniques. He, it will be remembered, had phrases like 'the calculus of probabilities' and 'algebraic analyses' constantly on his lips in the *Murders of the Rue Morgue* (1841) and *The Mystery of Marie Roget* (1842). Poe himself showed the way in which such techniques could be applied when surmising the future in *Mellonta Tanta*. There Amricca—the disguise is threadbare —is described a thousand years ahead as coming under:

> a fellow by the name of *Mob* who took everything into his own hands and set up a despotism, in comparison with which those of the fabulous Zenos and Hello fagabaluses were respectable and delectable . . . He was a giant in stature—insolent, rapacious, filthy; had the gall of a bullock with the heart of a hyena and the brains of a peacock. He died, at length, by dint of his own energies, which exhausted him.[23]

The same inductive reasoning was employed by Pelham in Bulwer Lytton's novel of that name and was used by Bulwer Lytton to descry *The Coming Race* (1871). Even 'the most perfect reasoning and observing machine' [*sic*] amongst these early detectives, Sherlock Holmes, seems to have been merely a re-hearsal for Conan Doyle's favourite character, Professor Challenger, a hero scientist, whose efforts, as told in *The Lost World* (1912) and *The Poison Belt* (1913), were supplemented by those of Dr. Maracot, another hero scientist, in Doyle's last work of fiction, *The Maracot Deep* (1929).[24] In attempts to explore even further, Doyle began to assault the psychic barrier. A fourth link between detection and prediction can be seen in M. P. Shiel's exotic Prince Zaleski who mixes deductions with prophecies, possessing 'the unparalleled power not merely of disentangling in retrospect, but of unravelling in prospect, able to relate coming events with unimaginable minuteness of precision'.

More contemporary deployments of the calculus of probability in imaginative detection and prediction were made by J. J. Connington (in real life A. W. Stewart, the professor of chemistry at Queen's University, Belfast, from 1919 to 1944), who wrote a number of detective stories and one outstanding tale of the future: *Nordenholt's Million* (1923), the story of the bacillus *diozotans* threatening life on earth.

G. K. Chesterton's use of the detective genre as an allegory of the search for God—in *The Man who was Thursday*—provided Karel Capek with the spur to write *Wayside Crosses* (1917). But as one character in it laments, 'God cannot be found by the technique of criminal investigation'.[25] Failing to find God in this book he discovered a sympathy for man. This sympathy he expressed in his play R.U.R. (1921), which gave the new word 'robot' to the English language. Indeed the original title, *Rossum's Universal Robots*, is in English, as if the author were anxious to have its significance debated—as indeed it was—at a public discussion in London between G. K. Chesterton and Bernard Shaw.[26]

Rossum (from the Czech *rozum* = reason), disbelieved in God, and, like a good nineteenth-century rationalist, tried to create life but had no thought of exploiting his discovery. His nephew, on the other hand, did, and began to mass-manufacture robots on an island. To this island comes Helena Glory, anxious to stimulate the robots to revolt. She first mistakes the directors for robots, and before she has been there, agrees to marry the managing director. But whilst she is there, she learns that man has lost his capacity to procreate and the robots have revolted. So she burns old Rossum's formula. The managing director tries to prevent the robots capturing the power plan of the factory by an electrified screen but the robots capture and kill all but the engineer, Alquist. He tries to discover Rossum's secret, but instead discovers that the robots have feelings, and indeed can procreate of themselves. They have supplanted man. In other words, love and life survive, technology only dehumanises men who wish to be dehumanised. As the author himself explained:

I ask whether it is not possible to see in the present social conflict of the world an analogous struggle between two, three, five, equally

serious verities and equally generous idealisms? I think it is possible
. . . instead of the struggle being, as we are so often told it is, one
between noble truth and vile selfish error.[27]

A year later he described how the exploitation of atomic energy
for industrial use released spiritual energy of the Absolute that
pervades matter. All involved in the process become 'possessed',
exhibiting all the syndromes of emotional conversion. Sceptically,
the Church stands off, but business demands that the exploitation
continue. And it does, with such alarming consequences that production soars, people forsake profit and the whole economic
system disintegrates. After world chaos and upheaval, the exploitation of atomic energy is abandoned: and a few men talking over
it in retrospect agree that the chaos was caused by man's desire
for the absolute and unwillingness to be relativistic. This was
translated five years later into English as *The Absolute at Large*
(1927)—two years after his second novel had appeared in England.

This second novel *Krakatit* (1924) also dealt with the misuse of
atomic energy. In his pilgrim's progress, the hero-engineer Prokop
passes through the temptations of self-satisfaction, self-will, and
power, all symbolised by a girl—in search of the mysterious veiled
beauty symbolising love of mankind, and not finding her, but
God, who warns him not to be a utopian large-scale, but a piece-
meal, engineer and to concentrate on harnessing energy.

A recent commentator has stressed Capek's preoccupation with
the destructive potential of energy and of siege. The latter is
especially true in *The War with the Newts* (1936), which appeared in
an English translation a year later. Here Capek says 'there is no
speculation about the future, but a mirroring of that which
exists'.[28] For his newts are really men corrupted by civilisation
serving the great Newt whole, 'god, ruler, employer, and spiritual
leader'. The story of these newts telescoping man's development
to outrival man and turn the water table against him is left in the
balance—as they begin to flood half Europe.

Capek's mirroring of two societies became a standard technique
in science-fiction. John Wyndham deserted the detective story in
which he had shown himself an adept with *Foul Play Suspected*
(1935) to flex his intellectual muscles in the American popular
magazines as John Beynon Harris, and later wrote, as John
Wyndham, a series of widely read fantasies like *The Day of the*

Triffids (1951), a story of a plant menace; *The Kraken Wakes* (1953), a story of the attempts of an alien race who have settled in the ocean to destroy humanity; *The Chrysalids* (1955), the story of a post-war remnant of civilisation which tries to destroy any organism deviating from the norm; *The Midwich Cuckoos* (1957), describing the illegitimate creation of great golden-eyed children of precocious intelligence and amorality; *The Outward Urge* (1959), unfolding the story of four generations of the Troon family exploring the moon, Mars, and Venus; and *Trouble with Lichen* (1960), which poses the problem of coping with a means of doubling life without creating a world catastrophe.[29] Lastly, Edmund Crispin's stories of Dr. Gervaise Fen, the donnish investigator of *Love Lies Bleeding* (1948), *Frequent Hearses* (1950), *The Moving Toyshop* (1951), and *Beware of the Trains* (1953), were but overtures to his brilliant exegeses of the new genre of science-fiction, whose name he did so much to popularise.

IV   THE COWBOY STORY AS PARADISE LOST

If the detective story (*pace* Raymond Chandler) was an allegorical paradise regained[30] (attracting political reformers like G. D. H. Cole and conservative theological writers like G. K. Chesterton and Dorothy L. Sayers), the cowboy story is a paradise lost. For the cowboy's unsophisticated honesty exemplifies the theme that earlier forms of social organisation are superior to later forms: agricultural society is better than industrial, pastoral better than agricultural, and a savage society is best of all.[31] As the harmony of Bulwer Lytton's vrilya was Victorian stability transposed, so the interplanetary conflicts of modern American space-fiction are developments of ideas in the novels of Ned Buntline, Bret Harte, Owen Wister, O. Henry, and Zane Grey. Indeed in the case of E. E. Smith, one could describe his novels as cowboys riding rocket-machines in space.

For he first set cowboys in space. Idaho-born E. E. Smith was a research chemist in Washington during the First World War, and his *The Skylark of Space*, though not published until over ten years later, set the frontier at the Milky Way.[32] Published by T. O'Connor Sloane, an associate of Gernsback and a scientific consultant in many law-suits about patents, and a prolific populariser of electricity, the *Skylark* series shows that, just as the detective story leant heavily on nineteenth-century chemistry and bacteriology (Sherlock Holmes was no mean chemist), so modern physics stimulated the rise of science-fiction.

From writing neo-cowboy stories like *David Star: Space Ranger* (1953), Isaac Asimov explored the moral problems confronting the contemporary technocrat. 'Above all a Technician must be dispassionate', is the motto of the hero of *The End of Eternity* (1955), since his role is to alter and monitor, where necessary, the cause-and-effect relationship of time. 'The Reality Change he initiates may affect the lives of as many as fifty billion people. A million or more of these may be so drastically affected as to be considered new individuals. Under these conditions an emotional make-up is a distinct handicap.'[33] Solaria, another fictional community designed by Isaac Asimov, is 'the first really new society; the first great social invention since the farmers of Sumeria and Egypt invented cities'. For its robots eliminated 'the action of social revolution and the reaction of guarding against such a revolution or combating it once it has begun'. Called in to help Solaria over a difficulty that has arisen over the interaction of robots and men, the hero reports back:

> 'The Solarians have given up something mankind has had for a million years; something worth more than atomic power, cities, agriculture, tools, fire, everything; because it's something that made everything else possible.'
> 'I don't want to guess, Bayley. What is it?'
> 'The tribe, Sir. Co-operation between individuals. Solaria has given it up entirely. It's a world of isolated individuals, and the plant's only sociologist is delighted that this is so.'[34]

The theme is even more extensively explored in his trilogy *Foundation* (1951), *Foundation and Empire* (1952), and *Second Foundation* (1953), where Hari Sheldon, the last great scientist of the first Empire of all the Planets, creates a new science of human behaviour—psychohistory—by reducing human psychology to a series of mathematical equations. Foreseeing anarchy, he sets up two Foundations of scientists at opposite ends of the Empire, one much publicised, and the other secret. The first two books tell the story of the first foundation, a small community of encyclopaedists in the outer periphery taking over the barbarised planets but falling before the Mule—a mutant which moulds men's emotions.

Both Mule and the first foundation look for the second, finding it at the centre of Seldon's Empire, at Trantor. Asimov's writing is requisitioned for inclusion in sociological readers.

V   THE IMAGINARY JOURNEY

At this stage science-fiction began to absorb an older genre: the imaginary journey—a medium through which, from the time of Lucian, Utopia or dystopia has been explored.[35] As one afficionado of the genre, L. Sprague de Camp, himself an engineer, has put it:

> Formerly they located their ideal commonwealths in the distant past or in undiscovered parts of the world. Now, however, that the unexplored places left on earth are few and uninviting and the history of the remote past is fairly well known, they prefer their Utopias in a distant future or even on other planets.[36]

The difference between the commonwealths presented in science-fiction and those before is that between dynamic and static systems. More sustained imaginary journeys into space on such a scale were made by Robert Heinlein (the stories of Dr. E. E. Smith were, in spite of their neo-Marxist outlook, rather raw emotionally), who modelled his Trollopian tomorrows on Sinclair Lewis's fictional State of Winnemac. For the technical data and sociological phenomena in Heinlein's stories conform to a developmental pattern being, as he says, 'of the what-would-happen-if sort, in which the "if", the basic postulate of each story, is some possible change in human environment latent in our present day technology or culture'.[37] The time-scale on which they are stretched extends from 1951 to the year 2600, and begins aptly enough with 'Lifeline', a witty tale about the dangers of knowing the future.

In a significant inversion of Archbishop Ussher's chronology, James Blish looks forward to the year A.D. 4004 in his quartet: *They Shall Have Stars*, *A Life for the Stars*, *Earthman Come Home*, and *A Clash of Cymbals*. Just as the Archbishop's laboriously computed time-scale from Eden onwards traced the stories of the cities of the plain, so Blish's traced that of cities in space. Ussher begins with Adam being expelled from Eden, Blish with the expulsion of a scientist from the U.S. Bureau of Standards. Both

Adam and Dr. Corsi are security risks. The exodus from the Earth Eden is explained by Senator Wagoner:

> The Soviets can have the Earth. As a matter of fact they will take it before very long, whether we give it to them or not. But we are going to scatter the West throughout the stars, scatter it with immortal people having immortal ideas.[38]

The exodus aid through space continues. Cities themselves take off, encountering Vegan tyrannies, battles between Government and Utopia, and the foundation of New Earth.

VI ANALOG AND ITS MODELS

This can be especially seen in the works of a young electrical engineer, John W. Campbell, who visited O'Connor Sloane in 1929 after submitting some stories whilst a student at M.I.T. For the next decade Campbell bombarded the magazines with stories of future physicists, exploiting power to work computers and explore the universe. These, alternating with entropic fantasies including some about atomic energy under the name of Don A. Stuart, became so popular that he was invited to edit a monthly magazine called *Astounding Stories*, founded in 1930. He changed its name to *Analog*, thereby indicating its role which was 'to describe a system which behaves in a manner similar to some other and less manipulable system, so that it is easier and more convenient to study'. Its contents were to be 'a convenient analog system for thinking about new scientific, social and economic ideas —and for examining old ideas'.[39] And so it became. Not only did it carry stories by Heinlein and Asimov, but A. E. van Vogt, Theodore Sturgeon, Henry Kuttner, and Catherine L. Moore as well. Most of these, later expanded as novels, represent Campbell's policy of 'subterranean education: to spread ideas which may help to break established patterns of thought', a policy that led to the magazine being nicknamed *Monologue*.[40]

By 1950 another significantly-named journal was *Worlds of IF*. Begun as *Galaxy Science Fiction* it acquired Frederik Pohl as editor in 1960, who changed its name. The change, as in the case of *Analog*, was symbolic. For just as models in physics represent more or less accurately what is going on in nature,[41] so Pohl's stories represented what might go on if certain decisions were taken. Such stories transcended normal mechanistic and biological models, by exploring psychological dimensions. If biologists and physicists regard systems 'as developing societies of trends, in which each trend describes events in a collectivity without predicting the behaviour of the individual elements out of which collectivity is made',[42] Pohl's authors explored that missing element. They were Utopian, dystopian, heuristic, paradigmatic, schematic, personificatory, or abstractive fictions. Before its change of name it carried three major modern dystopias: Ray Bradbury's *Fahrenheit 451*; Alfred Bester's *The Demolished Man*; and Pohl and Kornbluth's *Gravy Planet*.

As Pohl reminded his readers in May 1967:

> it's perfectly easy to project a world where bearded savages howl in the canyons of Wall Street. We're not suggesting that science-fiction writers should stick their heads in the sand and write a kind of twentieth century Pollyanna. We're suggesting that if you don't like the looks of the future, a very good story to write—and one that we get all too seldom—is the story of *how* the people of today after tomorrow learn how to avoid, prevent, terminate and/or cure whatever we think is going to be wrong. John R. Pierce says: 'There is only one future when it comes; the only chance we have to consider alternate futures is now, when we're still not sure what will turn up.'

Another such journal was *Fantasy and Science Fiction*. Begun in 1949, under Anthony Boucher, it commissioned a special series 'satirising one or another aspect of man's mortality'. Amongst the authors so enlisted was Howard Fast—whose story 'The Martian Shop' is in the tradition of his great hero Tom Paine.[43]

Further Asmodean fantasies were woven for the American magazine *Weird Tales*. Established in 1923, it became, as its name implies, a virtual arsenal of the Gothics. Two of its contributors were Howard Philip Lovecraft and Ray Bradbury. Lovecraft's stories of the Cthulhu were based on the myth that the former inhabitants of the world practised black magic and hovered on the outside, ready to take possession at any time. Even more self-consciously in the demonic tradition, Ray Bradbury provided a necklace of case histories strung around the colonisation of Mars at the beginning of the third millennium.

'Wouldn't Mr. Poe be delighted?' exclaims Mr. Stendhal, in the *Silver Locusts* (1951), as he contemplates his handiwork, the House of Usher, built after the burning of horror books in the great fire of 1975, 'when Once upon a Time became no more'. 'Poe and Lovecraft and Hawthorne and Ambrose Bierce,' he continued, 'and all the tales of terror and fantasy and horror and, for that matter, tales of the future were burned heartlessly. They passed a law. Oh, it started very small. In 1950 and '60 it was a grain of sand. . . . There was always a minority afraid of something, and a great majority afraid of the dark, afraid of the future, afraid of the past, afraid of the present, afraid of themselves and shadows of themselves.'[44] This diary of lost men and last men over the years 1999 to 2026 shows how the vandals and limited intelligences of earth destroy the civilisation of Mars. It is a fine example of Bradbury's avowed use of the medium. 'Science fiction', he wrote, 'is a wonderful hammer. I intend to use it when and if necessary to bark a few shins or knock a few heads, in order to make people leave people alone.'[45]

Equally astringent in his deployment of what he called para-normal kinetics, Clifford Simak describes a research station, Fishhook, founded on 'dribbles from metaphysical societies' taking shape in Mexico. By exploiting such techniques on a commercial scale, Fishhook is able to exploit the stars. Having started as a human crusade, Fishhook turns into 'one of the greatest mono-polies the world has ever known', and becomes a brake upon the advancement of the human race.[46] Shepherd Blaine dedicates him-self to destroying its monopoly. 'We must show the world that P.K. is a human ability and not a Fishhook ability. . . . Fishhook can't be the only contact man has with the stars.' In *Time is the Simplest Thing* (1961), Blaine explains that:

> Fishhook doesn't want you people. Fishhook isn't what you think it is. It has changed. . . . It has been the promised land. It has been the ultimate solution. The never-never land. But it's not like that at all. It is a country-house. It figures loss and profit.[47]

Harried and persecuted by Fishhook and by those who are afraid of para-normals, Blaine, at his wits' end, teleports himself and found himself 'lying on his face and beneath him was grass and the smell of grass and earth. The howling of the storm was gone and there was no rattle in the willows.'

> He rolled over and sat up.
> He held his breath at what he saw.
> He was in paradise![48]

Commenting on the assumption by these twentieth-century shamans of the role of the myth-makers, a European observer remarked:

In the other world all the improbability of mythology and biblical literature live again as real possibilities. Science fiction is tinged with a religious belief in wonders which religion itself has rejected as unrealistic.[49]

Many of the characters in these books are 'really us, magnified into what we hope or dread to be'.[50] In them are ideas that everyone will be forced to face, as well as the larger dreams—Jung's archetypes. They are examples of the maxim that 'reality thinking cannot operate without concurrent and supporting unconscious phantasies'.[51]

VII THE SPIRIT OF SORTILEGE

Fantasy, kindled outside the general orbit of the debate about the dynamo, animated the disciples of Charles Fort to form a society under the novelist Tiffany Thayer to remove the halo from the head of science and destroy scientists' faith in their own works. Aiming at a general return to the true scientific principle of 'temporary acceptance' by informing the general public of the political and self-preserving character of most work done under the ambiguous cloak of pure science, the Fortean Society published its own journal.

The English correspondent of this was Eric Frank Russell who became a science-fiction writer.[52]

Another such movement was actually started by a science-fiction writer, when in 1950, Lafayette Ron Hubbard claimed that he had discovered Dianetics, a mathematic of the mind, which dispensed with psychiatry and psychology. According to him, life is divided into ability and mechanics. Ability is the handling of matter, energy, space, and time, and mechanics is putting them together as an engine. The conscious mind is analytic, and the unconscious reactive but retentive. Such retention, especially of disorders—which he calls engrams—cause colds and neuroses. To eliminate such ailments, a patient must go to an 'auditor' (i.e. practitioner of Dianetics), who will put him into a reverie, and by identifying them, remove them. Dianetics developed into Scientology, which Hubbard described as 'a system of organised axioms resolving problems of life and thought, developed through the application of the methodology of the exact sciences, to the humanities'. Through 'auditors' and therapeutic groups, patients could increase their intelligence and be cured of ailments. Indeed, at one time John W. Campbell, Jr., rallied to the Dianetic movement.[53]

Other revelations came from a Polish-born engineer, Alfred Korzybski, who considered that undue pessimism might be proved to be as dangerous a religion as any other blind creed. As one preoccupied with the ethical implications of science, he pointed out how slowly metaphysical and social, as opposed to the natural sciences, were appreciated with the resultant revolutions and wars. He envisaged human engineering to be 'the science and art of directing human energies and human capacities to the advancement of human weal'. For to him humanity was the 'magnificent natural agency by which the past lives in the present and the present for the future'. It is civilised through 'the process of binding time'.

> There is indeed [he wrote] a fine sense in which we can, if we choose, apply the expression—survival of the fittest—to the activity of the time-binding energies of man . . . the development of the higher ideals is due to the *natural* capacity of humanity; the impulse is simply a time-binding impulse.[54]

Korzybski's 'non-Aristotelian systems' or Null A. were a new attempt to evaluate facts and worlds and exercised a powerful influence on A. E. van Vogt, a Canadian who in 1941 wrote the *World of Null A*, describing Venus as a centre for such activity training. In 1965 he wrote another, *The Players of Null A*, transferring the Null A world to deep space.

The mood infected theologians and poets too. Working in China on the remains of man's most ancient ancestor, Sinanthropos, Teilhard de Chardin, a Jesuit prehistorian, saw that the scientific solution of the problem of man cannot be determined 'by the study of fossils, but by a more careful consideration of the properties and possibilities in Man today which enable Man to predict the Man of tomorrow'. He told his sister in 1935, 'the Past has shown me the shape of the Future. And preoccupation with the future tends to sweep everything else aside.'[55]

Virgils of the Dynamo

'I have a Vision of the Future, chum,' wrote John Betjeman in *The Planesters Vision.*

> The workers' flats in fields of soya-beans
> Tower up like silver pencils, score on score.
> And surging millions hear the challenge come
> From microphones in communal canteens
> 'No Right! No Wrong! All's perfect—evermore'.[56]

VIII ANTIPODEAN ANTICIPATIONS

'Is it possible,' asked the first official statistician in the Commonwealth of Australia, Sir G. H. Knibbs, 'by envisaging the grave problems of the immediate future, to move toward a partial solution of them?'[57] He wanted 'to make prediction sure' so that 'with co-ordinated international effort, there would be no difficulty in so directing future statistical technique' in order that 'a more perfect study could be made of the drift of mankind'.[58]

That drift began increasingly to be mapped by the fantasts of the Southern Hemisphere. 'I sometimes wish that we had gone on treating these gentry [i.e. scientists] as they did Galileo in the long ago,'[59] said the hero of one of the earliest Australian fantasies: *Celestalia. A Fantasy A.D. 1975* (1933). The Australian naval officer, who wrote it under the pseudonym of A. L. Pullar, was obsessed by the movement of peoples. The Italians, decimated by a war in 1952 move to Queensland, Australia; the Japanese, evicted by an earthquake, colonise China and Brazil; whilst England becomes an aircraft carrier for British America—its coasts being lined with 'solid, solid concrete, from Plymouth, right round to the North of Scotland' as 'the last line of defence against the old Russian Bear'. It houses searchlights every few hundred yards and a hundred thousand planes. With her industry moved to Canada and America, England reverts to pastoral feudalism to such an extent that even the counties are renamed after noble families. Sussex and Surrey become Percy and Cecil. As the hero says, 'all the old estates have been restored and it now works well and happily. The black country is now no more . . . industrial England is practically extinct. They're welcome to it in British-America.'[60]

Pullar envisaged America as being 'taken over' in 1952 by the Canadians after a disastrous negro 'coup d'etat' in 1945. Another

145

Australian envisages America being dominated in 1999 by a woman messiah who sets out to evangelise the world and succeeds in every country—except Australia. There, the half million population were divided into two warring groups. Since these groups came together once a year at either end of the rusting ruins of Sydney Harbour Bridge, this Californian daughter of God decides to gas them from the air, but her plane is destroyed. Helen Simpson's fantasy *The Woman On The Beast* (1933) was followed by others like G. D. Mitchell's *The Awakening* (1937) and Erle Cox's *Fools Harvest* (1939), which foresaw invasion from the Orient. But by this time fact began to outrun fiction. The Second World War, followed by others in Korea and Vietnam, outran the wildest stretch of Australian imagination.

Chapter Ten

SECTARIAN SCIENTISM

I THE TECHNOLOGICAL IMPERATIVE

The fantasy of environmental change, which led Erasmus Darwin in Britain's first industrial spurt to suggest that icebergs should be rigged with sails so that they could drift southwards to moderate the heat of tropical climates, appeared in Russia too. As N. G. Chernyshevski anticipated in *What Is to Be Done* (1863) a time would come when the ploughman would live in a splendid club, always protected from wind and rain and only going out to set machines going. N. G. Chernyshevski became one of the 'fathers' of the revolution, exercising a great influence on Lenin, amongst others.

The Russians also read Grant Allen, Walter Besant, and Bulwer Lytton, as well as the 'new world' novels of Mayne Reed and Jack London.[1] By 1903 fantasy was becoming fact as K. E. Tsiolkovsky published an article on 'The probing of space by jet devices' in *Nauchnoe Obozrenie*. By 1920 he had outlined the construction of a large manned space station in which undiluted sunlight would be harnessed for factory processes, including the growing of plants for food.[2] His ideas influenced Alexsei Tolstoy, the novelist who put a Red Army man on Mars to effect a revolution against a decadent society there.

Tolstoy's *Aelita* (1923) presented one side of the picture. The other was drawn by Valerii Bryusov, in one of the earliest critical allegories of the new Soviet régime. Set in Star City in Antarctica, it describes the breakdown of a scientismic society. The author had had experience of the Soviets as a war correspondent as his story *The Republic of the Southern Cross* (1919) shows. Both assisted in the rise of P.F.L.: initials describing a popular magazine, *Priluchenchesko Fantasticheskaya Literatura*. This, to quote Robert

Milch, 'is dear to the ideologues of the Communist Party as a medium for propaganda . . . and as a means of propounding such socially desirable doctrines as the value of collective effort and faith in man's ability to control and harness nature'.[3] Or as that legislator of Socialist realism A. A. Zhdanov said at the 1st Soviet writers congress in 1930:

> Soviet literature must be able to show our heroes, be able to look into the future. It will not be a Utopia, for our tomorrow is being prepared by planned conscious work today.

11 'UNOFFICIAL FUTURES' IN THE SOVIET UNION

With the Soviet Government in power, the future acquired a new political significance, for there was one 'official' and several 'unofficial' futures. The scenarist of one such unofficial future was Alexsandra Cajanov, who writing under the name of Ivan Kremaev in 1920, visualised a peasant waking up in 1984 in a world divided into five closed power systems—the German, the Anglo-French, the American-Australian, the Sino-Japanese, and the Russian. His fellow peasants had put down the intelligentsia and destroyed the cities, whilst the Germans who had tried to put them down, were defeated and given reparation.[4]

An even more distinguished 'unofficial' future was a warning against simple extrapolations of present trends. For 'The Single State' of Evgeny Zamyatin's *We*, published for the first time in New York in 1925, is symbolised by a straight line, 'grand, precise and wise, the wisest of all lines'. Its citizens are known by numbers, its élite are mathematicians. One such indeed was D-503, engaged in building a rocket to take the party 'line' to the stars. *My* (it become *We* in translation), describes a world in which everyone is known by number, and regulated by the Hour Schedule. All have sacrificed privacy to live in a glass city, under the Benefactor and his Guardians. We see this world of A.D. 2600 through the papers of a participant, in this case a mathematician D.503, who is engaged on an interplanetary flying machine, 'The Integral'—which, as its name implies, is to introduce 'the system' to other worlds' 'The System' is based on group consciousness, logic, and mechanics. In it, there is no room for unregulated love, as we see from D.503's affair with 090, for which he has to get a pink ticket. But another woman upsets this and initiates a conflict between his rational self and his passion for her. This is I.330, the 'heroine' of the story. She takes him to 'the Ancient House', where the walls were not, as everywhere else, transparent, and introduces him to her fellow conspirators, who are irrational and show it by making a demonstration on the Day of Unanimity under her leadership. This D.503 finds hard, and tries to talk her out of her unreason but she asks him for the last number. He acknowledges there is none. 'The number of numbers is infinite.' She replies:

> 'Well, how can you speak of a last revolution? There is no last one, revolution is infinite. The last one—that's for children; children are frightened of infinity and must be allowed to sleep peacefully at night.'

Zamyatin's unique vision of the Brave New World inside Russia (where, of course, his book was banned), was based on parody of Soviet doctrine:

> Today negates yesterday, but then comes the negation of the negation—tomorrow; always the same dialectical path, bearing the world to infinity in a grandiose parabola. Thesis—yesterday; antithesis—today; synthesis—tomorrow.

Poor D.503! He cannot stomach the nakedness, irrationality and freedom of the revolutionaries, so when the Single State offers everyone the opportunity of having their imagination removed by an operation, he undergoes it. As a result, he can watch I.330 tortured to death by the Guardians without a qualm.[5] Significantly enough Zamyatin's American translator, G. Zilboorg, was an American psychiatrist.

The sight of America unnerved another Russian, Vladimir Mayakovsky—himself a futurist—who had been the driving force behind that creed in pre-war Russia. 'The futurism of naked technology with the superficial impressionism of smoke and wires which has the enormous task of revolutionising the paralysed, obese and ancient psyche—this elemental futurism has been definitely confirmed by America.' As Mayakovsky saw it, the Left Front of Literature (L.E.F.), the movement he and other futurists had founded after the Soviet Revolution, had not to hymn technology, but control it 'in the name of the interests of humanity. Not the aesthetic enjoyment of iron fire escapes, but the simple organisation of living quarters'. Three years earlier in *About This* (1923) he addressed a prayer to a chemist of the thirtieth century in the 'Future Workshop of Human Resurrection' asking for a keepership at a zoo—only to end up inside. 'Why am I alone in the cage?' he asked—and his reply came in his own play *The Bedbug* (1928). Here as Prisypkin, a lousy, vodka-soused member of the card-holding proletariat, he awakes in the year 1978 to find booze, sex, and tobacco abolished in a hygienic nirvana. He himself escaped to the bright lights of Paris only to commit suicide in 1930.[6]

III BERTRAND RUSSELL VERSUS J. B. S. HALDANE

The debate stirred outside Russia too. An English publisher commissioned a series of eighty-six volumes in a series called *Today and Tomorrow*. Each bore a Greek title and one of the most optimistic was *Daedalus, or Science and the Future* (1923) by J. B. S. Haldane which exhaled such optimism that Bertrand Russell countered it with *Icarus, or the Future of Science* (1925), pointing out that science could be used to promote the power of dominant groups rather than to make people happy. Russell was annoyed by the inhumanity of these projections. Though he agreed that 'science offers the possibility of far greater well-being for the human race than it has ever known before', he insisted that this could only come about by the even distribution of ultimate power, the abolition of war, and the limitation of population growth.[7]

Russell also continuously attacked the addition to technology, which he found to be 'indistinguishable from Calvinism'.

> Put [he wrote], the machine in place of God, the efficiency of the machine in place of the glory of God, the rich and the poor in place of the saved and the damned, inheritance in place of predestination; you will then find that every tenet of Calvinism has its counterpart in the modern religion of industrialism.[8]

Since he believed that 'the free intellect was the chief engine of human progress', Russell rejected the new secular religion of Communism: its hopes, he wrote, were 'as admirable as those instilled by the Sermon on the Mount; but they are held as fanatically and are as likely to do as much harm'.[9]

But Haldane's optimism was undimmed. 'The use, however haltingly, of our imaginations upon the possibilities of the future,' he wrote, 'is a valuable spiritual exercise.' In view of the tiny temporal and spatial scale of 'the older mythologies', he urged that attempts should be made 'to conjecture what purposes may be developed in the universe that we are beginning to apprehend'.[10] His wife Charlotte had tried just this in a Wells-type novel, *Man's World* (1926), picturing the elimination of politicians and philosophers in favour of an élite of scientists and geneticists.[11]

Equally optimistically, J. D. Bernal foresaw that physicists might one day control the world, biologists the flesh, and psychologists the devil, and together would become the élite of a world soviet, taking over the government through their organisations. 'Good' and 'evil' would be replaced by 'scientific' and 'unscientific'. They would in time progressively widen the distance between themselves and the masses—who though enjoying the 'appearance of perfect freedom' would have their energies siphoned off into harmless occupations. When the élite ultimately colonised space, the masses would be left behind on earth. 'The world might, in fact,' he wrote, 'be transformed into a human zoo, a zoo so intelligently managed that its inhabitants are not aware that they are there merely for the purposes of observation and experiment.'[12]

The hump to be got over was man's irrationality, and here Bernal hoped to overcome the limitations of the human body by substituting a man-made shell as a casing for the brain which, immersed in a constantly circulating fluid, and possibly linked to each other, would become parts of the whole 'in a way that completely transcends the devotion of the most fanatical adherent of a religious sect'.[13]

IV   THE LONG VISION OF OLAF STAPLEDON

Such great brains equipped with self-regulating pumps as a heart and chemical factories as digestive organs, electric fans as lungs, optic nerves growing out along five-foot-long probosces with ears on stalks, and housed in forty-foot-diameter turrets, becoming virtual factories of mind, were envisaged by Olaf Stapledon as taking shape over forty million years ahead. 'When your writers romance of the future,' writes one of the 'last men' in his *Last and First Men* (1930), 'they too easily imagine a progress toward some kind of Utopia, in which being like themselves live in unmitigated bliss among circumstances perfectly suited to a fixed human nature. I shall not describe any such paradise. Instead, I shall record huge fluctuations of joy and woe, the results of changes not only in man's environment but in his fluid nature.'[14] The 'huge fluctuations', on Olaf Stapledon's time-scale, cover 2,000 million years— nothing less than a history of man from his own time to the destruction of the solar system. In *Last and First Men* (1930), *A Story of the Near and Far Future* (1930), *Last Men in London* (1932), and *Star-Maker* (1937), Stapledon carried Darwinian ideas far further than Wells.[15] His method of dealing with the future was analogous to what Arnold Toynbee was currently doing for the past—envisaging the rise and fall of many civilisations—races and species even. Like Toynbee, Stapledon is concerned with unsuccessful attempts; like Marx, he was also concerned to show the dialectical reaction of one civilisation on another. Like Bernal he envisaged migrations from the earth to other planets, in Stapledon's case first to Venus, then to Neptune, but having gone through mutations of the Bernal kind, his final eighteenth race, appearing millions of years from now, being recognisably human again.

The mutations of man begin less than five thousand years after Newton, when the Sacred Order of Scientists, then running the Americanised world-state, fail to discover fresh supplies of energy, which even in the Antarctic are becoming exhausted. With no minerals either, mankind relapses for a hundred thousand years— indeed is reduced in number to a mere thirty-five. From the descendants of these a new human species arises in Asia, free of appendix, tonsils and other excrescences, with an expectation of life of a hundred and sixty. These second men are successively— over fifty thousand years—invaded by Martians, in the form of a horde of tiny cloudlets, and, after repelling the invaders, they find that their own vital units are poisoned and destroyed by the sub-vital remains of their dead enemies. Finally the second men breed a bacillus which destroyed the Martians and themselves.

After forty-million years of feline six-fingered, golden-eyed type—the third man—emerges to build a holy empire of music. These third men make the great brains which in turn become the fourth men, but they soon reduce their creators to the position of mere attendants. Departments of State were created to serve them, and in time cause other great brains to be built in various regions of the planets. Their 'lust of intellectualism' leads ultimately to their working on the surviving specimen of the fourth men to produce the fifth men—who destroy them.

In the push-button civilisation of the fifth men:

> . . . materially every individual was a multi-millionaire, in that he had at his beck and call a great diversity of powerful mechanisms; but also he was a penniless friar, for he had no vestige of economic control over any other human being.[16]

Not only was flying universal but a whole continent was kept as near as possible in a natural state for keeping contact with the primitive. An occasional decade of primitive living is a tonic to the fifth man with his three-thousand-year expectation of life and his capacity to communicate telepathically. But such longevity also leads them to make every attempt to recapture the past and so become a prey to a vast social melancholy.

But the supreme crisis of the fifth men was their discovery that the moon's orbit was narrowing in upon the earth. So they make preparations to colonise Venus. To produce the necessary oxygen on the planet a vast electrolytic apparatus is set up to split the hydrogen from the sea and eject it beyond the atmosphere at so great a speed that it would not return. In the oxygen thus liberated in the atmosphere of Venus vegetable life was introduced to prepare the planet for human habitation. Resenting this depletion of their aqueous world the marine inhabitants of Venus, the most developed of which were of the size and shape of swordfish, mount an offensive against these earthly colonists, undermining the great automatic electrolysing stations.

> Titanic explosions were engineered, which caused the invaders serious damage, but also strewed the ocean surface with thousands of dead Venerians. Secondly, it was found that, as electrolysis poured more and more free oxygen into the atmosphere, the ocean absorbed some of the potent element back into itself by solution; and this dissolved oxygen had a disastrous effect on the oceanic organisms.[17]

And as men came over in increasing numbers, they destroyed the rest of the native fauna by fleets of submarines.

Living on Venus for a longer time-span than on earth, man goes through yet further mutations. A species of seal-like submen, and a root-grubbing sixth man appeared, and in the next two hundred million years comes the seventh man—a kind of bat-like flying bird. An eighth man turns Venus into an engineers' paradise by drawing power from the planet's central heat. These eighth men detect the dwarfing of the sun and to escape freezing to death are prepared to migrate to Neptune.

For the migration, a new breed—ninth men—is prepared, one capable of supporting its own weight. Subhuman quadrupeds with some human traits start the next cycle. 'For instance there were certain grazers which in times of hardship would meet together and give tongue in cacophonous adulation; or, sitting on their haunches with fore-limbs pressed together, they would listen by the hour to the howls of some leader, responding intermittently with groans and whimpers.'[18] From these evolved the tenth man, until, after 600 million years from the first colonisation of Neptune the fifteenth man evolves—the highest species produced so far, who abolishes disease, toil, senility, misunderstanding, and ill-will, explores neighbouring planets, and designs his successor, the sixteenth man.

With artificial rigid atoms in its bone tissues to support great stature, with ample brains and with telepathic rapport, the sixteenth men are able to tap such unlimited energy that they can control their planet's course. By directing it into a wider orbit they temper its climate. Having possessed their world for fifty million years, in the next hundred million they devise a type of brain which would gain insight into the very heart of existence. Unfortunately their product, seventeenth man, is 'tortured by subtle imperfections beyond their makers' comprehension', and therefore, designs yet a more nearly perfect form—eighteenth man.

With their food factories on Jupiter and their automatic mining stations on the glacial outer planets reached by ether ships travelling faster than the planets themselves, eighteenth man lives in a microminiaturised world where microscopic tapes are played on instruments the size of a cigarette case. Everyone is potentially immortal, and the only reason for having children is to improve the type. Infancy lasts for a century, adolescence for a thousand years, and another thousand is spent in one of the antarctic continents known as the Land of the Young.

A million million citizens, grouped in over a thousand nations, live in perfect accord without the aid of armies or even of a police force . . . we have no government and no laws, if by law is meant a stereotyped convention supported by force, and not to be altered without the aid of cumbersome machinery. . . . Ours is thus in a sense the most democratic of societies. Yet in another sense it is extremely bureaucratic since it is already some millions of terrestrial years since any suggestion put forward by the College of Organisers was rejected or even seriously criticised, so thoroughly do these social engineers study their material.[19]

Twice in his long evolution man has been almost destroyed by astronomical events. Now, two thousand million years from the birth of Christ, a third calamity threatens, the continuous and increasing acceleration of the vital processes of the stars, a violent dissipation of its energy that was affecting even the sun. The Last Men now set about the forlorn task of disseminating among the stars the seeds of yet a new humanity:

> We are hoping to devise, [reports the last 'Last Man'] extremely minute electro-magnetic wave systems, akin to normal protons and electrons, which will be individually capable of sailing forward upon the hurricane of solar radiation at a speed not wholly incomparable with the speed of light itself.[20]

And the fabrication and projection of this human dust is the last men's last action—the last hope of immortality of this Brotherhood of the Condemned.

Stapledon's corollary to this book, *Last Men in London* (1932) and especially its sequal *Star Maker* (1937), are heavy with intimations of cosmic change. *Last Men* tells the story of the Last Man looking through the mind of a contemporary London schoolmaster. *Star Maker* comprises a tour of other worlds where evolution has taken strange forms: single-limbed humans, arachnoids, ichthyoids, avian, and plant-type men—all struggling for their particular utopia. Some planets can alter their orbits, others form their own sun, others colonise space.

Nor is this tour confined to space, for Stapledon takes his visitor forwards and backwards in time from the entropy of the universe to its creation. All are experiments of the Star Maker— the creator artist.

Stapledon's own Utopia was outlined in *Odd John* (1936). The hero, John Wainwright, was 'Odd' because he was a superman. Son of a physician, he develops along unusual lines. His slow but thorough intellectual development leads him to see behind accepted conclusions and to become imbued with a mission to found 'a finer human type'.

Thereupon he sets to work to make enough money to pursue his chosen path. Finding that a world war is imminent he prepares for his Utopia. First he goes to Scotland to brave the elements naked and alone and to establish telepathic communication with others throughout the world who share his powers. Then he seeks them out of the four corners of the earth, acquiring on the way the capacity to explore the future.

With the companions so acquired he makes for the South Seas where they begin to 'found a finer human type' by experimenting with human embryos. But their work is hampered by their capacity to see into the future, and thereby detect the growing antipathy of the rest of the world to their ideas. The rest of the world reacts as foreseen by sending a strong naval force against them. Although Odd John's group has mastered the secret of atomic power, they refrain from using it to defend themselves, arguing: 'When we had finished the great slaughter, should we be any longer fit mentally for our real work, for the founding of a finer species, and for worship?'

They prefer to sink their island in the sea.

V   C. S. LEWIS AND 'DEEP HEAVEN'

'I am a man rather prone to think of remote futurity,' wrote C. S. Lewis, 'a man who can read Mr. Olaf Stapledon with delight.'[21]

C. S. Lewis seized 'Deep Heaven', as he called space, as his theatre for re-assessing the pretensions of scientific humanism. The Silent Planet of his first story is Earth, where the hero, Dr. Ransom, like Lewis himself a literary scholar, is kidnapped by a Scientist, Dr. Weston, and taken to Malacandra (Mars) ostensibly as a sacrifice. Malacandra, however, is a stellar Heaven, where three distinct species had reached rationality, none of them having exterminated the other two. Ransom learnt that Earth's Oyarsa had been bound by Maleldil (God) in the air of his own planet—a Paradise Lost as it were—because he wanted 'to spoil other worlds besides his own'.

Lewis leaves no doubt of the main reason for earth being a paradise lost. The *Sorns*, one of the three forms of life on Malacandra, 'were astonished' at what Ransom 'had to tell them of human history—of war, slavery and prostitution'.

'It is because they have no Oyarsa, said one of the pupils.'

'It is because every one of them wants to be a little Oyarsa himself,' said Augray.

'They cannot help it,' said the old *Sorn.* 'There must be rule, yet how can creatures rule themselves? Beasts must be ruled by *Hnau,* and hnau by *eldila* and eldila by *Maledil.* These creatures have no eldila. They are like one trying to lift himself by his own hair—or one trying to see over a whole country when he is on a level with it— like a female trying to beget young on herself.'[22]

Ransom need not have told them, for when the scientist Weston was brought before the Oyarsa of Malacandra for killing some of the moon *hrossa,* he burst into a typical hubristic apologia:

'Life . . . has ruthlessly broken down all obstacles and liquidated all failures and today in her highest form—civilised man—and in me as his representative, she presses forward to that interplanetary leap which will, perhaps, place her for ever beyond the reach of death.

It is in her right, the right, or if you will the might of life herself, that I am prepared without flinching to plant the flag on the soil of Malacandra to march on, step by step, superseding, where necessary, the lower forms of life that we find, claiming planet after planet, system after system, till our posterity—whatever strange form and unguessed mentality they have assumed—dwell in the universe wherever the universe is habitable.[23]

The presumptuous Dr. Weston once more clashes with Dr. Ransom in *Perelandra* or *Voyage to Venus.* This retells the story of the Garden of Eden before the Fall with Weston as the Devil. Since Weston died on Perelandra, the next manifestation of evil Dr. Ransom has to fight is on earth—in the university town of Edgestow where one of Weston's friends, Devine (who had accompanied him to Malacandra and was now ennobled as Lord Feverstone), persuades the university to sell its 'holy wood' to an organisation called the National Institute for Co-ordinated Experiments. The poor don Curry—a classic example of the *trahison des clercs*—rhapsodises:

The N.I.C.E. marks the beginning of a new era—the *really* scientific era. There are to be forty interlocking committees sitting every day, and they've got a wonderful gadget by which the findings of each committee print themselves off in their own little compartment on the Analytical Notice-Board every half hour. Then that report slides itself into the right position where it's connected up by little arrows with all the relevant parts of the other reports. It's a marvellous gadget. The different kinds of business come out in different coloured lights. They call it a Pragmatometer.[24]

The anti-hero of the book, a sociologist, Mark Studdock, is lured into N.I.C.E. by flattering his sense of self-importance. He listens eagerly as the purpose of N.I.C.E. is revealed by Feverstone:

> Quite simple and obvious things, at first—sterilisation of the unfit, liquidation of backward races, selective breeding. Then real education, including pre-natal education. By real education I mean one that makes the patient what it wants infallibly: whatever he or his parents try to do about it. Of course, it'll have to be mainly psychological at first. But we'll get on to biochemical conditioning in the end and direct manipulation of the brain. A new type of man.[25]

Recruited to Belbury, the centre of these experiments, by Feverstone, Mark Studdock's incapacity to see the evil inherent in the system was itself a result of his poor breeding:

> It must be remembered that in Mark's mind hardly one rag of noble thought, either Christian or Pagan, had a secure lodging. His education had been neither scientific nor classical—merely 'Modern'. The severities both of abstraction and of high human tradition had passed him by: and he had neither peasant shrewdness nor aristocratic honour to help him. He was a man of straw, a glib examinee in subjects that require no exact Knowledge (he had always done well on Essays and General Papers), and the first hint of a real threat to his bodily life knocked him sprawling.[26]

Indeed, as one of the characters asked with justice, 'was there a single doctrine practised at Belbury which hadn't been preached by some lecturer at Edgestow?'[27]

The evil that Dr. Ransom had to fight at Belbury was the concentration of scientists on power, expressed by one of them, Professor Frost:

> It was not the great technocrats of Koenigsberg or Moscow who supplied the casualties in the siege of Stalingrad. The effect of modern war is to eliminate retrogressive types, while sparing the technocracy and increasing its hold on public affairs. In the new age, what has hitherto been merely the intellectual nucleus of the race is to become, by gradual stages, the race itself. You are to conceive the species as an animal which has discovered how to simplify nutrition and locomo-

tion to such a point that the old complex organs and the large body which contained them are no longer necessary. The masses are, therefore, to disappear. The body is to become all head. The human race is to become all Technocracy. . . . The great majority of the human race cannot be educated. Even if they could the day for a large population has passed. It has served its function as a kind of cocoon for Technocratic and Objective Man.[28]

VI   J. B. S. HALDANE VERSUS C. S. LEWIS

Because he thought Lewis would influence public opinion, and that of politicians, particularly in Britain, J. B. S. Haldane attacked him: 'More and more, among people who think about such matters,' he wrote, 'the division is appearing between those who think it is worth while working for a better future . . . and those who think the best thing we can do is to look after our immediate neighbours and our noble selves.'[29] Especially did he challenge Lewis's equation of science and diabolism, pointing out in *Auld Horne F.R.S.* that in all three books Lewis shows only one decent scientist and he was 'murdered by the devil-worshippers before the reader gets to know him'. If he scouted Lewis' poor view of scientists, he scorned his opinion that the human species was on the wrong road and in 'anti-Lewisite' challenged his view that 'Going back was the quickest way on.'[30]

Haldane's own long-range views of the future were summarised in 'Biological Possibilities for the Human Species in the Next Ten Thousand Years' (1963), in which he predicted that 'our descendants will be more interested in their own biology than we are, and have far more knowledge and content of it.' He considered that clonal reproduction as in *Brave New World* might have to come before educative methods are revised. But he considered that it was time systematic speculation was begun on the possibility of human beings living on planets, satellites, asteroids, or artificial vehicles.[31]

Bertrand Russell also returned to the attack with a futuristic satire on the pretensions of priesthoods. The descent of Zahatopolk in fiftieth-century Cotopasi, the highest mountain in Ecuador, is received by the Indians as a divine event, and inspires them to end the thousand-years' peace and conquer first America, then Africa and Europe. His Book of Sacred Law, completed before his death (or ascent) thirty years later became the basis of the New Incan Empire, as racially hierarchic as the Christian Empires of the Nineteenth century. Though forbidden to smoke and drink alcohol, the Peruvian élite alone could be admitted to the University of Cuzco.

The all-powerful priesthood restricted parents to having only three children—all above that number had to be eaten by their parents. Above the priests was the Inca—whose privilege it was to take the Virgin of the Year. One such Virgin, Diotina, refused as she disagreed with the whole theocracy. Though her fiancé, Thomas, was too cowardly to prevent her being burned at the stake, he was fired by her death to start a revolution with his friend Paul. Beginning at the University of Cuzco, the revolution broke out in 6022 at Kilimanjaro in the black African province of Sinistria, which then succeeded Peru as the centre of World Government. Gods and hierarchies were abolished and democracy reigned once more.

But Thomas died and Paul wrote a history of the revolution which became a sacred book. This sacred book acquired an interpreter, Gregorius, who pointed out that Thomas and Diotina were divine and slowly his interpretation supplanted the sacred book. Finally the wheel came full circle once again when in the sixty-seventh century a Maori called Tupia declared his intention of leading the world back to the ancient unfaith.[32]

VII   ORWELL AND ZAMYATIN

Post-Christian religions, whether sacred or profane, worried Orwell. 'No worthwhile picture of the future,' he told readers in the *Tribune* on 3rd March 1944, could be obtained unless they realised 'how much they had lost by the decay of Christianity'.

Zamyatin's story probably sharpened his own insight into the Russian Revolution and its overt endorsement by James Burnham as the paradigm of the new managerial technocracy.[33]

The motive behind the Party in Orwell's *Nineteen Eighty Four* (1949), is Power. As O'Brien, its leader, explains:

> The party seeks power entirely for its own sake. We are not interested in the good of others; we are interested solely in power. Not wealth or luxury or happiness; only power, pure power.

Orwell was the twentieth-century Swift, one of the authors whom he admired 'with least reserve'.[34] He first read *Gulliver's Travels* at the age of eight and not less than half a dozen times since. Its fascination seems inexhaustible. 'If I had to make a list of six books which were to be preserved when all others were destroyed, I would certainly put *Gulliver's Travels* among them.'

Like another secular prophet, Lenin, Orwell chose his 'public' name from a river, in his case, the Orwell in Suffolk, where he lived in the early thirties, watching Wellsian ideas (in his opinion) materialise in Nazi Germany where 'science was fighting on the side of superstition',[35] whereas the Marxists were 'suffering from a hypertrophied sense of order, wanting to reduce the world to something approaching a chessboard'.

Orwell sensed the recoil from Socialism as identified with mechanical progress. 'This essentially fat-bellied version of "progress" ' was, to Orwell, 'not an integral part of Socialism, but it has come to be thought of as one, with the result that the temperamental conservatism which is latent in all kinds of people is easily mobilised against Socialism.'[36] He saw Fascism as an expression of this and told his readers that:

> The only possible course is to examine the Fascist case, grasp that there is something to be said for it, and then make it clear to the world that whatever good Fascism contains is also implicit in Socialism.

Elsewhere he considered:

> All talk about democracy, liberty, equality, fraternity, all revolutionary movements, all visions of Utopia, or 'the classless society' or 'the Kingdom of Heaven on Earth' [to be] humbug (not necessarily conscious humbug), covering the ambitions of some new class which is elbowing its way into power.[37]

Even more definitely he regarded History as:

> ...a series of swindles, in which the masses are first lured into revolt by the promise of Utopia, and then, when they have done their job, enslaved over again by new masters.

At the turn of the war—November 1943 to February 1944—he had written a parody of Soviet Russia—*Animal Farm*—so called because the animals expel the farmer and his men and take over the farm. The old boar, Major, addresses them and, three days after he dies, two younger pigs, Napoleon (Stalin) and Snowball (Trotsky) take over: one the epitome of drive and unscrupulousness, the other of idealism and courage. Snowball drills the animals to repel the farmer's counter-attack, develops ideas for animal committees, and suggests a windmill, but Napoleon sets the dogs on him and drives him out, replacing him by his own lieutenant, Squealer.

Squealer operates behind the growing legend of Napoleon, growing because of the progressive concentration of feeling against Snowball as the 'betrayer' of the revolution, the very agent of the farmer Jones. Boxer (an archetype of the peasant), the great big simple carthorse who gives all for the revolution, is set upon by Napoleon's dogs and, when he gets too weak to work, is sent to the knacker's. But Squealer, the legend-maker, sees to it that the story gets around that he dies in hospital, exclaiming 'Long live Comrade Napoleon! Napoleon is always right.'

The seven commandments which Snowball put up on the end of the barn in the first flush of the revolution are now replaced by a statement: 'All animals are equal but some are more equal than others.' As Squealer rises to power on Snowball's exile, so he triumphs at Napoleon's death. The pigs, long the sole consumers of all the milk and apples produced by the rest, now begin to walk on two legs and wear clothing. For some time, too, they had been drinking whisky—they bought a case out of the money that the knacker paid for Boxer's carcase.

Now they entertain the neighbouring farmers at a dinner, earning unanimous plaudits from their human guests for ensuring that all their lower animals 'did more work and received less food than any animals in the country'. To the animals themselves, looking in on this dinner, as they 'looked from pig to man, and from man to pig, and from pig to man again' they found it 'impossible to say which was which'.[38]

'The exact opposite of the stupid hedonistic Utopias that the old reformers imagined' took shape in *Nineteen Eighty Four* (1949) under Big Brother, whose agent O'Brien, tells poor Winston Smith (who wants to be 'human'), that 'the world will grow more merciless as it refines itself'.[39]

As a thirty-nine-year-old civil servant in the Ministry of Truth —Mini-true in Newspeak—Winston Smith, like Zamyatin's D.503, keeps a diary to communicate with the future since communication with his present is virtually impossible. Police patrols snoop in people's windows, Thought Police plug into the wires of the telescreen in everyone's rooms, and even children are organised in troops of spies. Living in London, chief city of Airstrip One, the third most populous province of Oceania, Winston Smith meets a girl, a member of the junior Anti-Sex League. At first, as he watches her during the compulsory Two Minutes Hate, he fears and hates her. Then he slowly and furtively begins to respond to her. The slow progress of their affair is bound up with their increasing involvement with Emmanuel Goldstein, the Enemy of the People, who had advocated freedom of speech, of the press, of assembly, and of thought, but above all, freedom from the war which Oceania was waging with Eurasia. Followers of Goldstein—the Brotherhood—were ferreted out by the Thought Police and dealt with in the Ministry of Love—barricaded by barbed wire and machine-gun nests.

While the girl works a novel-writing machine, providing cheap pornography for the proles, Winston is employed in continuously doctoring the past to conform with the needs of the present. 'All history was a palimpsest, scraped clean and reinscribed exactly as often as was necessary.' As his involvement with the girl gets deeper he takes this work less and less seriously, regarding it as merely the substitution of one bit of nonsense by another. His continuous question—had it always been like this?—was reinforced by the sordidness of his meals in the canteen:

> . . . a low-ceilinged crowded room, its walls grimy from the contact of innumerable bodies; battered metal tables and chairs, placed so close together that you sat with your elbows touching; bent spoons, dented trays, coarse white mugs; all surfaces greasy, grime in every crack; and a sourish, composite smell of bad gin and bad coffee and metallic stew and dirty clothes. Always in your stomach and in your skin there was a sort of protest, a feeling that you had been cheated of something that you had a right to.[40]

Everyone wore overalls.

Ignited by his diary, Winston's revolt burns as he watches the proles, kept happy by the Lottery with its weekly pay-out of enormous prizes. 'If there is hope,' he wrote, 'it lies in the proles.' But he can't communicate with them. Winston's love affair becomes a political act. Intimations of the danger he is running crowd, one by one; his fellow workmates disappear into the cellars of the Ministry of Love. He himself is invited to join the 'Brother-hood'—the secret anti-Big Brother organisation—and is given a copy of Goldstein's book. Just after reading it to Julia, he too is arrested, and taken to the Ministry of Love for torture. Trapped and tormented by O'Brien who taunts him, 'If you are a man, Winston, you are the last man. Your kind is extinct; we are the inheritors. Do you understand that you are *alone*? You are outside history, you are non-existent', Winston abandons all pretence of being a nonconformist and slobbers his surrender to Big Brother.

VIII   A MINISCULE RUSSIA?

To the charge that *Walden Two's* 'behavioural engineering'[41] made it a miniscule Russia, its creator Frazier replied that, though it sprang from the same humanitarian impulses, his community had four advantages: the experimental spirit had not declined there, over-propagandization had not enslaved the working classes or alienated potential sympathisers; the 'hero principle' had not been inexpertly used, and political power was not unduly exploited.

This optimistic spirit radiates through B. F. Skinner's *Walden Two* (1949). As Frazier lies flat on his back with his arms stretched out, his legs lightly crossed, and his head a little to one side, Burris asks him if he is not comparing himself to God. Frazier acknowledges 'a curious similarity', but admits:

> Generally I've left things alone. I've never stepped in to wipe out the evil works of men with a great flood. Nor have I sent a personal emissary to reveal my plan and to put my people back on the track. The original design took deviations into account and provided automatic corrections. It's rather an improvement upon *Genesis*.[42]

But he does claim that he made a more explicit statement of his plan and could claim a more *deliberate* control:

> But [he continues], there's no doubt whatever that Walden Two was planned in advance pretty much as it turned out to be. In many ways the actual creation of Walden Two was closer to the spirit of Christian cosmogony than the evolution of the world according to modern science.

He is also accused of being 'a modern, mechanized, managerial Machiavelli', by Augustine Castle, a philosopher who 'in his preoccupation with Mind . . . has let himself put on too much weight'.[43]

Frazier discouraged 'any sense of history':

> The founding of Walden Two is never recalled publicly by anyone who took part in it. No distinction of seniority is recognised. It's very bad taste to refer to oneself as 'an early member'.

For history, to Frazier, obfuscated the evaluation of the present almost as much as a sense of destiny:

> Race, family, ancestor-worship—these are the handmaidens of history and we should have learned to beware of them by now. What we give our young people in Walden Two is a grasp of the *current* forces which a culture must deal with. None of your myths, none of your heroes—no history, no destiny—simply the *NOW!* The present is the thing. It's the only thing we can deal with, any-way.[44]

Castle is still not convinced. He accuses Frazier of blocking:

> . . . every path through which man was to struggle upward toward salvation. Intelligence, initiative—you have filled their places with a sort of degraded instinct, engineered compulsion. Walden Two is a marvel of efficient co-ordination—as efficient as an anthill. . . . Intellectually Walden Two is quite as incapable of a spontaneous change of course as the life within the beehive.[45]

IX ADAMIC FABLES

'Society reduced in size until it had attained the simplicity of a laboratory experiment'[46] was also the real subject of George R. Stewart's *Earth Abides* (1950), an Adamic fable centred round a young graduate biologist who survives the decimation of the world to begin the historical cycle again by mating with a semi-negress. Their offspring, reinforced by other strong survivors, become a tribe and he slowly tries to wean them from living as parasites on the ruins of civilisation to pioneering anew, from making their own bows to making their own laws.[47]

Over against man starting again, E. C. Large, an English biologist of repute, has the idea of God starting again. 'Suppose,' God asks Mother Nature, in *Dawn in Andromeda* (1956):

> We were to take a few humans off the earth, a few healthy ones without the worst kind of liars and start them off on another planet

—do you think they would survive . . . and prosper, and even make me something fairly complicated—say a seven-valve superhet—in one generation? If they did succeed, we might let them live to transmit something better than we've just been hearing.

So five men and five women walk out of the sea on the small uninhabited planet of Andromeda and start the whole evolutionary process all over again, building themselves a new society, a new school, a new university and a new religion. In twenty years they gallop through the history of man without priest or politician (aspirants to both offices had lost their lives on landing).

> Very early in their history the original ten had made an important empirical discovery. They found that if they met together in silence, and then each truthfully expressed his own view, they invariably had access to a spirit that was common to them all. . . . They came to know what they should do, and then, between them they went ahead and tried to do it. This simple process had given them their agriculture, their school, their village, their mill, their forge, their laboratory and their university. It could even—if they remembered it—give them a seven valve all-wave superhet in one generation, starting naked from the sea. . . .

But now with the rise of a new generation, a rival system of government threatens Andromeda—a system based on another empirical discovery—the uncanny power of money to work on its own in an unsuspecting community and to bring about desire for personal prosperity and personal advantage. The discovery leads to the division of Andromeda into West, East, and Centre. The discoverer, Azo, 'leads' the West, who are taught by Ferrous (who, in the same way as Azo has become a banker, has become a priest), how to:

> . . . get grand feelings without doing any work. They had only to sing his hymns and mutter his responses with fervour. Then they would go away, feeling very good and uplifted children.

Meanwhile, the East concentrates on building a steam ferry to take them up to coal, sulphur, and lava beds. Deprived of the sheaths of religion and property they are not insulated from reality and some of them begin to worship an abstraction they call science. The Centre, consisting of a few 'wobblers', wished to emigrate.

On the verge of war, a meteor destroys all this. They retreat to the caves just as the radio is built, and on it they hear a single voice from the throne of heaven that laughs and seems to say, 'And yet there is so much good in them.'[48]

X   RUSSIAN OPTIMISM

'There was a time when our ancestors in their novels of the future imagined us as weakly rickety things with overgrown skulls,' said Mveen Mass, the black African director of the Outer Stations in Ivan Yefremov's *Andromeda*. After originally setting it in the fourth millennium, the author subsequently reduced his projection to the third as 'the launching of the sputniks showed that the events related in the story could occur much sooner'. For these 'events' include the exploration of an iron star which virtually divides the Andromeda nebula from the Great Circle, of which earth is a part. Mveen Mass, of the Institute of Metagalactics, is in charge of attempts to communicate with the Andromeda nebula but, for undertaking an experiment on his own from the great Tibetan Station, he voluntarily resigns, and makes his way to the Island of Oblivion: the relegation centre for all those who can't cope with the labours of the world. For this is the Era of Common Labour. As Veda Kong, the historian who bridges the time-gap, explains whereas 'In the ancient Utopian dreams of a happy future great importance was attached to man's gradual liberation from the necessity to work'[49] the Era of Common Labour 'made it possible for a person to change his profession frequently, learn another easily, and bring endless variety into his work so that it became more and more satisfying'.[50]

By this time too, the life span reached 300 and the Academy of the Psychophysiology of Labour aided such adjustments. Planning was monitored by the Academy of Sorrow and Joy, cohered by the Academy of Productive Forces and guided by the Academy of Stochastics and Prognostications. The last-named indeed provided guidance even to the historian Veda Kong. She consults it over a problem in her excavations, imagining 'a gigantic human brain with its furrows and convolutions, alive and pulsating' although 'she knew that they were four electronic machines tended by a Prophetic Brain engineer'.[51] For the festivals of the world, where the melted icecaps had re-aligned human habitation on the shores of the warm seas round the 30–40° latitudes, included a Day of Scientific Audacity and Fantasy.

In a further novel about space, *The Heart of the Serpent* (1959), Yefremov was more directly propagandist. Its very title was an answer to Murray Leinster's account of a meeting between two highly technological civilisations in space in *First Contact*. Leinster's picture of the mutual suspicion (resolved by exchanging spaceships) was derided by Yefremov who maintained that any civilisation capable of making spaceships would be beyond the primitive stage of war and violence.

'The Russian picture of the future,' wrote one reviewer in 1967, 'viewed as a dynamic inspiration in the present, is far more refreshing and straightforward than even the best baroque productions of the West.' [51] And the West took the message: assessments [52] and translations [53] of their science fiction were issued in the fifties and sixties. Indeed the preoccupation of one writer, singularly enough a Pole, was with the moral and psychological problems of communicating with outsiders. This writer, Stanislaw Lem, found that his *Cosmonauts* (1957), *Invasion from Aldebaran*, and *The Invincibles* (1964) attacted such interest that he was included in a special French series on the future.

So the debate is now joined outside the Soviet Union. Contrasting an anthology of Russian stories with most Western ones the reviewer mentioned above concluded:

> In the west it is now more or less taken for granted by SF writers that the world of the future, and the imminent future at that, faces either inevitable devastation and catastrophe or a society more hideous in its technological inhumanity than ever George Orwell could dream up. In these Soviet stories neither possibility is even hinted at. Humanity has somehow (there is no looking back) solved all its outstanding political and social problems and is now united in its extension of scientific research and endeavour to remoter fields. This bland assumption sometimes leads to naivety in the writing but also gives an opportunity for idyllic lyricism . . . and also for humorous domestic anecdotes. [54]

At the present time the Russians have embarked on a twenty-year plan (1960–80), and the goals set need immunisation if they are to be attained. Such immunisation depends on conscience being soothed, doubts resolved, and contradictions accepted. Such double-think, or universal rationalisation, can, as many observers agree, only take place if the goal is constantly emoted upon. Comparing it to the bipolar power of the medieval church over the minds of men—heaven and hell, reward and punishment in the hereafter—one such observer wrote:

> Correspondingly in the communist world the spirit of the masses is anchored in anticipation of a terrestrial ideal—and anticipation that is strengthened by the utopian streak that has always been present in Russian thought.[55]

That streak enables them to discern currents in the evolutionary tide, without the complete information and rationality needed for such discernment. Even the Laplacean calculator itself (as adumbrated on page 31) could not do this. For as Professor Sir Karl Popper has pointed out, it is part of the physical world and could only predict the state of that world *after* the arrival of the time set for such a prediction.[56]

Yet though insisting that laws could not be deduced from history like the laws deduced by natural scientists, Popper suggested that social scientists might construct 'models' on the assumptions of complete rationality and information and compare actual behaviour with the model.

Such 'models' are now in various stages of construction ready for launching in the various 'think-tanks' constructed for this purpose in the western world.[57]

Let us now look at these 'think-tanks' or surmising forums.

Chapter Eleven

SURMISING FORUMS

I FORECASTING AS A LEGITIMATE SCIENTIFIC ACTIVITY

One of the earliest surmising forums was set up by the British Government at the beginning of the century, as a result of a forecast nearly forty years earlier that coal supplies would be exhausted. This Royal Commission on Coal estimated that exhaustion would begin at the earliest in A.D. 2100 and then only if the population had reached 130 million by A.D. 2091 and the export of coal had grown proportionately to what it was in the years 1890–5. But given economies in consumption and an average annual consumption rate of 250 million tons a year one estimator calculated it would last for four centuries. The Commission opted for three.

Such surmises were also the responsibility of the U.S. Natural Resources Committee to whom it seemed in 1937 no reason 'why one should not use science in estimating the future, as in any other business'. Articulated earlier by a committee of scientists appointed by President Hoover to survey American society, which reported in 1932 on *Recent Social Trends*, this attitude was explicitly and officially adopted in the N.R.C.'s report on *Technological Trends* and *National Policy* (1937). Described as 'the first major attempt to show the kinds of new inventions which may affect the living and working conditions in America in the next ten to twenty-five years'[1] it indicated 'some of the problems which the adoption and use of these inventions will inevitably bring in their train'. Facts and facets of recent developments were followed by an analysis of nineteen major inventions. It found that the average interval between the formulation of the basic idea and the granting of the patent was a century and three quarters; the average interval between the patent and its practical use a quarter of a century; from practical use to commercial success 14 years and for important use another 12. The assumptions behind all this was, as one commentator remarked; that forecasts of the effects of inventions 'even if only approximate', would, 'prepare man for their arrival, and help him, while it is still easy and before the new interests created by the new inventions have crystallised, to avoid unnecessary social disorganisation and draw the maximum benefit from his own achievements'.

After the second world war (which they had done so much to win), physicists turned to prediction: three especially.

'With our present knowledge of the world and of the things in it,' wrote Darwin's grandson in 1952, 'though we cannot see all the detail, we can foresee the general course its history is almost certain to take over a long period. It is certainly not possible to predict anything like a detailed history of the world, but nevertheless it is now possible to foresee a good deal of what I may call its average history.' So, in *The Next Million Years* (1952) Sir Charles Darwin confessed that 'the final stimulus' for his forecast came from his 'studies in the physical sciences'. Another was more definite and, in *The Foreseeable Future* (1955), Sir George Thomson looked forward to a bleak, laborious, and over-crowded world. A third, Professor Dennis Gabor, lamented the failure of such forecasts to prepare us for the Utopia of Science as 'treason by omission': to him *Inventing the Future* (1963) was a psychological necessity.

Not that such forecasts were lacking, especially from scientists who claimed that in a few decades it might be possible to remould the inadequate intellectual and emotional equipment of our present average human being. Sir Macfarland Burnett, a Nobel Prize winner in 1960, forecast that research into molecular biology must produce micro-organisms of hitherto unknown virulence, which might escape and wreak havoc amongst human beings. Characteristically, he concluded: 'no-one has ever headed the words of a Cassandra'.[2]

Both singly and in sodalities, scientists donned the mantic mantle with a flourish as if the future were in their bones. At one such sodality, the American Association for the Advancement of Science, a case was made, in 1955, for the establishment of chairs of the future, to provide visions of the fine detail of what man might be. And universities, especially in America, have listened. Dr. Charles Osgood at Urbana is conducting a 'computerised exploration of the year 2000', to other people a series of possible choices and indicate the consequences of such choices. Buckminster Fuller's World Resources inventory is being supported by Southern Illinois University and Professor Daniel Bell of Columbia is in charge of a commission on the year 2000 that is supported by the American Academy of Arts and Sciences. Those well-endowed non-churches of the modern world, the great foundations, have caught the mood. The Wenner-Gren Foundation assembled a kind of ecumenical council of biologists, to consider 'Man's Role in Changing the Face of the Earth'.[3]

Looking up in 1967 from the equivalent of their crystal balls the A.A.A.S. Commission on the year 2000 described an America that would be dominated by three megalopolitan and cultural aggregations: Boswash (housing of a telescoped Boston, Washington, and New York), Chipitts (a Bible Belt Complex between Chicago and Pittsburgh) and Sansan (a hipster, new Left Bar-B-Q sprawl from San Francisco to San Diego). Inhabited by couples practising birth control and a smaller number of families devoted to child rearing, policed by exquisitely penetrative eavesdropping techniques and structured as a highly competitive meritocracy, America will be a society in which solitude will be at a premium, and fortunes would be made by providing, on a monthly, weekly, daily or even hourly basis, 'a room of one's own'.

One of the most recent of these groups is Mankind 2000, an International Foundation initiated in 1964 by Dr. Robert Jungk of Vienna, author of *Tomorrow is Already Here* (1954) and of that remarkable 'moral and political history' of the atomic scientists: *Brighter than a Thousand Suns* (1958). A memorandum *Mankind 2000—A Vision of Tomorrow* was circulated in 1965 and elicited some seventy sponsors from Western and Communist countries, including Lord Boyd Orr. They hope to co-operate not only with Professor Charles Osgood's project, but with Professor I. Glagolev's group (which is supported by the Economic Commission of the Soviet Peace Committee and the Peace Research institute in Oslo); with Dr. Arthur Waskow's 'Simulation Technique' project for presenting different aspects of life in the anticipated future; with the Magenta project based on the International

Centre of Science in Italy, and with the International Interdisciplinary Study Centre near Deauville in France (the Mont Canisy Project). Dr. Jungk indeed is at present writing a book outlining the whole 'future' movement.

Yet another sodality, alerted by the menace of uncontrolled radio-activity, chose a clock of doom for the cover of their journal, *The Bulletin of the Atomic Scientists* (first issued in December 1945), indicating that the midnight hour was about to strike. In this several extrapolatory and minatory fables were published. One by Louis N. Ridenour, a physicist at the University of Illinois, was set 'some years after all the industrialised nations have mastered the production and use of atomic power'. Another, in 1956, by Harrison Brown, a geologist at the California Institute of Technology, urged readers to look 'beyond the narrow sights which the government all too frequently sets for us to sights which embrace not only the world of the next decade, but also the world of the next century'.

Harrison Brown considered that he and his colleagues at the California Institute of Technology 'had at least a reasonable chance of forecasting more accurately than did Malthus' since they 'know more than he did about the extent, the potentialities and the limitations of the world in which we live', as well as about the 'potentialities and the limitations of our technology'.[4]

The continued success of international conferences of scientists on world affairs like COSWA which first began in 1956, and was attended unexpectedly, by a four-man Soviet delegation, was such that in June 1960 the Bulletin's editor, Eugene Rabinovitch, set back the clock five minutes. It no longer points to midnight.

II HERMAN KAHN: A MODERN MERLIN

Such declarations by socially-conscious scientists were too idealistic for Herman Kahn. So were novels like Nevil Shute's *On the Beach* which, in his opinion, was 'interesting but badly researched'.[5] 'More serious and sober thought on various facets of the strategic problem' seemed to be necessary, so he wrote three vivid conjectural scenarios: *On Thermonuclear War* (1960), *Thinking about the Unthinkable* (1962), and *On Escalation* (1965).[6] In the first, dedicated to 'the goal of anticipating, avoiding and alleviating crises', he used anticipatory techniques derived from collaborative analysis to explore implications of future world wars. He foresaw ten prototype situations up to 1973: Armageddon, Camlan, 1871–1914, Pearl Harbour, Munich, Hacha, Rotterdam, Berlin, Korea, and the Reichstag Fire.

The ghost of Merlin still walks beside him.

> Camlan refers, of course, to the last battle of King Arthur. It seems that King Arthur's son, Mordred, revolted against his father. After some fighting the two contenders met, with all their troops, on the field of Camlan to negotiate. Both sides were fully armed and desperately suspicious that the other side was going to try some ruse or stratagem. The negotiations were going smoothly until one of the knights was stung by an asp and drew his sword to kill the reptile. The others saw the sword being drawn and immediately fell upon each other. A tremendous slaughter ensued. The chronicle *Morte d'Arthur* is quite specific about the point that the slaughter was excessive chiefly because the battle took place without preparation and premeditation. When the battle was over everybody except King Arthur, Mordred, and a couple of knights lay dead.[7]

These long-range scenarios, suggested Kahn, should be drafted out by an interdisciplinary team of from a hundred to a thousand members.

> The idea of doing such long-range research is not new. It is now conventional for the military to plan five, ten and even fifteen years ahead. This planning or analysis is done in detail when possible, in broad brush when it is not. The plans or views that are developed must often be scrapped as the uncertain future emerges, but good or bad it is at least essential to do the analysis. Even a poor analysis itself is educational.[8]

As weapons have escalated from megaton to multimegaton to gigaton, capable of killing every man, woman, and child in the world many times over, a paradoxical situation has developed. Max Lerner noticed it in 1962:

> While the psychic fears and needs which feed the building of the deterrent power on each side are basically non-rational, the operation of the deterrence principle in preventing war depends on almost flawless rationality on both sides. Thus, the pressures build up because men are fearful, but their resolution is premised on the assump-

tion that their fear leads them to be rational—which is not always the case.[9]

It is safer, in other words, to trust a computer than a political head of state.

III   INDUSTRIAL ISAIAHS

'In the computer field, the moment of truth is a running programme; all else is prophecy'.[10] So H. A. Simon, one of the most convincing and realistic exponents of that new tool. But he also forecast that, in twenty years, machines would be capable of doing any work that a man could do.

For it looks safer, too, to trust a computer than a captain of industry. Increasing use of computer simulation threw up further extrapolatory models of tomorrow, some of which reached laymen in the form of books written with an eye to industrial policy.

The Unilever picture of 1984 as drawn by Ronald Brech depends on a fourfold increase in generating capacity, to cope with a threefold increase in demand. Houses will discard water-central heating in favour of pumped warm air from heat-storage systems charged in off-peak hours. Coal will not be for burning (consumers' requirement will drop to 140 million tons a year), but for chemicals, since other forms of energy, solar, nuclear, heavy hydrogen, fuel cells, and nuclear power will be operational. Natural materials at present used for plumbing, piping, guttering, insulation, doors, walls, and ceilings, will be supplemented and supplanted by the efforts of molecular engineers. Metals elsewhere will be used in alloy forms. Routine operations will be eliminated by automatic controls, rationalised by greater use of pipelines, roads on stilts, nuclear-powered ships, and rockets for postal services, whilst present novelties like telewriters, telephones with vision and personal walkie-talkie sets will become necessities.

Those who service and improve this new world will cause the shape of our society, once a feudal pyramid, to look less like a diamond than an onion. For as Brech rightly points out, to tax the rich alters the top of the diamond and to subsidise the poor rounds the bottom. But above all it will be a society geared to planning its future. Here Brech, by his own admission, places himself in the biocratic tradition.

By 1984 the managerial revolution will have affected most firms, and the well-trained, knowledgeable, professional manager will at last have come into his own. He will have at his disposal various scientific techniques and statistical aids to reduce the area of guessing. He will still require business acumen, or hunch, but this will be reserved for those problems that defy scientific or quasi-scientific analysis. His management information will have built-in probability calculations enabling him to see the likely results of decisions even before he has taken them. It will be based on sampling techniques so that the actual quantity of information he has to deal with will be greatly reduced, but the information will be more meaningful. The manager will also have at his disposal various techniques such as operational research (which by 1984 will be standard management practice), to help him achieve greater operational efficiency.[11]

In America the cybernated parousia of the industrialist has its scarifying side. There Donald N. Michael foresees in twenty years that though a larger proportion of better educated children will be available, they will be unable to understand the cybernated world in which they live, and 'the research realm of scientists, the problems of government and the interplay between them will be beyond the ken even of our college graduates'. He foresees 'a small, almost separate, society of people *en rapport* with the advanced computers' who will have to be trained from childhood 'as intensively as a classical ballerina'. He allows that a proportion of the rest 'will be productively engaged in human-to-human or human-to-machine activities requiring judgment and a high level of intelligence or training', but asks, 'what will the rest do?' No-one, he considers, has seriously envisioned what activities the rest will pursue. 'Their activities,' he continues, 'must be adequate enough to avoid frustration and desperation, and resentment of technological change.'[12]

IV ANTI-MANDARIN MANIFESTOES

Round the selection involved in such societies a further literature of dissent has grown up. Ever since Wells described the selenites being bred in jars for their various vocations, and Aldous Huxley intimated the horrors of the Central London Hatchery, this has been a constant theme of future-fiction, or futopias. An early post-war protest was Gerald Heard's picture in *Doppelgängers* (1948) of the year 1997 when the class structure would be determined by psychologists.[13] A future World Conference on Special Aptitudes in the Middle East where Hindus abandon caste in favour of occupational selection and Christians allow their priests to be selected by psychological tests by atheistic, and therefore impartial, psychologists, was envisaged by C. H. Sisson.[14] A World State Planning Commission in the twenty-fifth century is described by Geddes MacGregor, in the epistles of a twenty-fifth century St. Paul written to Timothy—a historian studying the scholasticism of the scientists of the twentieth century. In MacGregor's new world of the twenty-fifth century, the inhabitants of airborne cities speak logic-lingo, a language adapted for the use of machines, and life embodies the worst features of Russian Communism and American democracy. The Papacy has been transferred to Quebec. Thinking and programming have, for four centuries, been regarded as identical activities. Those infected by the communicable disease of Christianity are forbidden to leave their ghettos: hence the title of MacGregor's fantasy: *From a Christian Ghetto: Letters of Ghostly Wit. A.D. 2453* (1954).[15]

Sin has become error against the state, and everyone speaks in the third person in David Karp's state of the twenty-first century. To the new priesthood of psychologists and bureaucrats, spies of the Department of Internal Examination report, for, as Chief Inquisitor Lark explains:

> The benevolent state has a long way to go, whole areas of supervision ahead of it. Our Society is slowly being poured into the mould. If we cannot successfully remove heresy at this stage of the game, then we may as well give up any idea of continuing the creation of a new society.[16]

One of the spies, Professor Burden, of Templar College, is summoned for questioning, and afterwards is reported as dead, but really he is endowed with a new identity as a clerk—Hughes— and emerges 'purged of heresy'.

'Here in this Utopia we are all mad, mad and frightened,' confesses a character of John Iggulden. 'I am happy to believe that this world needs no God.' A tyrant, Dr. Bronstern, by means of a capsule implanted in every leading citizen's body that can be exploded by remote control, is overthrown by an Australian hero.[17]

Other bleak pictures of an élite of engineers at odds with a group of ghettoed mutes, are drawn by Heinlein. All believe in 'Jordan's Plan', that their spaceship is homing heavenwards to far Centaurus. But the chief engineer tells the hero:

> That stuff is all right to keep the peasants quiet and in their place, but don't fall for it yourself. There is no Plan—other than our own plans for looking out for ourselves.

Exploring the dark upper-decks of the ship, the hero discovers that the control room is completely unmanned. Helped by the 'mutants', he tries to get the ship moving towards Centaurus, but, when opposed by the engineers, escapes with a few friends.[18]

These gloomy apocalyptics are redeemed by mocking pictures of what a psychologically-dominated world might become. The mania for averages leads to the choice of the completely average man as President of the United States, then as President of the world. Under him the absence of political or miliary excitement produces a rapid technological retrogression. The United States sinks into a national trance as the first non-Platonic system of politics, or doctrine of the Lowest Common Denominator, spreads. Preferential university scholarships are given to students nearest the age-group median-attainment quotients. In an attempt to preserve the traditions of *homo sapiens* a small group of intelligent people retreat to Egypt, but fall out amongst them selves. *Homo abnegus* reigns unchallenged for a quarter of a million years, until a highly sophisticated canine civilisation, developed in the Arctic, sweeps down to enslave him as a stick-thrower for their traditional sport—until they devise a stick-throwing machine.[19]

A converse picture of the evils attendant upon classification was presented by Kurt Vonnegut: a fearful anticipation of the time when everyone has to take the National General Classification Tests at eighteen in order to get into college. Rejects literally become Reeks and Wrecks as the Army and the Reclamation Corps are known. One such wreck is Rudy Hertz, whose skills have been copied by a machine at the fully-automated works at Ilium, whose director Dr. Paul Proteus is made uncomfortably aware of the General Classification Tests when he meets a fellow manager with three children.

> It's a trial watching your kids grow up, wondering if they've got what it takes, seeing 'em just about killing themselves before the

General Classification Tests, then waiting for the grades'—The sentence ended with a sigh. 'I've just gone through that G.C.T. business with my oldest . . . and I've got to live through the whole nightmare twice more still.[20]

Drawn into the leadership of the anti-managerial Ghost Shirt Society, Dr. Proteus finds himself working to overthrow EPIPAC XIV, the national electronic computer in Carlsbad Caverns, which decides how many of everything America and her customers can buy and consume, and how many engineers, managers, researchers, and civil servants will be required.

Watching it in the Carlsbad Caverns, the Shah of Bratpuhr (who, with his entourage and interpreters, appears throughout the book as a chorus), compares it to the mud-and-straw idols of one of his own infidel tribes. As a revolt of the Ghost Shirt Society begins, the Shah comes to Ilium to be persuaded to allow an American technical mission to draw up blueprints for modernising his country. He replies: 'Before we take this step would you ask EPIPAC what people are for?' That question is not, alas, adequately answered by Kurt Vonnegut, for as soon as EPIPAC XIV is destroyed the rebels begin grubbing about among the ruins to build it up again.

In England, the author of the most notable of such fantasies, *The Rise of the Meritocracy* (1958) became, eight years later, the first chairman of the Social Science Research Council.

V   THE SPIRIT OF REVOLT

Contemporary nihilism, having shed all transcendental trappings, has led man to realise how absurd is his condition. Engendered by Nietzsche and to a lesser extent Hegel,[21] this contemporary nihilism calls for a reconsideration of the myth of the eponymous hero of both technology and prophecy, whose name, Prometheus, means forethought. Prometheus stole fire from the Gods for men and yet further endowed them with the skill to interpret omens. In revenge, he was tempted by Zeus with a woman made of clay —Pandora—and when he rejected her, his brother Epimetheus took her and her box. This contained all the evils and sicknesses Zeus wished mankind to inherit, and when Epimetheus opened it they all flew out to afflict mankind. All, that is, except hope, which remained at the bottom of the box. Prometheus himself was crucified to a rock for thirty-thousand years and tormented by an eagle. His story was presented by Camus in *L'Homme Révolté* (1951), as 'le plus grand mythe de l'intelligence révolté'.[22] Such revolt against man's specific condition and against the 'ends' of his creation he sees as necessary. Subsequent 'revolts' against God (as in the French Revolution), against reason (as in Hegel), and against revolt itself (as in Nietzsche), have made it necessary to start the process again.

Myths of 'starting the process again', like Walter M. Miller, Jr.'s picture of the twenty-sixth century *A Canticle for Leibowitz* (1959) have a strong theological bias. A Runaway Planet known as 'Rejoice in Messias, the Day is at Hand', is the subject of *Wolfbane* (1959) by C. M. Kornbluth and Frederik Pohl. Since their new sun—the Moon—needed rekindling every five years, population shrank and the remainder adopted a way of life designed to save calories. Since the rating of the total available calories to the population was not sufficient to maintain an adequate Artistic-Technological Style, engineering disappeared and earth came under the control of a computerised 'Pyramid'. People became so inhibited that they developed cults of behaviour designed to emphasise this.

A non-inhibited wolf, Glenn Tropile, penetrates and destroys the programmed fastness of the Pyramid and restores, to the world of A.D. 2200, a rekindled Sun. But he has to sacrifice himself.[23]

Another great mythic theme, that of the periodic destruction of the world followed by a new world and a new regenerated mankind, has been shown by Mircea Eliade to go back to the Graeco-Oriental Great Year which opened with a creation and concluded with a chaos. The cosmic cycle includes a 'creation', an 'existence' (or 'history', wearing-out, degeneration), and a return to 'chaos' (*ekpyrosis, ragnarok, pralaya*, submergence of Atlantis, or apocalypse).[24] Man's need of the myth of eternal renewal is seen in Kurt Vonnegut's sketch of a gerontocratic world in 2158. As one of his characters complains of the new life-lengthening drug 'anti-gerason':

> Sometimes I wish folks just up and died regularly as clockwork, without anything to say about it, instead of deciding themselves how long they're going to stay around. There ought to be a law against selling the stuff to anybody over 150.[25]

The possibility of instant nuclear ekpyrosis has given ample scope for rewriting the book of Genesis. One such attempt describes a graduate student in ecology finding himself alone and alive after such a catastrophe and deciding to re-people the world with the help of a semi-negress.[26] Another, by Rex Gordon, centres round the director of a new community created after the 'Great Rift'. Its director Leibnitz, asks a time traveller in 2050:

> What kind of super-man will the emergent species be when the Rift, the Discontinuity, the period of radiation ends? What do we want him to be? A man like you archaics, a toolmaker with mechanical genius who is skilled in war? Or something still more fiendish and effective. A master of treachery, savagery, heartless and fiendish in all his actions? Those are the survival virtues? That is what may come out of human selection in its next stage! But we impose on life our will, our purpose. It is time that man took charge of his own destiny, and did not leave it in the hands of a God called Nature![27]

Coming from pre-catastrophic times, the traveller, Judgen, is selected for this breeding centre for his 'archaic' body structure as he conforms to none of the five main types: albino, wide-shouldered, squat, big-head, or chimpanzee. He realises his companions are the last representatives of humanity as he had known it. 'We were like creatures in a zoo, the last products of an all but extinct and dying species, yet kept obviously as things of value for breeding purposes.'[28] Embedded in the commentary on Center City is the oblique criticism of Judgen's own world, its 'specialists in Security whose business it was to prevent some scientists knowing what others did'; its 'élite of knowledge without power, and an electorate priding themselves on their stupidity and ignorance'; its specialisms whereby 'people who did know facts about the world knew them separately, in isolation, as separate facts, that, because of the division of the sciences, were never put together'. Such were the faults in Judgen's world which he saw caused the great catastrophe. For not realising that the earth itself was an atomic pile they started up the earth's internal atomic forces by exploding atom bombs underground in Nevada.

On his return to the contemporary world, Judgen manages to secure the transfer of the bomb tests from Nevada to space, but the dilemma still remains: 'The world of Center City will be hanging over us always now.' Judgen finds the mohole boring, down through the seabed where the crust of the earth is thin, has begun, and 'the people I talk to seem happy to go on knowing nothing. They prefer quite blindly to take the risk.'

VI SCIENTISTS AND THE FUTURE

That such sociological fables or shamanistic tales should be woven by those with a scientific training indicates that a new operational ethic was emerging. This was so absorbing to other scientists that when Asimov was orally examined for his Ph.D., it is said that his examiners were more interested in his science-fiction than his thesis. There is nothing new in this. Robert Louis Stevenson was the son of an engineer; H. G. Wells was a graduate of the Royal College of Science, and John Munro, author of *Trip to Venus* (1897), was a professor of engineering at Bristol. Stanley G. Weinbaum, an original contributor to *Wonder Stories*, who died in 1935, was a graduate chemical engineer; John W. Campbell, Jr., the editor of *Astounding Science Fiction*, a physics graduate of M.I.T.; L. Sprague de Camp holds three technology degrees and was an Assistant Editor for the American Society of Mechanical Engineers (1937). T. L. Sherred is a Detroit automobile engineer; Lee Correy is a rocket engineer; Chad Oliver an anthropologist; George O. Smith an electronics engineer; Richard McKenna was a naval machinist who has become an anthropologist, whilst Philip Wylie, one of the best known pre-war writers, had a degree in physics.[29] Heinlein graduated at the U.S. Naval Academy of Annapolis and practised engineering; E. E. Smith was a food chemist engaged in the mass manufacture of doughnuts.

There was, however, a real political bite from the eminent English mathematician, Fred Hoyle, whose fantasies about the future are virtually political tracts. One, set in the year 1965 as seen from 2020, invests Christopher Kingsley, a Cambridge astronomer, with a supra-political power at Nortonstowe, a Cotswold fastness, to cope with a cloud of gas that shuts off the sun's rays from earth: *The Black Cloud* (1957). It has a two-fold significance. First, it portrays a conflict between the politicians (who wish to destroy the cloud by rockets), and the scientists (who wish to communicate with it). Secondly, the scientists concerned are Russians, Americans, and English, while the neutral civil servant, Parkinson, virtually deserts his political masters for their point of view, gaining thereby, increasing influence in government circles. It is really a sermon on the evils of scientists 'doing the thinking', 'for an archaic crowd of nitwits' and 'allowing themselves to be pushed about in the bargain'.

In another story two years later, a young Cambridge mathematician of 1970 investigates the activities of an industrial group in Southern Ireland, I.C.E. (Industrial Corporation of Eire), based on a new prime mover which enables industrial material to be obtained from water, air, and fairly common rocks. He finds that the personnel of I.C.E. are really an alien folk who have deserted another planet because, owing to the increasing power of the sun, it had become a blazing slagheap. Having plumbed their secret, Thomas Sherwood is told by one of the aliens:

> What's the point of it all? It'll be just the same here. The Earth is already half-way along exactly the same road to extinction. The sun will get inexorably brighter as the years roll on, just as our star did, and life on the Earth will just as surely come to an end.[30]

Even more forcefully the physicist Leo Szilard, founder and co-chairman of the Council for a Liveable World, pressed home, in five fables, a similar concern that political problems could be more speedily solved if they were subjected to the same kind of discussion as scientific ones. In one a man returns from the deep freeze to the world after ninety years to learn how fast science has progressed in the interval. He discovers that twenty-five million others have been rendered redundant and followed him into *statu dormiendi*. Among those who remain, teeth have been dispensed with, the oesophagus bypassed so that they don't have to watch their diet, and artificial insemination has resulted in a few donors becoming millionaires. One such millionaire donor wants to retard the rapid progress of science so Szilard's hero suggests he should establish a foundation to do so. The satire on the National Science Foundation is explicit.

> First of all, the best scientists would be removed from their laboratories and kept busy on committees passing on applications for funds. Secondly, the scientific workers in need of funds would concentrate on problems which were considered promising and to lead to publishable results. For a few years there might be a great increase in scientific output; but by going after the obvious, pretty soon science would dry out. Science would become something like

a parlour game. Some things would be considered interesting, others not. There would be fashions. Those who followed the fashion would get grants. Those who wouldn't would not and pretty soon they would burn to follow the fashion too.[31]

Leo Szilard's fear of fossilization was shared by Fred Hoyle. Both entertained operational views of the future based on criticism of projected models. As Hoyle wrote:

> A truly Utopian society would be one, not as usually imagined with impossible static perfection, but one endowed with the property of feedback control mechanism. Temporary perfection is not so important as a procedure for removing inconsistencies as soon as they arise; a procedure whereby an inconsistency itself sets in operation the means for its own correction.[32]

VII   THE THEOLOGY OF TOMORROW

As physicists moved into biology and the mathematicians into games theory and stochastic processes, it seemed as if Henry Adams's prediction that the 'future of thought and, therefore, of history, lies in the hands of physicists'[33] was on the verge of being fulfilled. Nicholas Rashevsky, a Russian physicist who migrated to the Westinghouse Laboratories in 1924, began increasingly to preoccupy himself with the mathematical biology of human behaviour. His fellow countryman, Anatol Rapoport, carried forward his ideas in *Science and the Goals of Man* (1950) and *Fights, Games and Debates* (1960).

But what physicists might do a hundred years from now was visualised by Professor (now Lord) Ritchie Calder. He described a world conference as it might take place at Alert on the North Coast of Ellesmere Island—four hundred miles from the North Pole. Northern darkness would be dispelled by man-made sunlight, beamed from sodium in the vacuum beyond the earth's envelope. This would serve the additional purpose of reflecting T.V. waves, thus enabling people all over the globe to see and hear the President of the United States of Africa, Dr. Okoboyko, taking the chair inside a great dome of transparent plastic, where the delegates would be able to debate in the calmness of a controlled climate, having arrived from all quarters by remote-controlled rocket-airlines. By then, too, seafarms would be supplementing the food reserves of the world, harvested by an atomic-powered mechanical-whale. The seas themselves would be extended by unfreezing areas like Hudson's Bay with atomic energy.[34]

Theologians caught the mood. After watching a cyclotron at the University of California in 1952, Teilhard recognised it as a true revelation. 'For fifty years,' he wrote, 'we have been present, without being much aware of it, at the birth all over the world of veritable generators (or focussers) of human energy.' These were now 'focussing upon each other' so that one could now speak of a 'psychozoic era'. Elsewhere he wrote: 'To a Martian capable of analysing sidereal radiations psychically no less than physically, the first characteristic of our planet would be, not the blue of the sea or the green of the forests, but the phosphorescence of thought.'[35]

This phosphorescence is especially visible in the pragmatic, future-oriented community based upon function and contract described by Harvey Cox as 'technopolis' or 'the secular city'. In an afterword to the debate his book evoked in the United States, he describes 'the problem which dogs all forms of strictly Utopian eschatology' as what a temporary future fulfilment does mean for the individual.

> Unrequited hope [he wrote] produces corrosive cynicism unless the future is experienced as present now in a significant way. We need not just the idea of future hope, but also something very like the Johannine idea of 'eternity', the present presence of the future, if such cynicism is to be avoided. Jesus' insistence that the New Time is *both* here *and* coming dramatises this tension.

Cox considered that God's *avant-garde* had four roles: Kerygmatic, diakonic, koinoniac, and cathartic. As kerygmatics they proclaim the freedom of man as against the principalities and powers seeking to engulf him. As diakonics, they confront social ailments with the therapy of a social gospel. As koinoniacs they are 'harbingers of a reality which is breaking into history not from the past but from the future'. As cathartics, or better still as cultural exorcists, they hope to free man from the 'narcotic vagaries through which they wrongly perceive the social reality around them, and from habitual forms of action or inaction stemming from these illusions'.[35]

The secretary of the World Council of Churches also urged Christians to restore their own sense of proportion in the face of what he called 'futurology'—the systematic study of trends which enable us to forecast the shape of things to come—with these words:

> The ecclesiastical and even theological issues on which they spend much time are unsignificant compared with the tremendous issue: what will become of man in the civilisation of the future?[36]

He acknowledged that the Kingdom will not come after the conclusion of the historical process in which we are now involved but will manifest itself in history whenever men obey the Divine Call.

VIII PHYLOGENY AND PROPHECY: THE NEW BESTIARIES

The potential acceleration or sidetracking of evolution stimulated the composition of new bestiaries as didactic as anything in Aesop or Phaedrus. Even before Hiroshima, with ants, skilled as mathematicians and sociologists, ruling over degenerate man in F. H. Ridley's *The Green Machine* (1926), and the cats seated in millions which watch the evolution of man from 1933 to A.D. 12,000 in John Gloag's *Tomorrow's Yesterday* (1932). But other ant-fables like those of A. G. Bennet, *The Demigods* (1939), and R. L. Fanthorpe, *Fiends* (1959) or cat fables like those of C. D. Simak, *City* (1954), D. Wallop *What has Four Wheels and Flies* (1959), or even K. Capek's celebrated *War with the Newts* (1937) now tend to be overshadowed by speculations of man's genetic future in the world of uncontrolled radiation.

Many phylogenic avenues were explored. From Edmond Hamilton's androids (C. Simak, *Time and Again* (1956) and E. Cooper, *That Uncertain Midnight* (1958)), humanoids (J. Williamson in a novel of that name in 1953), mutants (Henry Kuttner also in a novel of that name in 1954) to slans (A. E. Von Vogt, *Destination Universe* (1953)) and yuccas (G. Goodchild, *Dr. Zil's Experiment* (1953)). Most of these explorers posed the question, set earlier by H. G. Wells in *The Island of Dr. Moreau*: was man rolling the evolutionary chart backwards instead of forwards? As seen by A. E. van Vogt these *pseudo-people* (as they were called in an anthology of that name subtitled *Androids in Science Fiction*, edited by William F. Nolan, in 1965) had a more didactic role:

'a mirror in which science-fiction writers reflect a part of mankind's unending search into the roots of human behaviour' (p. 14).

Quite a specialist bestiarist is Clifford Simak. In *The City* (1952) men have passed away from the earth leaving it to dogs and robots. Round the hearth fires, dogs ask 'What is man? What is a city? What is war?' The Websters, who have produced intelligent talking-dogs, go with mankind to Jupiter in order to live longer. After centuries the last of the Websters revisits earth and finds the world controlled by dogs and robots. In *They Walked Like Men* (1962), he shows aliens expropriating the human race by assuming human shape and buying up human property. These aliens have protean powers that prompt a science journalist, after outwitting them, to confess (p. 138):

> It was almost as if we, the three of us, were acting out an old morality play, with the basic sins of mankind enlarged a millionfold to prove a point of exaggeration.

In this case the exaggeration is the weakness of the aliens—an overdeveloped sense of smell. For though they could change themselves into any form they wish—rolling balls, odorous liquids, or dolls—they were the slaves of the sense of smell. They so abandoned themselves to it, that it enabled them to be detected, unmasked, and destroyed.

The possibility of reaching an evolutionary cul-de-sac, and 'the ultimate boredom that only Utopia can supply' drives one of A. C. Clarke's characters to escape to the cold twilight beyond Pluto in a flying refrigerator. It outlasts eons. Ultimately returned to earth by the refrigerator's robot controls, he wakes to find that he has no more riddles to ask of Time. 'For in the last moment of his life, as he saw those waiting round him, he knew that the ancient war between them and insect had long ago been ended, and that man was not the victor.'[38]

The complete cessation of reproduction in most species, including man, as a result of experiments with The Bomb, is described in Brian Aldiss's *Greybeard* (1964). A group of homidically-selfish old people exists on the banks of the Thames in a society ruled by a military dictator and docile professors, whilst packs of stoats roam the countryside. The overpowering question hangs over the book—will man be born again?

As a form of apocalytic intuition, peculiar to our age, that the human race may be a biological misfit doomed to extinction like the gigantic reptiles of an earlier life,[39] such fiction seemed to Arthur Koestler unduly preoccupied with the end products of evolution.

'Why,' playfully asked an eminent British scientist, 'cannot man set up a community like an ants' nest . . . with the help of recent and probable future biological discoveries, some sort of imitation by man of the ants' nest cannot be quite excluded from consideration.' This might, he thought, enable man to carry out a sex revolution and free himself from the urgency of the sexual impulse so that he could lead a contented celibate life. But Sir Charles Darwin then consoled us by pointing out that it would need a new phylum of the animal kingdom. He also considered the possibility of breeding humans, like dogs, for special purposes.[40]

IX   THE NEW RIGHT: AYN RAND

The veteran science-fiction writer Heinlein suggested the formation of a 'Patrick Henry League', taking a full page advertisement in the Colorado Springs *Gazette Telegraph* on 13th April 1958 to do so. In his subsequent novels one critic sees this feeling at work: *Starship Troopers* (1959) reads to him like a recruiting pamphlet for the marines, while *Farnham's Freehold* (1964), with its dark intimations of a future Negro ascendancy is, to him, part of the Conservative warning.[41]

Dark pictures of tomorrow were thrown up by Ayn Rand. In the future society in *Anthem* (1954) everyone is zoned and known by an occupational number. 'We' and 'they' replace 'I' and 'thou', and Hymns to the Collective Spirit are sung. Amenities are reduced to such primitive levels by Communism that the local science institute has just invented candles. One scientist, hoping to join it, is, for asking too many questions, given a 'Life mandate' as a street-sweeper. But he discovers some old electrical equipment in a tunnel and gets it to work. The scientists are so angry that he escapes to the forest and becomes an 'I'. 'To be free,' he reflects, 'a man must be free of his brothers. That is freedom; that and nothing else.' So, with a girl, he finds a house and carves 'Ego' above the portal. Ego is his new Anthem. Ego comes even more to the fore in *Atlas Shrugged* (1957), the story of a group of business men, scientists, and doctors who find the world so saturated and top heavy with welfare-state ideology that they shrug it off like Atlas and withdraw to a mountain fastness. Their leader, John Galt, asks as a post-Christian secularist:

What is the nature of the guilt that your teachers call his Original Sin? What are the evils man acquired when he fell from a state they consider perfection? Their myth declares that he ate the fruit of the tree of knowledge—he acquired a mind and became a rational being. It was the knowledge of good and evil—he became a moral being. He was sentenced to earn his bread by his labor—he became a productive being. He was sentenced to experience desire—he acquired the capacity of sexual enjoyment. The evils for which they damn him are reason, morality, creativeness, joy—all the cardinal values of his existence. It is not his vices that their myth of man's fall is designed to explain and condemn, it is not his errors that they hold as his guilt, but the essence of his nature as a man. Whatever he was—that robot in the Garden of Eden, who existed without mind, without values, without labor, without love—he was not a man.[42]

He castigates the:

... grotesque little atavists [who] stare blindly at the skyscrapers and smokestacks around [and] dream of enslaving the material providers who are scientists, inventors, industrialists. When you clamor for public ownership of the mind, I have taught my strikers that the answer you deserve is only: 'Try and get it'.

The Gaderene descent to hedonism in a world where hunger and poverty have been eliminated and death has lost its terrors, might involve, as James Gunn showed in *The Joy Makers* (1961), the sacrifice of free will and personality. In this Hedonics, institutionalised, so succeed in cocooning human beings that the envoy from Venus to Earth only prevents himself being enslaved by losing his temper.

X   THE NEW LEFT: WILLIAM BURROUGHS AND
J. G. BALLARD

Further criticism was proffered by those who saw life as a surrealist fantasy. Following the mazy itinerary of the great routemaster of the subconscious, James Joyce, who used a single moment of existence as a lens in which to see endless perspectives of reality, others tried to show how 'the past is consumed in the present and the present is living only because it brings forth the future'.[43] For just as Bloom experiences 'the cold of interstellar space, thousands of degrees below freezing point'[44] and *Finnegan's Wake* is 'one continuous present-tense integument slowly unfolding all marryvoising moodmoulded cyclewheeling history',[45] so more experimentally, and certainly excrementally, William Burroughs presented a Swiftian satire on megalopolitan America in *The Naked Lunch* (1959). Through the hallucinations of one withdrawing from drug addiction we see the totalitarian country of America, where the sinister scientist Doctor Benway interrogates, brainwashes, and controls. We see, too, 'Liquificationists', 'Senders', and 'Divisionists', all tragically perverse in their quest for pleasure, power, and love, crowd into a vast box of a bulging building in the City of Interzone. It justifies Burroughs's claim:

> . . . to make people aware of the true criminality of our times, to wise up to the marks. All my work is directed against those who are bent, through stupidity, or design, on blowing up the planet or rendering it uninhabitable.[46]

In *Nova Express* (1965) he presents Inspector J. Lee's Nova Police preventing the Nova Mob from blowing up the planet.

If Burroughs confessed that he was most closely akin to C. S. Lewis (the idea of conspiracy in *The Hideous Strength* being 'very similar to many of the conspirators . . . in *Nova Express*'),[47] his own work has evoked the admiration of the British author J. G. Ballard,[48] who jettisoned physical ideas like interstellar travel for biological ones. To Ballard 'the only alien planet is Earth' and his self-acknowledged 'oblique style, understated themes, private symbols and vocabularies' are seen in *The Drowned World* (1962).[49] 'We know all the history of the next three million years,' says Kerans as the temperatures at the equator rise to 180° and the rainbelts are continuous up to the 20th parallel. Solar flares have melted the polar icecaps, the major cities of the world are either lagooned or smothered in silt. Iguanas and basilisks squat in former boardrooms, and all around is the hatred that one zoological class feels towards the other that is succeeding it. All the world is reverting to its Palaeozoic past and the only transit avenues for the United Nations military units are lagoons through colonies of miasmic vegetables, built up in what had once been the Arctic circle, now a sub-tropical zone with an annual mean temperature of eighty-five degrees. As mammalian fertility declines, amphibian and reptile forms obtain superiority. As Kerans observed, 'the geological tree of mankind was systematically pruning itself, apparently moving backwards in time, and a point might ultimately be reached where a second Adam and Eve found themselves alone in a new Eden'.[50]

Ballard's heroes seem so occluded from science that one might regard them as literary incarnations of the helpless intellectual in a world hurried along by technocrats. As Algis Budrys, himself a skilful draftsman of futuristic scenarios, remarked in *Galaxy* (December 1966), 'in order to be the protagonist of a J. G. Ballard novel or anything more than a very minor character therein, you must have cut yourself off from the entire body of scientific education. In this way when the world disaster—be it wind or water—comes upon you, you are under absolutely no obligation to do anything about it but sit and worship it'.

Ballard uses the horrors of nature to show up the sickness in ourselves and his other stories, like the *Wind from Nowhere* (1961), *The Voice of Time* (1962), *Billennium* (1962), *The 4-Dimensional Nightmare* (1963), *The Terminal Beach* (1964), and *The Drought* (1965) led one critic to claim that he was, with William Burroughs, 'the only s.f. writer worth reading'.[51]

XI THE NEW MODERATE: ALDOUS HUXLEY

As if to lower the temperature of speculation on the future of the brave new world that he had done so much to kindle, Aldous Huxley sketched, in his last novel *Island* (1962), a South East Asian island where the mynah birds sing 'Attention. Here and Now Boys' in an Erewhonian manner. Here the techniques of Mendel and Pavlov are as well known as the ideas of Darwin. His traveller, William Asquith Farnaby, is told on reaching Pala:

> Darwin took the old Totemism and raised it to the level of biology. The fertility cults reappeared as genetics and Havelock Ellis. And now its up to us to take another half-turn up the spiral. Darwin was the old Neolithic Wisdom turned into scientific concepts. The new conscious Wisdom—the kind of wisdom that was prophetically glimpsed in Zen and Taoism and Tantra—is biological theory realised in living practice.[52]

Pala survives amongst aggressive outside neighbours because of its oil. As the sinister ambassador of the most threatening neighbour-state reminds Farnaby:

> Any clear-sighted observer could have seen that for three-quarters of the human race, freedom and happiness were almost out of the question. Today, they're completely out of the question. And meanwhile the outside world has been closing in on this little island of freedom and happiness. Closing in steadily and inexorably, coming nearer and nearer.[53]

This freedom and happiness were achieved by a veritable dynasty of biocrats. The great grandfather of Will Farnaby's interlocutor began it by an alliance with the Raja in setting up a kind of eastern Rothamsted, to strengthen the alliance between man and nature. By so doing, they found it 'quite easy to pass from mutual aid in a village community to streamlined co-operative techniques for buying and selling and profit-sharing and financing. . . . Even co-operative financing.'[54]

With electricity they made their next leap forward, since reliable refrigeration enabled them in the late twenties to keep a deep-freeze bank of human semen; thereby enabling families to enrich their stock with new physiques and temperaments—a process justified in terms of Karm and reincarnation. 'Give us another century,' proudly boasts a father of two who had resorted to the bank for his next child, 'and our average I.Q. will be up to a hundred and fifteen', whereas Farnaby gloomily replies: 'whereas *ours*, at the present rate of progress, will be down to eighty-five.'[55]

To this was coupled a policy of birth control—a thirty-night supply of contraceptives was delivered at the beginning of each month—and of *Maithuna*—the yoga of love. So the 'problem' of population did not exist since Pala's grew at the rate of one third of one per cent per annum.

As Dr. MacPhail, Farnaby's interlocutor, put it:

> Lenin used to say that electricity plus socialism equals communism. Our equations are rather different. Electricity minus heavy industry plus birth control equals democracy and plenty. Electricity plus heavy industry minus birth control equals misery, totalitarianism and war.[56]

Pala's kind of Democracy was based on the rule that nobody was allowed to become more than four or five times as rich as average. Pala had no omnipotent politicians or bureaucrats, but was 'a federation of self-governing units—so there's plenty of scope for small-scale initiative and democratic leaders. . . .' With no established church and a religion stressing 'immediate experience' and deploring 'belief in unverifiable dogmas and the emotions which that belief inspires', Pala escaped the twin plagues of popery and fundamentalist revivalism.[57]

Destiny Control was encouraged in the schools. The 'Muscle People' and the 'Peter Pans' who cause all the trouble in the world were diagnosed early, and by the humane use of Pavlovian techniques ('Food plus caress plus contact plus good equals love. And love equals pleasure, love equals satisfaction'),[58] the 'Muscle People' and 'Peter Pans' were guided into the Way of Disinterested Action by appropriate therapeutic activities. Together with other 'types' like 'guinea-pigs' (the gentle and friendly), 'cats' (the solitaries), 'sheep' (the gregarious), and 'martens' (the doers). In schools they played logic games—Evolutionary Snakes and Ladders, Mendelian Happy Families, or Psychological Bridge—and indulged in bridge-building sessions to cross theory and practice.

Such 'conditioning' was fortified outside the school by Mutual Adoption Clubs providing a series of deputy fathers and mothers to compensate for the shortcomings or absence of real ones. These M.A.C.'s yet further hybridised the micro-culture of the families. The Doctor's daughter-in-law told Farnaby:

> It's as beneficial, on its own level, as the hybridisation of different strains of maize or chickens. Healthier relationships in more responsible groups, wider sympathies and deeper understandings. And the sympathies and understandings are for everyone in the M.A.C. from babies to centenarians.[59]

That is why, when Farnaby saw a marionette show of *Oedipus* in Pala, Jocasta was talked out of suicide and Oedipus out of blinding himself.[60]

Though Dr. MacPhail was murdered by the apostles of 'Progress, Values, Oil and True Spirituality', Will Farnaby is converted to the need for compassion 'in the great world of impersonal forces, of proliferating numbers, of collective paranoias, of authoritative hypnotists, of tribes of buffoons and hucksters and of the purveyors of entertaining irrelevances'. Huxley considered that his new model was 'Darwinism raised to the level of compassion and spiritual insight'.

XII MALTHUS WALKS ABROAD

Beside the ghost of Merlin was the ghost of Malthus.

> Our recent mastery of global statistics [wrote two biologists] has tended to go to our heads; and until we become acclimatized to living in a statistically comprehensible world, we shall continue to suffer from a kind of nervous strain. We can never again be ignorant. A mass of global statistics, slowly collected and refined over the last half-century, has suddenly transformed our outlook on the world. the revolutionary nature of this change has not yet been realised.[61]

Amongst these global statistics none were more impressive than those concerned with the mounting population. These statistics were most noticeable in places equipped neither to feed nor to educate them. China, it was predicted, would reach a billion by 1980, the U.S. by 2050.

Such arithmetic was all the more impressive in that it was carefully worked out.[62] Yet such extrapolatory curves have long preoccupied the ingenious.[63] Population forecasting implicates disciplines other than those of mere demography. So, at the suggestion of Dr. Pincus, whose work on hormones has contributed a great deal to the development of the oral contraceptive, a conference was convened by the CIBA foundation in 1963 on the future of man; to 'stir the imagination, speed the flow of information and generally hasten the progress of work in medical and biological research'.[64]

A year or so earlier one of the speakers had been invited to deliver the Reith Lectures for the B.B.C. Concentrating on the 'process of foretelling rather than what was actually foretold', he agreed that 'a man can influence posterity by other than genetic means, that nature does not know best, and that neither fatuous good humour nor liverishness will solve the problems for ever being posed, only continuous exploration and extension of our knowledge of nature'.[65]

A minatory scenario of New York in 1999 was sketched by Harry Harrison in *Make Room! Make Room!* (1966). As a city of 35 million people grubs a living by growing food in window boxes, hoards razor blades and soylent steaks, hunts rats for food and drinks water that's brackish when not saline, the full import of the extrapolatory fable is borne in: not only the U.S.A. is so crowded. In Britain the last Tory gets shot defending the last grouse woods when they come to plough it up, and a regular Gothic line defends the larder country of Denmark. The policeman hero admits the need for animal trainers rather than policemen. And having whetted the reader's incredulity, Harrison then obligingly refers him to a bibliography at the end which includes Malthus and his latter day successors. It serves indeed as an overture to any serious demographic discussion, fulfilling one of the basic roles of science-fiction in modern society.

To promote the discussion of research findings in the social as well as the natural sciences in so far as they affect 'possible futures', Bertrand de Jouvenal established *Futuribles*. This aimed at initiating a permanent discussion of the future, a discussion which, by giving advance notice of unfavourable and favourable possibilities, might help in guiding policies away from dangerous paths. Eliciting individual speculative essays from experts in various disciplines, he convened the first inter-disciplinary conference on long-term speculation, at Geneva (June 1932). Another followed in Paris (July 1963) and the third at Yale (December 1964). The number of essays were carried through the bulletin S.E.D.E.I.S. (now *Analyse and Prévision*), starting in April 1961. By 1966 research groups dedicated to the study of the future began in various countries.[66]

Some amongst these high-pressure haruspical groups entertain near millennial expectations. Emmanuel Mesthene of Harvard is quoted as saying that 'man may have finally expiated his original sin, and might now aspire to bliss'. Such confidence is perhaps one reason why speculation about the future will continue to concentrate on what *might* go amiss.[67]

Galtonian preoccupation with the need to plan the arrival of the fittest continues up to the present day. It is manifest, for instance, in the works of C. M. Kornbluth. Citing his story *The Little Black Bag*, first published in *Astounding Science Fiction* in 1950, one editor has said that he was 'persecuted by a persistent premonition that mankind was debasing itself by the absence of any attempt at selective breeding, plus a horrifying kind of auto-intoxication called 'popular education'.[68] A similar scepticism tinges the writing of Dr. D. H. Fink, whose story *Compound B* (which makes the black races more intelligent) ends with the sombre reflection:

> It seems strange to us today that anyone could want to keep secret . . . a discovery that has done for mankind just what Dr. Murdock said it would do, namely, make the human race intelligent enough to govern itself. But we must remember the twentieth century was the age of secrecy . . . no one believed it possible that he might be stupid . . . people even thought that the possession of a television set and atomic weapons was evidence of their sanity and wisdom.[69]

XIII MULTIPLE PROGNOSES

To define the boundaries within which possible futures must lie, one of the most prolific of the post-war fabulists, A. C. Clarke, suggested in *Profiles of the Future* (1962), some technological advances that would take place by the year 2100. For by then, he considered, 'politics and economics would cease to be as important as they have been in the past', and that the time would come when 'most of our present controversies on these matters will seem as trivial, or as meaningless, as the theological debates in which the keenest minds of the Middle Ages dissipated their energies'.[70] By the twenty-second century he thought that travel speeds approaching that of light would be reached, enabling man to meet extraterrestrials and to colonise the planets. On earth a Wellsian 'World Brain', climate control, artificial life, and a Stapledonian system of replacing defective parts of the human body would be common, to say nothing of telesensory devices.

As a prophet, Clarke had already made a name by predicting the first communications satellite[71] and the first manned satellites.[72] In addition, his numerous science-fiction stories of the future[73] sharpened appetites for more fare of this kind.

The enormous popular appeal of this and other prophecies was not lost on journals and newspapers. The *New Scientist*,[74] a very enterprising interpreter of new science to the general public, made the most ambitious attempt in 1964 by asking nearly 100 distinguished scholars and scientists for their personal medium-range forecasts, thereby achieving a comprehensive approach. But since all of them revealed their names and the institutions with which they were associated, their forecasts were judicious and eminently unstartling, even to the extent of virtually ignoring the possibility of another major war.

A smaller but bolder group of vaticinal skirmishers made *1990* —a special number 126 of the *Weekend Telegraph* on 3rd March 1967—more stimulating and lively. Whether it was the further date, or the year's preparation, it certainly considered that the total control of present and future would be provided by Scientism. Decayed cities like Bradford, Huddersfield, Leeds, and Manchester would have been resited, Britain with six million immigrants would have been expelled from the Commonwealth but 'in' Europe (the European Economic Union headquarters would be at Brighton), manual labour would have disappeared and the increased use of 'psycho-scientismic methods' of employee-control would have weakened the great traditional unions. The great problem of democratic control, would, however, not be solved even by equipping the opposition with data-processing equipment. With mood-controllers on every wrist, swamis on call in India, and rocket transport to Mecca, the inhabitants of the great South Eastern linear city of 30 million people would have few worries.

What made *1990* an interesting variant of the usual type of prophecy was that it contained a prophecy within it. For in *1990* it was agreed to build a three-mile-high city, the top 200 floors of which would house a psychosocial cognitor. This, as Kingsley Amis wrote, would show 'that we have advanced for ever into the Age of Pure Scientism, that we have put behind us for ever the hybrid schizophrenic age of the two cultures. Then human beings will be able to face the future with confidence, because they will know exactly what the future holds'.[75]

XIV PSYCHOMANTICS

Kingsley Amis in fact deserved great credit for pointing out that one does not read science-fiction to discover scientific truths, any more than one reads Westerns to learn about ranching methods. Nor does one read it as 'prophecy' even though, by the very number of the prophecies made, some are bound to be right. As he sees it, its real value is as 'a means of dramatising social enquiry', as 'providing a fictional mode in which cultural tendencies can be isolated and judged'.[76]

Since he wrote, this fictional mode of isolating and judging cultural tendencies has spread to other countries whose writers have not hitherto impinged on our story. Thus, for instance, from Norway came a welcome reinforcement to this select cadre of commentators (for Kingsley Amis considered that science-fiction 'only did this at its most ambitious, and even then, presumptuously'), Axel Jensen's insignificantly named subject, *Epp* (1965) is anything but presumptuous. He lives in a solitary cell on the fourteenth floor of Block 982 in Oblidor. He is a Bloom of tomorrow's world. Before his window passes his namesake and nephew 'quite pale from sitting in the teaching machine'.[77] Beside him live those displaced by the robotisation of the mines, or the wallpaper industry. As a citizen of Gambolia he watches 'the Box' and finds his country's new war machines 'very interesting, . . . because they raise the war in Om to a spiritual level by transforming or rather beautifying the Omesians' death rattles and death cries into Gambolian military music'. He rejects the idea of going on holiday since he must apply to the Recreation Selection Board for a transfer to the coast. Around him sniffle several thousand sociologists 'making a survey of us dimwits'. Regularly his pills come through the post-tube valve and he flushes them down the loo. Apart from speculating about neighbours whose condition is even more parlous than his own, he projects all his feeling on to a solitary plant —which stings him. In a world where the conveyor-pavements are packed with pensioners, Epp keeps his individuality by staying in his room.

Certainly contemporary social problems can be effectively posed by laterally extending them into the future. B. A. Young's picture of Britain under a marijuana-smoking West Indian Prime Minister in 1996—*Cabinet Pudding* (1967)—is more than Othello in modern dress. The pound is worth 1*s.* 5*d.* of what it is in 1967, the school entry age raised, a population of 80 millions, Buckingham Palace an Open House. And when 'A' levels are a major criteria of achievement, and the British foreign secretary (Curzon by name!) is compromised in an indiscreet frolic in Africa, we realise its pungent relevance to our own times.

A psychomantic mood was even visible on the London stage. At the time of writing (1967) the Duchess was staging *After the Rain*. The 'rain' in the title begins in 1967 and lasts for three years; sweeping away everyone except six men and three women who happen, as an advertising stunt, to have embarked, before the rains began, on a raft stocked with breakfast cereals. They become the ancestors of a new race. Their adventures are portrayed as a play within a play by a university lecturer of the twenty-second century who sets players to re-enact them. These players embody the 'original sins' of the raft group as they float through the phases of democracy, autocracy, and theocracy. The God of the theocracy is Arthur Henderson, the leader of the raft party, who ultimately demands a human sacrifice. The actor playing Henderson is purging himself of the 'sin' of 'individualistic thinking', just as the actor playing the mutineering cook is purging himself of 'psychosomatic asthma': both 'sins' of the future and both to be purged by psychodrama.

XV GAMING AND THE EDUCATION OF THE FUTURE

Participation in a remarkable exercise in collaborative prognosis was organised by the Kaiser Aluminum and Chemical Corporation to inaugurate its twentieth anniversary in the light metal industry. Instead of the usual lavish 'history' looking back in retrospect, it took a 'new-wide-angle look' to tomorrow by introducing a game called 'Future'.

In this, the probability percentages of some sixty 'events' of 1986 were listed. Players were asked, after playing the game, to give their estimates of the probability percentages, and, if necessary, to 'write-in' other events not given in the printed sixty. The events and their interaction on other events in the game, were worked out by Dr. Olaf Helmer of the Rand Corporation who has devoted much time to the methodological aspects of long range forecasting, and T. J. Gordon, Director of the Advanced Saturn and Large Launch Systems of the Douglas Aircraft Company. The layout, equipment, and mechanics of the game were worked out by Dr. Goldschmidt, who is a gaming expert.[78]

'Let there be no mistake about it,' wrote Nigel Calder, a British Science writer, 'a game there must be.' He put forward the Environment game as a fourth method of planning for the future since the existing three (the Utopian, the opportunistic, and the problem-solving approach) tended either to emphasise ends above means or means above ends. Games, on the other hand, would enable the players to see what was under study as 'a process on the midst of other processes', and to look for 'a harmony between them all'. Being honest he admitted that 'this quest for harmony is Utopian in the sense that if the manifold activities of man, and of nature too, can be better integrated, the Earth will be a safer and more congenial planet'.

So the composer who plans such 'themes of the future' would have to adopt a 'somewhat Utopian stance', and 'like the Utopia-builder' look at the basic assumptions about human society.[79]

Such 'Environment games' would, in Nigel Calder's opinion, become possible when large areas of the earth's land surface would be released from food growing. In the wildernesses so created games would enable players to foresee problems of environmental development. He also argued that 'Only when the social scientists boldly start setting up game—like experiments with human volunteers', would they achieve a stature comparable to that of their colleagues in the natural sciences. He also suggested that in time the political scientists would follow suit and that their chief concern would be with the merits of rival systems of games 'instead of present tinkering with the institutional rules of an obsolescent game'.[80]

Model-making, management control, and intelligence games will be played by people of all ages so that education 'will cease to be a socially necessary preamble to real life, but the real stuff of human existence'.[81]

XVI THE PRECEDENCE OF FRANCE

A nation-wide discussion of the French Fifth Plan was also encouraged as having 'a scope and significance extending beyond the borders of France'. For it is 'an *indicative plan*; and is, so far, the only conscious and methodical realisation of such a plan in the world. Indicative planning is an original institution, contrasting both with the imperative Plans of the East and with those capitalist societies which reject the whole notion of planning'.[82]

Here the debate about tomorrow seems to be most sanely and sensibly staged. Here too the 'hermeneutic of prospective' does not consists of extrapolation alone but of a search for new mutations whether social or technical. Avoiding the technocratic optimism of their forebears or the coagulant processes of consensus of the American surmising forums, French speculation, whether conducted in Group 85 or Horizon 80, plays upon the national plan, itself an exercise in operational provision.

It is no accident that a French scholar has given us one of the best accounts of Utopian thought in England[83] and that since his time there has been a radiant commentary on the significant of 'prospective' (an English word introduced by Gaston Berger to describe a method of looking at the future to which the word prevision was inaccurate). There is also an excellent series of reprints and translations in the series 'Presence du futur,' issued by Editions De Noël in Paris, which includes, not only the standard American science-fiction writers, but Lino Aldani of Italy and Stanislaw Lem of Poland.

France has re-entered the forum of science-fiction with Pierre Boulle who, having given a sharp satiric picture of a wrong way evolutionary development in *The Monkey Planet*, confessed in the *Garden of the Moon* (1965) (*le jardin de Kanashima* 1965) that whilst not intimidated by making a prophecy covering a thousand years ahead, he was circumspect when it was a question of six to seven years. 'What I dread', he confessed, 'is to see the history of tomorrow bring to pass the very absurdities I have tried to avoid.' His picture of 1970 was extrapolated from Peenemunde and tells the story of the Japanese anticipating the Americans and the Russians to land on the moon.

Chapter Twelve

OPERATIONAL ESCHATOLOGIES

I   THE FUTURE AS CAUSE OF THE PRESENT

To some modern sociologists 'The future *is* the cause of the present in substantial degree, and it is only the failure of sociologists to come to terms with human purpose that has hidden this verity from their view'.[1] This sociologist, Wendell E. Moore, foresees a demand for monitoring the social changes that result from this.[2]

Such 'monitoring' he envisages as being effected by counter-utopias which 'encourage prior preventive action to dampen and redirect trends of change'. Suggesting that sociologists themselves might be more indulgent to such monitoring, he closed his presidential address to the American Sociological Society at Miami Beach on 31st August 1966 with the words, 'A little activism of this ambitious kind will do us no harm at all'.[3]

Such activism has in fact been long visible. The foregoing pages are more than a lightning tour of what R. K. Merton called 'the thickly populated graveyard of soft-hearted Utopias'.[4]

For the consideration of such futures has been enhanced by the leap from our planet. To involve others in its implications, the RAND Corporation, the best known interdisciplinary operational oracle in the United States, convened a Conference on 22nd–23rd October 1959 on the International Political Implications of Outer Space. Amongst the papers delivered was one on 'A Look to 1988' by Professor Karl W. Deutsch of M.I.T. and Yale, in which he suggested some means whereby national capabilities could be raised. One of these he defines as 'a climate stressing the values of playfulness and curiosity . . . supporting the intellectual forays of the young'.[5]

Such activism has also manifested itself in numerous newspaper supplements on the future, e.g. and most noticeably in the last film made by Walt Disney explaining his Experimental Prototype Community of Tomorrow (EPCOT) which, as he said 'will never be complete—it will never cease to be a blueprint of the future and there will always be new materials, new systems and new ideas introduced'. EPCOT will develop in Florida—a forty-three acre complex in which cars and lorries will go underground and surface transport will be limited to monorails and electric carts.[6]

Noticing the fashionable growth of such 'futurists' and of the tendency for business men to retain science-fiction writers 'for much the same reason that medieval monarchs used to like having a court astrologer about', *The New York Times Magazine* of 9th April 1967 raised three doubts posed by such practices. Firstly, the possibility of closing more than they open, or perhaps opening all the wrong doors whilst closing the right ones. Secondly, the tendency to induce 'moral simple-mindedness' since the 'leap into the future is too often a bolt away from the stubborn, the grubby, the unfathomable and the infuriating complexities of the present into a sort of carefree playland in which the shorter week appears to promise more water skiing (but not more alcoholism) and a helicopter is pictured on every suburban roof-top (rather than in more Vietnams)'. Thirdly, they asked, who listens? Here they cited J. Robert Oppenheimer: 'Our problem is not only to face the sombre and grim elements of the future, but to keep them from obscuring it!' *The Times* of London followed this up on 3rd June 1967 with a shorter but more deferential article on Simulation and Forecasting Studies in which they cited Dr. Olaf Helmer of the RAND Corporation as saying 'Fatalism has no longer become a fatality. The future is no longer viewed as unique, unforeseeable, and inevitable. There are instead, it is realised, a multitude of possible futures, with associated probabilities that can be estimated, and, to some extent, manipulated'.

This 'activism' has been accompanied by an enhanced awareness of what are the social effects of prediction, an awareness which Professor Dorothy Emmett summed up as introducing

a new variable into a situation which can effect the outcome in more than one way. If it produces complacency or fear, it might discourage people from acting in the way required for it to be fulfilled—this is called the boomerang response.[7]

One might develop this metaphor. There seems to be developing a technique of staging such boomerang sessions, whereby a
group of specialists from widely differing fields are convened or
sponsored by large-scale industrial organisations to anticipate
reasonable possibilities and open up unfamiliar areas of speculation. Of the ten specialists who accepted the invitation of the
Esso Petroleum Company to consider 'Britain in the 1990's' one
hit the mark when he confessed how 'notoriously difficult it is even
to size-up current events'. He continued:

> An impression that the change is for the worse may therefore be
> a false translation, into pseudo-objective terms, of the observer's
> subjective difficulty in digesting so great an amount of change,
> whether the change is in truth for the worse or for the better.[8]

Or as the great French planner, M. Massé, wrote in 1959:

> Every agency in charge of making decisions must avoid two
> dangers. One is to put too much trust in mechanical projections based
> on the past; the other is to accept too eagerly anticipated situations
> which lack date, substance and definition. Prospective must avoid
> both dangers. . . . Provided with a temporal radar which scans the
> ramifications of what is possible, its role is to sketch with a light but
> sure touch the shape of the future.[9]

Global warnings, however, still need sounding. Dr. Lloyd
Berkner estimated that in the next thirty-three years the world's
population would more than double—from 3,300 million to
7,400 million. By then, the average calorie intake per person would
have fallen from 2,121 to 1,340 calories a day as the absolute
starvation level. He saw no prospect of the world producing sufficient food for its inhabitants without a limitation on population.
But, he said, 'people being what they are, no significant change
can be expected (in this direction) until humankind has toppled
over the brink, and widespread starvation with all its suffering
and death is a reality'.

His gloomy forecast was based on the fact that world food production would have to increase above one per cent a year—a virtually impossible target since, in his opinion, the amount of uncultiv-
able land available was not adequate. 'We are probably already
beyond the critical point at which a sensible solution is possible,'
he wrote. 'By about 1980, some of us will avoid starvation, but at
the expense of others.'[10]

11 PREDICTION AS A HEURISTIC DEVICE

With allegory, fable, and proverb, the parable has played an important role in moral dialogues. Such dialogues have shifted from theological to sociological questions, because their hortatory and argumentative component has increasingly relied on scientific techniques of prediction, extrapolation, and model-making. But the consequent weakening of the eschatological component has led to millenial apprehensions or expectations being secularised, becoming indeed operational eschatologies. The very variety of names applied to these predictive fantasies indicates that the changing issues round which the dialogue is evolving.

Since Tarde's time the influence of the future on the present is becoming a significant factor in human evolution. C. Wright Mills pointed out how people:

> ... may become aware of predictions made about their activities, and that accordingly they can and often do re-direct themselves; they may falsify or fulfill the predictions. Which they will do is not, as yet, subject to very good prediction. In so far as men have some degree of freedom, what they may do will not be readily predictable.[11]

For sociologists indeed, predictions can be heuristic devices, large plans without which little ones cannot be made. 'Far easier it is indeed,' wrote David Riesman, 'to concentrate on programmes for choosing among lesser evils, even to the point where those evils can scarcely be distinguished, one from the other.' As he says, 'many lawyers, political scientists, and economists occupy themselves by suggesting the minimal changes which are necessary to stand still; yet today this hope is almost invariably disappointed; the *status quo* proves the most illusory of goals'.[12] He considered that a revival of futurist, even utopist, thinking ('a human ability to transcend the ideologies provided by the culture'), was necessary to counter mid-twentieth century pessimism, which he saw to be as complacent as Victorian evolutionary optimism. Yet long-range tales of tomorrow tend to balance both moods. 'Those who brood much on the remote past or future, or stare long at the night sky' were, in C. S. Lewis's view 'less likely than others to be ardent or orthodox partisans'.[13] To him they were manifestations of an imaginative impulse as old as the human race working under the special conditions of our own time and modified his own space trilogy accordingly: 'I took a hero once to Mars in a space-ship but when I knew better I had angels convey him to Venus.'[14] Round Lewis's own views quite a thriving sectarian industry is developing.[15] Just as sects protested against the ever-more centralised church, trying to influence decisions of structural consequence, so proponents of value views of tomorrow continue the great eschatological debate waged in Macaulay's Bethels. That this debate must be continued was the last message of the great 'preaching' sociologist, C. Wright Mills, and is the latest message of the great 'preaching' historian, Arnold Toynbee.[16]

A recent French writer has suggested that these predictive fantasies be called 'futopias'.[17] Certainly their number has led to them adding a new dimension to the traditional category of utopia.[18] Events tend to happen at once in circular and probabilistic ways, thereby making it increasingly difficult to live meaningfully in a world trained to think in sequences of cause and effect.[19] Daniel Bell thought we are experiencing the end of what he calls 'the rational vision'. In his opinion 'one seeks "pre-vision" as much to "halt" a future as to help it come into being, for the function of prediction is not, as often stated, to aid social control, but to widen the spheres of moral choice.'[20]

III THE TOO-REPRESSIVE SUPER-EGO: FREUD

Pictures of future society can well be a protest against a too-repressive social super-ego—assuming, of course, that there is a community super-ego analogous to that in the individual. One of Freud's disciples suggested that:

> If we could imagine the id with a time sense at all, it would be a future sense—that is, the drive toward total gratification is pure future, and leads, if not inhibited, to death. The ego's function is to arrest future by means of past, to make the present moment a unity of past and future. The result of this process is to slow down the drive towards death.[21]

Holding that Freud would be honoured as the pathfinder towards a humanism of the future and that his science of the unconscious would become a therapeutic method overarching mere case histories, Thomas Mann wrote:

> Call this, if you chose, a poet's Utopia; but the thought is after all not unthinkable that the resolution of our great fear and our

great hate, their conversion into a different relation to the unconscious which shall be more the artist's, more ironic and yet not necessarily irreverent, may one day be due to the healing effect of this very science.[22]

Though Freud had no sympathy with mantic practices, he acknowledged that:

> The ancient belief that dreams represent the future is not entirely devoid of truth. By representing a wish as fulfilled, the dreamer certainly leads us into the future; but this future, which the dreamer accepts as his present, has been shaped in the likeness of the past by the indestructible wish.[23]

Some of his followers, however, have been too pessimistic, like N. O. Brown, who thought that:

> Current psychoanalysis has no utopia; current neo-orthodox Protestantism has no eschatology. This defect cripples both of them as allies of the life instinct in that war against the death instinct which is human history.

and that:

> Mankind today is still making history without having any conscious idea of what it really wants or under what conditions it would stop being unhappy; in fact what it is doing seems to be making itself more unhappy and calling that unhappiness progress.

He considered fantasy to be the 'opaque shield' protecting the ego from reality and through which it sees reality.[24]

Certainly Freud has sparked off speculations about the future by some remarks in *Civilisation and its Discontents*.

> Man has become a god by means of artificial limbs, so to speak, quite magnificent when equipped with all his necessary organs; but they do not grow on him and they still give him trouble at times. However, he is entitled to console himself with the thought that this evolution will not come to an end in A.D. 1930. Future ages will produce further great advances in this realm of culture.

Building on this, Bernard's Wolfe visualised America, known as the Inland Strip, in 1990 inhabited by amputees and under a dictator. Though their limbs have been lopped off to deprive them of aggressive instincts, they still restlessly search for Columbium (out of which new artificial limbs can be made) and are at war with the Union (the U.S.S.R.). The hero, Dr. Martine, who has withdrawn to an unmapped island where lobotomy has been practised from ancient times, makes a brief return to witness the final holocaust.

Wolfe's purpose was a serious one:

> I am writing [he declared] about the overtone and undertone of *now* – in the guise of 1990 because it would take decades for a year like 1950 to be milked of its implications. . . . On the spurious map of the future presented herein, on the far side of the pinpoint of now, I have to inscribe, as did the medieval cartographers over all the terrifying areas outside their ken: HERE LIVE LIONS.[25]

He also confessed it was 'satire (or today-centred)' and not Utopia (or tomorrow-centred) and that his intellectual creditors included Max Weber, Ruth Benedict, Nietzsche, and Dostoyevsky as well as Freud.

From this bleak story it may be argued that an optimistic utopia represents the author's longing for the idleness of the womb, or the passivity of childhood from which he has been exiled, and a plea for an illusionary return to such a condition, yet Freud, as David Riesman has shown, was ambivalent. He faced the possibility that 'a fundamental alteration of the social order will have little hope of success until new discoveries are made that will increase our control over the forces of nature, and so make easier the satisfaction of our needs'.[26] Man must act to 'make an effort to change the destined course of the world'.

Karen Horney also decried Freud's physiological-biological determinism in favour of an interaction theory between man and his environment:

> Man is no longer an instinct-ridden creature, but a being capable of choice and responsibility. Growing up under favourable conditions he will develop his inherent constructive forces, and like every other living organism, will want to realize his potentialities.[27]

IV ANXIETY OVER THE FUTURE: MARX

Freud satisfied the first component of what W. H. Auden called the basic human problem—'man's anxiety in time': namely 'his present anxiety over himself in relation to his past and present'. The other two—man's present anxiety over himself in relation to his future and his neighbours (Marx) and his present anxiety over himself in relation to eternity and God (Kierkegaard)[28]—draw in the historians and the theologians.

Since Marx, historians have been writing prophecy in reverse, some even consciously. Amongst his voluminous notes and collections, Acton hoped to forge an instrument of action and power that would indicate the future. A more modern historian, E. H. Carr, thought historians could not escape being prophets: 'for whether they like it or not,' he wrote, 'they have the future in their bones. Besides the question "why?" the historian also asks the question "whether?".'[29] And from Tocqueville to Toynbee, the natural history of man has been so written.[30] Even to criticise the prophet Toynbee, Professor Hugh Trevor-Roper asked his readers to 'transport themselves a century ahead in time' and interpose what he called 'the cooling concept of an imaginary century' between themselves and the Toynbeean millennium when Western Civilisation, long declining, has been preserved and pickled in the 'universal world-state with its universal world-religion of Mish-Mash'.

He then pictures the training college for the Mish-Mash Clergy at Wootton Court (Toynbee's prep. school); the great Toynbeeum in California housing Toynbee's Study; the 'Stations' or centres of the new religion where the founder experienced his direct historical revelations; Oxford becoming Arnoldopolis, and a jewelled reliquary at the Athenaeum housing the three volumes of Grote's Plato consulted by the master.[31]

American historians are no less unwilling to don the mantle. Optimistically E. P. Cheney predicted the diffusion of moral progress and democracy. Pessimistically Henry Adams saw the year 1921 as a time when man's power of thought would reach the 'limits of its possibilities', though he thought that it might ultimately take place in 2025. A third American historian recently urged his fellows that 'to meet the future and help others meet it lies within our power and is indeed our responsibility . . . the historical process is no ultimate, and it explains nothing by itself. We must assume the task . . . of tentatively advising mankind of the range of the possible that lies before it.'[32]

Indeed, there has been much discussion of the phenomenon

of post-historic man. First identified by Roderick Seidenberg in *Post Historic Man* (University of North Carolina, 1950) and best described in taxonomic detail by Lewis Mumford in *The Transformations of Man* (George Allen and Unwin 1957) this poses the final control of man's conscious intelligence over his instincts. Having begun by controlling his physical activities, man has now extended this control to his biological and social life. By so doing, argued Mumford, man now must adapt himself to the machine, if he wishes to be selected for survival. Having applied to himself the canons he once applied to the physical world, man is producing a society 'similar to that of certain insect societies, which have remained stable for sixty million years; for once intelligence has reached a final form, it does not permit any deviation from its perfected solution'.[33] In other words life itself is becoming predictable, mechanically conditioned and controlled, with incalculable elements removed. Even the imaginative forays into the future (which he describes as 'post-historic fantasies, erupting out of the unconscious') have 'ceased to be merely prophetic', and 'have already taken command of mechanisation and have been channelled into the most obstructive and pitifully obsolete of human institutions, war'.[34]

Indeed post-historic man won't wait to look back at history but wants to evaluate his own actions. Hence the writers of many tales of the future propel themselves into the future in order to write history. Science-fiction also switches from flash forward to flash back for the same reason.

As 'a way of controlling, of ordering, of giving shape and significance to the immense panorama of futility and anarchy which is modern history', Eliot himself juxtaposed myth and contemporary scenes in order to heighten his moral. His Tiresias, 'though blind, throbbing between two lives' foresees the triviality and meaninglessness of the mechanical seduction by the cheap house agent's clerk. The sterility of secularism forced him to explore other mythic avenues to the future, like the Tarot cards used by Madame Sosostris.[35]

As he said in *The Dry Salvages*:

> Man's curiosity searches past and future
> And clings to that dimension. But to apprehend
> The point of intersection of the timeless
> With time, is an occupation for the saint—

and again:

> Time past and time future
> Allow but a little consciousness.
> To be conscious is not to be in time
> But only in time can the moment in the rose-garden . . .
> Be remembered; involved with past and future.
> Only through time time is conquered.

The rest of popular addictions:

> To communicate with Mars, converse with spirits,
> To report the behaviour of the sea monster,
> Describe the horoscope, haruspicate or scry,
> Observe disease in signatures, evoke
> Biography from the wrinkles of the palm
> And tragedy from fingers; release omens
> By sortilege, or tea leaves, riddle the inevitable
> With playing cards, fiddle with pentagrams
> Or barbituric acids, or dissect
> The recurrent image into preconscious terrors—

he saw as 'usual pastimes and drugs, and features of the press'.[36]

V ANXIETY OVER ETERNITY: KIERKEGAARD

Here, the third or Kierkegaardian element of man's predicament, his 'present anxiety over himself in relation to eternity and God' is particularly relevant. Believing that 'life must be understood backwards, but lived forwards', Kierkegaard thought that a second belief was needed in relation to belief: the belief that one believed. He considered that everyone 'had to travel over the bridge of sighs to eternity'. To him pure thinking was a 'phantom': all thinking should be committed thinking. Life being a process of sustained 'becoming' through moral strife and tension, Man had to be a perpetual seeker, suffering perpetual unrest, unpeace of mind and insecurity.[37]

In the Church, said Kierkegaard, Christianity perishes in palaver, and his plea for non-church religion has been amplified by Bernard Shaw and H. G. Wells. Shaw, though he confessed to having been always a mystic and a believer in the life force, nevertheless insisted that:

> To attempt to represent this particular will or power as God – in the former meaning of the word – is now hopeless.[38]

and never wrote the 'gospel of Shavianity' proposed in *Androcles and the Lion*.[39]

Wells went further and proposed the constant revision of the whole Bible, providing a new book of Genesis in the *Outline of History*, a new Leviticus in the *Work, Wealth and Happiness of Mankind* and a new Deuteronomy in *The Shape of Things to Come*. To him:

> Every new religious development is haunted by the precedents of the religion it replaces, and it was only to be expected that among those who have recovered their faith there should be a search for apostles and disciples, an attempt to determine sources and to form original congregations, especially among people with European traditions.
>
> These dispositions mark a relapse from understanding. They are imitative. This time there has been no revelation here or there; there is no claim to a revelation but simply that God has become visible. Men have thought and sought until insensibly the fog of obsolete theology has cleared away.[40]

Wells described the new religion of his day as having 'no revelation and no founder' but 'appearing simultaneously'.

> It has no church, no authorities, no teachers, no orthodoxy. It does not even thrust and struggle among the other things; simply it grows clear. There will be no putting an end to it. It arrives inevitably, and it will continue to separate itself out from confusing ideas.[41]

'Belief in God as the Invisible King,' wrote Wells, 'brings with it almost necessarily a conception of this coming Kingdom of God on earth.'

> Each believer, as he grasps this natural and immediate consequence of the faith that has come into his life, will form at the same time a Utopian conception of this world changed in the direction of God's purpose . . . Christian thought struggles towards it (i.e. the true religion), with the millstones of Syrian theology and an outrageous mythology of incarnation and resurrection about its neck. . . . The coming of God is a kind of internal consciousness. It is the attainment of an absolute certainty that one is not alone in oneself.[42]

Olaf Stapledon reported from the future through the mind of Paul in *Last Men in London* (1932), since he epitomised:

> . . . in his character, his circumstances and his reaction to my influence, the spiritual crisis of your age, and indeed the doom of your

'species'. It would not be true to say he was an exceptionally average member of his race, far from it. . . . Yet he is typical in that he illustrates very clearly the confused nature of his species, and the disorder of its world. . . . In Paul the old Simian nature was undisguised and insisted, while the new human nature had defined itself with precision and emphasis.[43]

As glands and genes took over from God, the need for reassurance and protection 'in an unfathomably cruel world' increased. 'Contradictory, primitive and superstitious religions may have been,' wrote Koestler, 'but they at least invested what happened to man with transcendental causality and justice.'[44] Such transcendental causality and justice is freshly explored in science-fiction, seen by Edmund Crispin to be:

> 'sceptical about man. It cannot trust him to investigate even such harmless, amorphous creatures as the prott without bringing the universe down on his head like a ton of bricks.'[45]

Edenic conflicts between forces of good and evil, as in the myth of the Cthulhu, occur in some of the Gothic tales of H. P. Lovecraft who believed that the world was at one time inhabited by evil ones who now live on the outside ready to take possession at any moment.[46]

Stapledon's vehicle for his message influenced C. S. Lewis to whom myths were hints of history to be. Ransom, his experiencing hero of *Perelandra*, suspects that 'what was myth in one world might be fact in some other', a suspicion confirmed when he realises that his name was no accident:

> Before his mother had borne him, before his ancestors had been called Ransoms, before *ransom* had been the name of a payment that develops, before the world was made, all these things had so stood together in eternity that the very significance of the pattern at this point lay in their coming together in just this fashion.[47]

Lewis also deployed elements of the Arthurian myth to elaborate the conflict between religion (Logres) and secularism (Britain). More optimistically Teilhard de Chardin suggested that today a religion of the future is indeed possible:

> We continue from force of habit to think of the Parousia, whereby the Kingdom of God is to be consummated on Earth, as an event of a purely catastrophic nature—that is to say, liable to come about

at any moment in history, irrespective of any definite state of Mankind. But why should we not assume, in accordance with the latest scientific view of Mankind in a state of anthropogenesis, that the parousiac spark can, of physical and organic necessity, only be kindled between Heaven and a Mankind which has biologically reached a certain critical evolutionary point of collective maturity?[48]

VI AFTER UTOPIA

Old static utopias have disappeared[49] together with their variants 'aipotu' and 'uchronia'. The new state of 'after utopia'[50] is, as Teilhard de Chardin suggests, the dynamic one:

> It is finally the Utopians, not the 'realists', who make scientific sense. They at least, though their flights of fancy may cause us to smile, have a feeling for the true dimensions of the phenomenon of Man.[51]

Even the existentialists, whom Teilhard described as morbid, agree that the real dilemma is to ingest and live with the future.[52] Kafka was afraid of it.[53] Sartre met it halfway by acknowledging 'the continual possibilization of possibles'.[54] For to Sartre, just as the past was invested with meaning by the present, so the present is invested with meaning by the future and consistently turns into the future. Hence his philosophy of the future is one 'in which the past is abandoned, obliterated to make room for seemingly impossible new creations'.[55] The past has to be abandoned because it cannot be recaptured, only distorted, and its meanings vary with future projects. Sartre thought of the future so consistently that he considered the very nature of consciousness to be a progression into the future.[56]

Such concern for the future prevents experience relapsing into mere existential responses. Indeed, one of the pioneers of the new school of existential psychiatry considered that 'whether or not a patient can even recall the events of the past depends upon his decision with regard to the future'. This school stressed that only by coping with our anxiety about the future, and becoming relatively positive about it, could past and present obstacles be negotiated.[57]

For we should not forget that 'Futurelessness' was one of the most serious aspects of life in a concentration camp.[58] 'We are made wise,' said Zoo in *Man and Superman*, 'not by the recollections of our past, but by the responsibilities of our future.'[59] And Cassirer agreed: 'To think of the future and to live in the future is a necessary part of man's nature,' he wrote.

> We live much more in our doubts and fears, our anxieties and hopes about the future, than in our recollections or in our present experiences. This would appear at first glance as a questionable human endowment, for it introduces an element of uncertainty into human life which is alien to all other creatures. It seems as though man would be wiser and happier if he got rid of this fantastic idea, of this mirage of the future. Philosophers, poets and great religious teachers have at all times warned man against this source of constant self-deception. Religion admonishes man not to be fearful of the day to come, and human wisdom advises him to enjoy the present day, not caring for the future. *Quid sit futurum cras fuge quaerere*, says Horace. But man never could follow this advice.[60]

One 'unashamed propagandist' of this idea of a more sophisticated version of Wells's Open Conspiracy is Kenneth Boulding who sees its members as 'critically accepting' the process at work whereby man is creating his own successor. Boulding warned that the process can be suppressed by adopting fixed ideas which, though generating motive power in the individual, can also inhibit the feedback mechanisms in the process itself. The ideal, as he says, is 'an image of the world which can provide motivation without impairing the capacity for learning about what is the best direction of change'.[61]

Learning the best direction of change involves perpetual scrutiny and criticism of the 'models'. As Wells said:

> There will be many Utopias. Each generation will have its new version of Utopia, a little more certain and complete and real, with its problems lying closer and closer to the problems of the Thing in Being.[62]

Wells suggested that 'only teachers could recondition' human life by lifting man out of self-preoccupation, and releasing him 'into a wider circle of ideas beyond himself in which he can at length forget himself and his meagre personal ends altogether'. As one of them, Job Huss, says in *The Undying Fire*, 'we can open his ideas to the past and the future and to the undying life of man. So through us and only through us he escapes from death and futility.' As another teacher pointed out, it also involves patience with human imperfections:

> The Perfectibility of Man! [exclaimed D. H. Lawrence], Ah heaven, what a dreary theme! The perfectibility of the Ford car! The perfectibility of which man? I am many men. Which of them are you going to perfect? I am not a mechanical contrivance. . . . The perfectibility of man, dear God! When every man as long as he remains alive is in himself a multitude of conflicting men. Which of these do you choose to perfect, at the expense of every other?[63]

But the process should avoid institutions, it should not become yet another church. As a devout German physicist argued: 'the Church should not in any way lead the process of history; indeed it should not even know it, as this process is self-destructive, or at least alien to the Gospel'.[64]

It also should be based on man's traditional awareness of time, which as a professor of religion reminds us:

> . . . renders him incapable of complete immersion in present experience; it causes him ever to be looking ahead beyond the immediate moment, and from that disposition stems his abiding sense of personal insecurity, which in turn inspires him to seek such a form of refuge as represents his idea of safety from all that he fears as the conservation of all that he desires.[65]

Lastly, it must be a collectivist image:

> We cannot build our individual ladders in heaven and leave the total human enterprise unredeemed of its excesses and corruptions [wrote Reinhold Niebuhr]. In the task of that redemption the most effective agents will be men who have substituted some new illusions for the abandoned ones. The most important of these illusions is that the collective life of mankind can achieve perfect justice.[66]

Nor need it be joyless: 'The chattering of one's teeth,' Arnold Green reminds us, 'is often mistaken for the approaching hoofbeats of the Four Horsemen of the Apocalypse.'[67]

And in the Church, theology has registered the change. 'We have renounced the idea of Hell,' the Bishop of Bradford told his diocesan conference in 1952, 'and have lost belief in Heaven except as a desirable but probably fictitious residential neighbourhood.' 'If hell offends,' said Canon Bezzant three years later, 'Heaven bores.' Or as J. G. Ballard wrote in 'Visions of Hell'

(*New Worlds*, March 1966, p. 48), 'Hell is out of fashion—institutional hells at any rate. The populated infernos of the twentieth century are more private affairs, the gaps between the bars are the sutures of one's own skull.' Indeed theology itself seems to have concentrated on justifying meaninglessness: Paul Tillich regarding the acceptance of meaninglessness as itself a meaningful act[68] and Karl Jaspers considering that it is only by men facing tragic situations that they can rise above them.[69]

VII PSYCHOMETABOLIC MAN

Just as nature's raw materials are serviced for man's biologically operative system, so myths, theories, commandments, and codes as well as abstractions like truth are used to build up man's psycho-socially-operative organisations of thought and feeling. Sir Julian Huxley describes this as man's psychometabolic system, which produces patterns of ideas out of chaos, enabling complex situations to be grasped and the trend of history to be appreciated. As Sir Julian said in another context:

> It is the forces of the internal environment of the human species that are now causing distress and bewilderment and are being felt as Destiny to be propitiated or otherwise manipulated. Here our ignorance and lack of control are now most glaring. . . . Science will be called on to advise what expressions of the religious impulse are intellectually permissible and socially desirable, if that impulse is to be properly integrated with other human activities.

Or, as he epigrammatically observed: 'Purposes in life are made, not found.'[70]

We have been enlightened by John Dewey who put it in another way by stressing not a planned society, but a continuous planning society. The first was based on rescripts from above, the second on continuous inquiry and investigations to discover the best method of solving present and future problems. The first relies on the frozen intelligence of some past thinker, sect, or cult. The latter regards all theories as tentative until verified.[71]

Far from 'the great conversation about the future' (as Dennis Gabor calls it), diminishing, over the last generation it has increased.[72] For the need, detected by J. O. Bailey 'for books I cannot define, because I have not seen them yet—books to present a graphic, convincing study of the paths we ought to follow'[73] is being fulfilled and the suggestion he made that:

> . . . the most fruitful further development of scientific fiction will be in . . . psychological and ethical studies, efforts to discover the right adjustment to the Machine Age and the Atomic Age and to see guidingly into the future of the race, in the best light of science[74] . . .

is being implemented.

For though Gabor detected a new *trahison des clercs*, 'the hostility of many artists to the future', and though he considered it would be impossible for even Shakespeare or Tolstoy to display their talents in a world from which injustice had been abolished,[75] yet mankind is being psychologically prepared for the age of science, by the very proliferation of projections of tomorrow.[76]

These tentative or conflict models[77] of utopias represent the feeling articulated by Koestler that 'It *is* impossible to turn back to the languages and symbols of a past epoch, of a mental climate which is no longer ours.'[78] Or, as D. K. Price saw, there is 'no hope in trying to get back into the Garden of Eden'.[79]

The new dialectic is the interaction between images of the future and the present from which they spring.

> Positive images of the future conceived in each present time are co-determining for the future of that time. Conversely the projected future is already exercising its influence on the present through these images, and by continuous interaction it is also affecting the construction of revised images of the future.[80]

Such tales can become models for testing certain philosophical ideas about society; part of the generalised viewing of the future now so essential in operational research, useful as posing potentially desirable ends, and as testers of such ends with models.[81] The process rather than the specific is important. The process is analogous to sloughing off specifies as one takes off one's coat, or changes one's shirt. Indeed the model must never become the Nessus shirt and kill Hercules. They may be culs-de-sac, 'underprophecies' and perhaps neuroses, sometimes discards in the process of human growth. But occasionally, as in *Brave New World* and *1984*, they shape the thought of generations.

VIII THE ROLE OF FANTASY IN A LOGICAL WORLD

The dark power myths of Prometheus, Daedalus, Frankenstein, and Faust have explored man's use of the technology stolen from Heaven. Daily, as we recombine genes and viruses to skirt the creation of life itself, more is being stolen and the limit to such discoveries in the foreseeable future seemed to be set, according to an American physicist, 'only loosely by nature, more tightly by the abilities of exceptional minds, but most tightly of all by human desire and its balance of values'.[82]

That 'balance of values' is struck in these operational theodicies: theodicies in that they recognise evil in worlds conjured up in order to illustrate the potential for good in the world today. Leibnitz would have approved of them, since in his own *Theodicy* he wrote:

> It is true that one may imagine possible worlds without sin and without unhappiness, and one could make some like Utopian or Severambian romances: but these same worlds again would be very inferior to ours in goodness.[83]

Himself gnawed by the advantages of *not* knowing the future, he envisaged his monads 'big with the future'. As a mathematician of movement, he wrote to a friend:

> When I speak of the force and action of created beings, I mean that each created being is pregnant with its future state, and that it naturally follows a certain course, if nothing hinders it; and that the Monads, which are the true and only substances, cannot be naturally hindered in their inner determinations, since they include the representation of everything external (to them). But, nevertheless, I do not say that the future state of the created being follows from its present state without the co-operation (concours) of God, and I am rather of opinion that preservation is a continual creation with an orderly change.[84]

Using post-Leibnitzean laws of evolution, of complexity-consciousness and of solidarity in space-time, Teilhard de Chardin argued that man is evolution become reflective. 'I am thinking,' he wrote in 1952 'of writing . . . on "The end of the species" (human): a disguised criticism of the apocalyptics and an open attack on the myths (Marxist, etc.) of a golden age in the future.'[85] Yet he also felt 'We must take up again, on a sounder scientific basis and as a more exact philosophical concept, the idea (or, if you prefer it, the "myth") of progress. This is the essential setting in which I see the simultaneous rebirth of humanism and Christianity.'[86] This rebirth he saw coming, especially from the evolutionary humanism of Sir Julian Huxley: 'the exact essence of what I have been dreaming of for such a long time'.[87]

Some such coming together seems inevitable now that Christianity has been demythologised, dekerygmatised and exhausted till it is merely a philosophy of existence. For if myth, in Bultmann's words, is the expression of the other-worldly in terms of this world, 'the divine in terms of human life, the other side in terms of this side',[88] these forays into the future represent a valid modern mythology. Indeed a modern exegete of Bultmann considers it 'certainly the vehicle of a self-understanding . . . the reverse of the biblical myth of the Tower of Babel', giving not only 'vivid and concrete embodiment to the popular belief in the omnicompetence of science' but leading 'back in turn to a deeper belief, which is the modern secular man's understanding of himself as self-sufficient'. Indeed this exegete considers that it is 'almost like the apocalyptic literature of a religion which represents the consummation as already here', encouraging man 'along the path he has chosen—the path towards godlike power'.[89]

This is too hard. For if the pattern of debate outlined in the foregoing pages is accepted, it constitutes a more relevant and reverent escape from 'the power and service of transitory things' than the more conventional avenues of the theologians.

IX ALICE: MADONNA OF THE MODERNS

Perhaps this is why Alice has become the white Madonna of economists and psychologists and revered by the future-oriented middle classes of the West.[90]

Having originated as the outcome of the investigation and refutation of successive Utopian proposals, economics is[91] today very much concerned with games and simulated models.[92] Psychologists are also seized of the value of symbolic experience. Only through symbolic experiences do our temporal perspectives really develop and ever become 'capable of conceiving a future which is a creation in relation to our own history. This creation itself is only possible for those who are carried beyond the present situations by the dynamism of their own activity. Generally speaking the future only unfolds in so far as we imagine a future which seems to us to be realisable.'[93]

As Paul Fraisse pointed out, 'Our future perspectives remain fairly similar to those of a child for whom the entire future is located in the interdeterminate domain of tomorrow.' He (and other psychologists like Hull, Miller, Lewin, and Cohen) has indicated that there is an approach as well as an avoidance gradient to our goals. The temporal distance between the present moment and the future situation affects our emotions. This is a profound biopsychological problem.[94] He concludes that it is only by 'keeping the past available through memory and conquering the future in advance through anticipation' that man remains free.[95] Perhaps the truest assessment is to consider the modern exfoliation of science fantasy as an exploitation of our illogical world. The wonderlands on the other side of the mirror are perhaps best explored by those who never accept the habitual. Thus Lewis Carroll, who as a mathematician lived in a world of abstract space, created beasts like the snark and the jabberwock. Since his time the modern world has come to depend more and more on the abstract, to bend time and space and twist logic and causation. The layman, looking at certain modern physical concepts, might well feel that he is living on the other side of the mirror. So contemporary fantasy tends to become a Universe where solitude does not exist and the madhatter's tea-party provides the only explicable story of what is going on. This is evident not only in the more fantastic science-fiction writers like Lewis Padgett, Frederic Brown, and Catherine Moore[96] but in the atonal music of Bartok and Schonberg, to say nothing of the paintings of Paul Klee. Indeed fantasy might well be proved in the scientific world to be the inevitable antidote to the crushing logic of *1984*.[97]

NOTES

I THE MANTIC HERITAGE

1. J. A. Gunn, *The Problem of Time* (1929); Adolf E. Jensen, *Myths and Cult among Primitive Peoples*, translated by T. Choldin and Wolfgang Weissleder (Chicago, 1963), 30.

2. Adolf E. Jensen, *loc. cit.*, 30.

3. Joseph Klausner, *The Messianic Idea in Israel* (1956), 15.

4. R. Martin-Achard, 'Prophecy', in J. J. von Allmen (ed.), *Vocabulary of the Bible* (1958).

5. Voltaire, *Dictionaire Philosophique* (1785 edition), quoted C. E. Vulliamy, *The Anatomy of Satire* (1950), 112.

6. H. W. Parke and D. E. W. Wormell, *The Delphic Oracle* (1946); Joseph Fontenrose, *Python: A study of the Delphic Myth and its origins* (Berkeley, 1959).

7. Robert Flacelière, *Greek Oracles* translated by Douglas Garman, (1965), 87.

8. *Ibid.*, 20; A. Bouché-Leclercq, *Histoire de la divination dans l'Antiquité* (Paris, 1879–82); W. Warde Fowler, *The Religious Experience of the Roman People from the Earliest Times to the Age of Augustus* (1911), 299.

9. W. H. S. Jones and E. T. Withington (ed. and trans.), *Hippocrates* (1931).

10. Martin P. Nilsson, *Greek Popular Religion* (1947), 127. He considers that their role in influencing public opinion when an important issue was pending has not been sufficiently appreciated.

11. John Boodin, 'Roots of Scientific Thought', ed. P. Wiener and Noland (New York, 1957), 71.

12. W. Warde Fowler, *The Religious Experience of the Roman People* (1911), 293 ff.; Franz Cumont, *After Life in Roman Paganeum* (New Haven, 1922).

13. An excellent translation of his *True History* has recently (1955), appeared by Paul Turner.

14. See Joseph B. Mayor, W. Warde Fowler, and R. S. Conway, *Virgil's Messianic Eclogue* (1907), full discussion.

15. J. A. McCulloch, *Early Christian Visions of the Other World* (1912); *The Harrowing of Hell. A Comparative Study of an Early Christian Doctrine* (1930); *Medieval Faith and Fable* (1932).

16. Theodore Silverstein, 'Did Dante Know the Vision of St. Paul?' *Harvard Studies and Notes in Philology and Literature*, XIX (1937).

17. Domenico Comparetti, *Virgil in the Middle Ages*, translated by E. F. M. Benecke, (1895); Fr. Klaeber, 'Aeneas und Beowulf', in *Archiv. für das Studium der Neveren Sprachen und Literaturn* (1911), Band 126; Charles Godfrey

Leland, *The Unpublished Legends of Virgil* (1899); Omera Floyd Long, 'The Attitude of Alcuin towards Vergil', in *Studies in Honour of B. L. Gildersleeve* (Baltimore, Md., 1902); W. P. Mustard, *Classical Echoes in Tennyson* (New York, 1904); Rev. R. D. B. Rawnsley, 'Tennyson and Virgil, by a Lincolnshire Rector', *Macmillan's Magazine*, 1875; Paul Stapfer, 'Shakespeare and Classical Antiquity', translated from the French by Emily J. Carey, *Shakespeare's Classical Knowledge* (1880, Ch. IV); J. S. Tunison, *Master Virgil, the Author of the Aeneid as he Seemed in the Middle Ages* (Cincinnati, 1888); Georg Zappert, *Virgils Fortleben im Mittelalter* (Vienna, 1851); John Webster Spargo, 'Virgil the Necromancer', *Harvard Studies in Comparative Literature*, X (1934).

18. *Jewish Encyclopaedia* article 'Golem'. John Cohen, *Human Robots in Myth and Science* (1966).

19. The most recent biography of Geoffrey of Monmouth is by J. E. Lloyd in *English Historical Review*, lvii (1942), 460–8.

20. Rupert Taylor, *The Political Prophecy in England* (New York, 1911), quoting from Thomas Wright, *Political Poems relating to English History Composed during the period from the accession of Edward the Third to that of Richard the Second*, Rolls Series (1859–61); J. J. Parry and R. A. Caldwell in R. S. Loomis (ed.) *Arthurian Literature in the Middle Ages* (1959), 72–93.

21. P. Sumthor, *Merlin le Prophète* (Lausanne, 1943); Margaret E. Griffiths, *Early Vaticisation in Welsh with English Parallels* (Cardiff, 1937); Jacob Hammer, 'A Commentary on the Prophetia Merlini (The Seventh Book of Geoffrey of Monmouth's Historia Regum Britanniae)', *Speculum* X (1935), 3–30.

22. Laura Keeler, *Geoffrey of Monmouth and the Late Latin Chroniclers 1300–1500* (Berkeley and Los Angeles, 1946) confirms this from a study of thirty chroniclers.

23. Sebastian Evans, *The Prophecy of Merlin* (1904), 178; J. A. Giles (ed.), *Geoffrey of Monmouth's Historia Regum Britanniae* (1944), 129–30.

24. R. Taylor, *The Political Prophecy in England* (New York, 1911), XII.

25. E. G. H. Tausenfreund, *Vergil und Godfried von Monmouth* (1913).

26. J. J. Ign von Döllinger, translated by Alfred Plummer *Prophecies and the Prophetic Spirit in the Christian Spirit* (1873), 25.

27. *Ibid.*, 30.

28. Lucy Allan Paton, *Les Prophécies de Merlin. Edited from MS 593 in the Bibliothèque Municipale of Rennes* (New York, 1927), ii, 346–7.

29. 'Alanus de Insulis', in Taylor, *op. cit.*, 88.

30. W. Shakespeare, *Henry IV*, Part I.

31. Thomas Heywood, *Life of Merlin sirnamed Ambrosius. His Prophesies and Predictions Interpreted and their Truths made Good by our English Annals* (1641), 1–2.

32. R. Freyhan, 'Joachism and the English Apocalypse'. *Journal of the Warburg and Courtauld Institutes*, XVIII (1955), 214.

33. Morton W. Bloomfield, *Piers Plowman as Fourteenth Century Apocalypse* (New Brunswick, N.J., 1961), 99.

34. *Ibid.*, 102.

2 EXTRAVAGANCE TO EXTRAPOLATION

1. Elizabeth Sewell, *The Orphic Voice* (1961), 236, quoting D'Arcy Thompson's *On Growth and Form*.

2. Gilbert Highet, *The Anatomy of Satire* (1962), 160.

3. Howard Rollin Patch, *The Other World* (Cambridge, Mass., 1950), 31, 58, 160, 165–6, 232.

4. Sir T. More, *Utopia. A Fruitful and Pleasant work of the Best State of a Public Weal and the New Isle called Utopia* (first published at Leyden in Latin in 1516 and in London in English in 1551). As A. L. Morton reminds us in his spirited and lively book, *The English Utopia* (1952), the Utopia of the Folk was clearly manifest in the early fourteenth-century English poem *The Land of Cockayne*. Indeed, a 'large body of myth and fable ... cannot be discounted in any attempt to study the minds of Renaissance voyagers', Boies Penrose, *Travel and Discovery in the Renaissance 1420–1620* (Cambridge, Mass., 1952), 10.

5. Russell Ames, *Citizen Thomas More and his Utopia* (1949), gives and analyses fourteen such interpretations; Thomas More, *Utopia* (Penguin Books, 1965), gives a good translation by Paul Turner. François de Dainville, *La Geographie des Humanistes* (Paris, 1940) offers a Catholic background to man's widening vision.

6. R. W. Gibson, *St. Thomas More: A Preliminary Bibliography of His Works and of Moreana to the year 1750* (New Haven, 1961); J. H. Hexter, *More's Utopia. The Biography of an Idea* (Princeton, 1952).

7. Certainly the seclusion of Japan, which began in 1624, offers a curious parallel to Bacon's Bensalem, as A. B. Gough's edition of the *New Atlantis* (1915) shows. The possibility of a larger influence on Bacon, that of William Adams, the first English resident in Japan, is discussed by D. W. Thompson, 'Japan and the *New Atlantis*', Studies in *Philology*, xxx (1933), 59–68.

8. Howard B. White, 'Bacon and the Orphic Myth', *Social Research*, xxvii (1960), 22–38.

9. F. Bacon, *Of Prophecies*. Mother Shipton was, in fact, first mentioned in a tract of 1641 as prophesying the death of Cardinal Wolsey. The tract was much read and imitated and a 'life' was published in 1677 by a notorious gambler Richard Head. Subsequent prophecies fastened to her included by 1862 those of the steam engines and the telegraph. Another such person was 'discovered' by the Whig historian, John Oldmixon in the person of Robert Nixon, the Cheshire prophet. Long suspected—and not without cause apparently—of harbouring treasonable designs against Queen Elizabeth, Henry Howard, Earl of Northumberland, wrote a three hundred and thirty page *Defensive against the poyson of supposed prophecies. Not hitherto confuted by the Pen of any Man* (1583). Himself a concealed Catholic, he argued that 'warnings of our frail and slippery state "were" not so rare and dainty that one needed to repair to the closets of false oracles to become more wary in abstaining from offence'. He deplored the 'old wives' tales' as being 'in overmuch use with us', citing Mother Joan of Stowe. He might well have cited Mother

Demdike of Lancashire, Mother Redcap of urban Kentish town, and Mother Shipton of Yorkshire.

> '*Chariots without horses shall go*
> *And accidents fill the world with woe*
> *Around the world thoughts shall fly*
> *In the twinkling of an eye.*'

See Charles Hindley, *Life of Mother Shipton* (1862) and Charles Mackay, *Memoirs of Extraordinary Popular Delusions* (1841), i, 168–203.

10. J. Spedding, R. L. Heath, and D. D. Heath, *Works of Francis Bacon* (1857), III, 156.

11. Howard B. White, 'Bacon and the Orphic Myth', *Social Research*, xxvii (1960), 22–38; Basil Willey, 'Bacon and the Rehabilitation of Nature', in his *Seventeenth Century Background* (1934); F. R. Jones, *Ancients and Moderns* (St. Louis, 1936); G. Bullough, 'Bacon and the Defence of Learning', *Seventeenth Century Studies presented to Sir Herbert Grierson* (1938); F. H. Anderson, *The Philosophy of Francis Bacon* (Chicago, 1948); R. P. Adams, 'The Social Responsibilities of Science in *Utopia, New Atlantis* and After', *Journal of the History of Ideas*, X (1949), 374–98; E. Zilzel, 'The Genesis of the Concept of Scientific Progress', *ibid.*, vi (1945), 346 ff.; Moody E. Prior, 'Bacon's Man of Science', *ibid.*, XV (1954), 348–70 and Judah Bierman, 'Science and Society in the *New Atlantis* and other Renaissance Utopias', *P.M.L.A.* (1963), 492–500.

12. See the translation by William J. Gilstrap in G. Negley and J. Max Patrick, *The Quest for Utopia: An Anthology of Imaginary Societies* (New York, 1952), 325.

13. Geoffrey Strachan (ed.), 'Cyrano de Bergerac'. *Other Worlds* (Oxford University Press, 1965) 80, 88, 136, 208.

14. F. E. Held (translator), *Johann Valentin Andreae, Christianopolis* (1916), 154–5.

15. Pierre de la Juilliére, *Les Images de Rabelais* (Paris, 1912); J. G. Bourke, *Scatalogic Rites of All Nations* (Washington, 1891), 163.

16. A. L. Morton, *The English Utopia* (1952), 97.

17. Rabelais' first three books were translated by Sir Thomas Urquhart (1611–1660), author of the 'Admirable Crichton', and completed by Peter Anthony Motteux (1660–1718), the translator of Don Quixote. This is from Vol. I, pp. 324–5 of the 1897 edition edited by A. Wallis.

18. J. Max Patrick, 'Robert Burton's Utopianism', *Philological Quarterly*, xxvii (1948), 345–58.

19. Glenn Negley and J. Max Patrick, *The Quest for Utopia: An Anthology of Imaginary Societies* (New York, 1952), 353–5.

20. Hall protested in his day against the 'strange abortions of some particular prophesies to private interests'. He saw great danger in 'that train of strange paradoxes and uncouth consequences' consequent upon 'vainly imagining this Reign of the Saints' had already begun. *The Revelation Unrevealed. Concerning the Thousand Years' Reign of the Saints with Christ upon Earth. Laying forth the Weak grounds and strange consequences of that plausible, and too much received opinion, Works*, iii (1662), 892 ff.

21. Huntingdon Brown (ed.), *Joseph Hall, the Discovery of a New World* (Cambridge, Mass., 1937); *Rebelais in English Literature* (Cambridge, Mass., 1933), 164.

22. Peter Heylyn, *Cosmography* (1652), 195.

23. J. Middleton Murry, *Jonathan Swift* (1954), 432–48; Aldous Huxley, *Do What You Will* (1929), 94; William Empson, *Some Versions of Pastoral* (1935), 60; P. Greenacre, 'The Mutual Adventures of Jonathan Swift and Lemuel Gulliver', *Psychoanalytic Quarterly*, xxiv (1955), 20–62.

24. Jonathan Swift, *Tale of a Tub* (in *Prose Works*) (1939), i, 102.

25. Jonathan Swift, *A Discourse Concerning the Mechanical Operation of the Spirit* in *Prose Works* (1939), i, 186.

26. Norman O. Brown, *Life against Death. The Psychoanalytical Meaning of History* (1959), 185, to which I owe much in this connection.

27. *Gulliver's Travels*, ed. H. Williams (1941), 243.

28. *Ibid.*, 256.

29. *Ibid.*, 262.

30. John M. Mullitt, *Jonathan Swift and the Anatomy of Satire* (Cambridge, Mass.), 15, who argues that it was to make human beasts wince that Swift employed satire, and describes him (p. 192), as 'England's—and perhaps the world's—greatest satirist'. Being unable to justify God's ways to man, he viewed God's purposes on earth as inscrutable and terrible.

31. James Preu, 'Swift's Influence on Godwin's Doctrine of Anarchism', *Journal of the History of Ideas*, XV (1954), 371–83.

32. Mankind's likeness to the animals, used in the written homiletics of the Bible as well as the mouth-to-mouth teaching of African tribes, was perhaps the oldest method of showing up man's imperfections. Sir Roger L'Estrange, press censor, pamphleteer, and editor, made the most extensive collection of animal fables in existence: *The Fables of Aesop and other eminent Mythologists, with Moral Reflections* (1692). Swift's use of the animal fable had been tellingly exploited by Bernard de Mandeville in *The Fable of the Bees, or Private Vices, Public Benefits* (1714), showing that the mutual rapacities of a beehive, like those in society, made it thrive. The sombre message of such teachings alarmed the more serious clergy and William Law wrote a refutation of it in 1723, following it with his *Serious Call to a Devout and Holy Life*, which by Wesley's own acknowledgment was a kindling influence in the formation of Methodism. Law increasingly stressed the importance, as Tolstoy did later, of the Kingdom of Heaven within each person.

Irvin Ehrenpreis, *The Personality of Jonathan Swift* (1958), argues (p. 99 ff.), that the Houyhnhnms 'do not represent his moral ideal for mankind' since they combine deistic and stoic views of human nature to which Swift, as an Anglican clergyman, could not subscribe. He argues that Swift had in mind a particular exponent of deistic thought whose name was borne by Swift's own horse: Bolingbroke. He goes on to conclude (p. 109), that 'If the Houyhnhnms are a false idea for humanity, the yahoos are a false debasement of our nature. The representation of men as apes suggests Calvinist doctrines.' In other words Ehrenpreis sees Swift's imagination working in terms of people, not values or ideas, and whilst he admits it is an ancestor of *Erewhon* and *Brave New World*, he sees it more as a series of detached characterisations of individuals.

33. Margaret Cavendish, *Observation upon Experimental Philosophy to which is added, The Discription of a New Blazing World* (1666).

34. Henry Nevile, *The Isle of Pines* (1668) reprinted in *Shorter Novels*, Vol. 2 Everyman Library No. 841, pp. 225–35.

35. Simon Berington, *The Memoirs of the Sig^r. Gaudentio de Lucca* (1737).

36. Robert Paltock, *The Life and Adventures of Peter Wilkins* (1751) ed. with an introduction by A. H. Bullen (Everyman Library, 1914).

37. C. Oman (ed.), *The Reign of George VI 1900–1925. A forecast written in the year 1763* (1899), xxviii.

38. *Ibid.*, 99.

39. *Ibid.*, 100.

40. *Ibid.*, 94–5.

41. Norman O. Brown, *Life against Death. The Psychoanalytical Meaning of History* (1959), 296–7.

42. Francis Godwin, 'The Man in the Moon', *Smith College Studies in Modern Languages, XIX* (1938).

43. Marjorie Nicolson, *Voyages to the Moon* (New York, 1948).

44. Marjorie Nicolson, 'English Almanacs and the New Astronomy', *Annals of Science*, iv (1939), 19–20 and Hubert Davis (ed.), *The Prose Writings of Jonathan Swift* (1940), ii, 139–72.

45. W. H. Barber, *Leibnitz in France. From Arnauld to Voltaire. A Study in French Reactions to Leibnitzianism 1670–1760* (1955), 95.

46. John Dillenberger, *Protestant Thought and Natural Science* (1961), 125–6.

47. Robert Hooke, *Philosophical Collections*, No. 1, 1679, 18.

48. Richard D. Altick, *Richard Owen Cambridge: Belated Augustan* (Philadelphia, 1941).

49. Gwen J. Kolb, 'Johnson's 'Dissertation on Flying' and John Wilkins' Mathematical Magick', *Modern Philology*, xlvii (1949), 24–31.

50. Joseph Priestley, *An Essay on the First Principles of Government; and on the Nature of Political, Civil, and Religious Liberty* (1771), pp. 4–5 quoted Carl L. Becker, *The Heavenly City of the Eighteenth-Century Philosophers*.

51. Erasmus Darwin, *The Botanic Garden* (1791), 178.

52. 'Ideas of a Perfect Commonwealth' in David Hume, *Political Essays*, ed. Charles W. Hendel (New York, 1953), 145 and 158.

53. Robert Wallace, *Various Prospects of Mankind, Nature and Providence* (Edinburgh, 1761), 114.

54. Such a compilation was made in 1867 in anticipation of the centennial of the United States. When its compiler, Charles Sumner, garnered them for the aptly named *Atlantic Monthly*, he showed that by the nineteenth century literate Americans were riding on a wave of destiny. It was subsequently published as a book: *Prophetic verses concerning America* (Boston, 1874).

3   THE DEBATE BEGINS: FROM NOBLE SAVAGE TO LAST MAN

1. Melchisédec Thévenot, *Relations de divers voyages curieux qui n'ont pas esté publiées* (Paris 1664, augmentées et réimprimées, 1666).

2. Geoffroy Atkinson, *The Extraordinary Voyage in French Literature before 1700* (New York, 1920); *The Extraordinary Voyage in French Literature from 1700–1722* (New York, 1922); van Wijngaarden, *Les odyssées philosophiques en France entre 1616 et 1789* (Haarlem, 1932).

3. W. E. Mann, *Robinson Crusoe en France* (Paris 1916). Not all these travellers' tales were Robinsonaden. The French diplomatist, Benoit de Maillet, presented his contemporaries with an Indian philosopher who confronted a missionary with the view that constant evaporation (3 feet every thousand years) would so dry up the Atlantic that ultimately the earth would incandesce like the suns. On the other hand his better-known fellow countryman Buffon held that it would cool. His *Telliamid ou Entrétiens d'un Philosophe Indien avec un Missionaire Francaise* (1748) was followed by his fellow countryman Buffon's *Théorie de la Terre* (1749) and *Epoques de la Nature* (1778).

4. G. Chinard, *L'Amérique et le rêve exotique dans la littérature française au XVIIe et au XVIIIe siècle* (Paris, 1913).

5. There was an average of at least one such publication per year.

6. H. N. Fairchild, *The Noble Savage* (New York, 1928).

7. M. Pierre Martine, *L'Orient dans la littérature française au XVIIe et au XVIIIe siècle* (1906); M. P. Conant, *The Oriental Tale in England in the 18th Century* (New York, 1908).

8. H. Temple Patterson, 'Poetic Genesis: Sebastian Mercier into Victor Hugo', in *Studies on Voltaire and the Eighteenth Century*, ed. Theodore Besterman (Geneva, 1960), 39.

9. His English translator, William Hooper, a Liverpool medical practitioner, also published *Rational Recreation, in which the Principles of Numbers and Natural Philosophy are . . . elucidated by a series of . . . experiments* which ran to four editions from 1783 to 1902.

10. Shelby T. McCloy, *French Inventions of the Eighteenth Century* (Lexington, Ky., 1952), 39–40. J. B. Bury, *The Idea of Progress* (1920), 193, regarded it as 'the first prophetic utopia' but considered (p. 179) that he showed 'curiously little resource' in his scanty prophecies of what science might effect.

11. M. Lanson, 'Le rôle de l'expérience dans la formation de la philosophie du XVIIIe siècle en France', *Revue du Mois*, IX (1910).

12. Frank E. Manuel, *The Prophets of Paris* (Cambridge, Mass., 1962), 65; M. J. Laboulle, 'La Mathématique sociale: Condorcet et ces prédécesseurs', *Revue de l'histoire littéraire de France*, XXXVI (1939).

13. Gilles-Gaston Granger, *La Mathématique sociale du marquis de Condorcet* (Paris, 1956).

14. James Frazer, *Condorcet on the Progress of the Human Mind* (1933), 13.

15. J. L. Talmon, *Political Messianism. The Romantic Phase* (1960), 86–90.

16. Barthélemy Enfantin, *Mémoirs d'un industriel de l'an 2240* (1829); Jean P. Alem, *Enfantin, le prophète aux sept visages* (Paris, 1963).

17. *Œuvres Complètes* (1886), vii, quoted E. W. Barnes, *Scientific Theory and Religion* (1933), 578.

18. Talmon, *op. cit.*, p. 143.

19. Talmon, *op. cit.*, 156 and D. O. Evans, *Social Romanticism in France 1830–1848* (1951).

20. J. Déjacque, *L'Humanisphère* (Paris, 1899), quoted in George Woodcock, *Anarchism. A History of Libertarian Ideas and Movements* (1963), 226.

21. C. M. Le Roy de Bonneville, *Etude Biographique et Littéraire sur Cousin de Grainville* (Havre, 1863); A. J. Sambrook, 'A Romantic Theme: The Last Man', *Forum for Modern Language Studies*, II, No. 1 (1966), 25 ff.

22. A. Richard Oliver, *Charles Nodier. Pilot of Romanticism* (1964), 126.

23. Pierre-Georges Castex (ed.), *Charles Nodier, Contes* (Paris, 1961), 393–462.

24. August Viatte, *Victor Hugo et les illuminés de son temps* (Montreal, 1942).

25. Camille Flammarion, *Les Mondes Imaginaires et les Mondes Réels* (1865).

26. Ingvald Raknem, *H. G. Wells and His Critics* (1962), 178–9, 384, 408–9.

27. I. O. Evans, *Jules Verne* (1965), 27.

28. P. G. Gove, *The Imaginary Voyage in Prose Fiction* (1941), 372; Marc Chadourne, *Restif de la Bretonne ou le Siècle Prophetique* (Paris, 1958); Hélène Tuzet, *Le Cosmos et l'Imagination* (Paris, 1962).

29. Winwood Reade's *The Martyrdom of Man* (1872) ran to eight editions in twelve years. This is from the 1934 reprint, p. 413.

30. Gustave Flaubert, *Bouvard et Pécuchet* (1881).

31. J. Bollery and P.-J. Castex (ed.), *L'Eve Future par Villiers de l'Isle Adam* (Paris, 1957).

32. *Revue de Métaphysique et de Morale*, Part IX, 119; René Sudre, *Treatise on Parapsychology* (1960) describes it as 'very original' (p. 375) and adds, 'This strong idea does not completely resolve the problem of precognition, but it provides a rough sketch of a solution by removing the theoretically impenetrable character of future events.'

33. Gabriel Tarde (1843–1904), began as a provincial magistrate, becoming director of criminal statistics at the Ministry of Justice and later professor of Modern Philosophy at the Collège de France. He held that the causes of crime were social, but the responsibility was the psychology of the criminal. He rejected the law of evolution for that of transformation, e.g. *Les transformations du droit* (1892) *Les transformations du pouvoir* (1899). He believed that some individuals are inventors, others repetitors (*Les lois d'imitation*, 1890). These clashes of waves of influence could, in Tarde's view, lead to peaceful change and his Utopia envisaged an ideal society based on disinterested love, with no coercion. Michael M. Davis, *Psychological Interpretations of Society* (Columbia, 1909), 84–163; H. E. Barnes, 'The Philosophy of the State in the Writings of Gabriel Tarde', *Philosophical Review*, XXVIII (1919), 248–79 writes: 'Of all French writers upon systematic sociology since the time of Comte probably no other author has been as influential in shaping the general body of sociological thought as Gabriel Tarde.'

34. Gabriel Tarde, *Underground Man* translated by Cloudesley Brereton (with a preface by H. G. Wells) (1905), 41–2, 52.

35. For other novels on the extinction of the race see: J. E. Flecker, *The Last Generation* (1908); W. H. Hudson, *The Night Land* (1912) and J. L. Tayler, *The Last of my Race* (1924).

36. Koenrad W. Swart, *The Sense of Decadence in Nineteenth Century France* (The Hague, 1964); Richard Chadbourne, *Renan as an Essayist* (Ithaca, 1957), 96–7. Renan was influenced by his fellow Breton, the almost equally prolific,

but austere, Emile Souvestre, whose *Le Monde Tel qu'il sera* (1846) influenced Renan to write *L'Avenir de la Science, pensées de 1848*. This outlined the law of the three stages of history; myth, curiosity, and synthesis, and humanised the story of the Fall. Man left Paradise (the age of myth), to satisfy his curiosity; then, alienated from his fellows and from God, finding his own way back to Paradise through 'the scientific organisation of mankind' to put him beyond the realm of material want. It had an enormous appeal to intellectuals, and was translated into English by A. D. Vandam and C. B. Pitman in 1891.

37. Anatole France, *The White Stone* (1905), translated by C. E. Roche (1925), 148.

38. *Ibid.*, 195.

39. *Ibid.*, 196, 198.

40. *Ibid.*, 201.

41. *Ibid.*, 220–1.

42. Jules Verne, *Yesterday and Tomorrow* (1910). See also the Verne Scholarship industry that has been expertly documented by Mark R. Hillegas in *Extrapolation* II (1960), 5–16.

43. Other nineteenth- and early twentieth-century science-fiction writers were Paschal Grousset (André Laurie), Paul D'Ivoir, Georges Price, Albert Robida, G. Le Faure, H. de Grattigny. For a recent assessment see Pierre Versins 'Une porte peut être ouverte et fermée', in *Fiction*, 140, 126–133; 141, 130–139; and 142, 147–159 (July, August, and Sept. 1965).

44. For an excellent modern discussion of this see C. C. Gillespie, 'Intellectual Factors in the Background of Analysis by Probabilities', in A. G. Crombie (ed.) *Historical Change . . . Symposium on the History of Science University of Oxford 9–15 July, 1961* (1963), 431–453.

45. P. S. Laplace 'Essai philosophique des probabilités', in *Œuvres*, VII (Paris 1878–1912).

46. S. D. Poisson, *Recherches sur la probabilité des jugements* (Paris, 1837).

47. A. Cournot, *Exposition de la théorie des chances et des probabilités* (Paris, 1843).

48. Joseph Lottin, *Quetelet, Statisticien et sociologue* (Louvain, 1912).

49. *Macmillan's Magazine*, 12th November 1859.

50. P. E. M. Berthelot, *Science et Philosophie* (1886), *Science et Morale* (1897). For his correspondence with Renan see *E. Renan et M. Berthelot Correspondance 1847–1892* (Paris, 1898).

4   THE GOTHIC IMAGINATION

1. Signe Toksvig, *Emmanuel Swedenborg. Scientist and Mystic* (New Haven, 1948).

2. D. J. Sloss and J. P. R. Wallis (ed.), *William Blake's Prophetic Writings* (1926), 1, 450.

3. F. B. Evans, 'Platonic Scholarship in Eighteenth Century England', *Modern Philology*, XLI (1943); S. T. Coleridge (ed., Kathleen Coburn), *The Philosophical Lectures* (1949), 318.

4. Frank B. Evans, 'Thomas Taylor, Platonist of the Romantic Period', *P.M.L.A.*, LV (1940), 1060–79.

5. George Mills Harper, *The Neoplatonism of William Blake* (Chapel Hill, 1961), 17–33.

6. Ross Greig Woodman, *The Apocalyptic Vision in the Poetry of Shelley* (Toronto, 1964), 11; James A. Notopoulos, *The Platonism of Shelley* (Durham, NC., 1949).

7. Woodman, *op. cit.*, ix and 11–12.

8. John F. Newton, 'Hindoo Zodiac', *Monthly Magazine*, xxxiii (March, 1812), 109.

9. T. Hutchinson (ed.), *Complete Poetical Works of Percy Bysshe Shelley* (1956), 825.

10. H. B. Forman (ed.), *The Poetical Works of P. B. Shelley* (1882), 11, 448, 518.

11. Donald Macrae, *Ideology and Society* (1961), 129. Not the forward prospect but the backward look over seven centuries appealed to Horace Walpole whose *Castle of Otranto* (1764) set the vogue for such 'Gothic' novels that specialised in flesh-creeping stories of horror.

'I almost think, he wrote, 'there is no wisdom comparable to that of exchanging what is called the realities of life for dreams. Old castles, old pictures, old histories and the babble of old people make one look back into centuries that cannot disappoint one. One holds fast and surely what is past. The dead have exhausted their power of deceiving.'

The time swing is important for it underlies the point that the novel itself is the art form of the scientific method developing as it did when physics and biology were making fundamental advances. Its chief claim to scientific method is that 'it is an observational form of art' and has 'both drawn upon and contributed directly to psychology, social anthropology and even physics and biology': Rex Comfort, *The Novel and our Time* (1948), 14; Edith Birkhead, *The Tale of Terror* (1921), 18; see also: Emo Rails, *The Haunted Castle* (1927); Montague Summers, *The Gothic Quest* (1938); D. P. Varma, *The Gothic Flame* (1957); and M. P. Conant, *The Oriental Tale in the Eighteenth Century* (New York, 1908); F. G. Black, *The Epistolary Novel in the Late Eighteenth Century* (Eugene, Oregon, 1940); Dorothy Scarborough, *The Supernatural in Modern English Fiction* (New York, 1917); J. T. Taylor, *Early Opposition to the English Novel: the Popular Reaction from 1760 to 1830* (New York, 1943).

12. Muriel Spark, *Child of Night. A reassessment of Mary Wollstonecraft Shelley* (Hadleigh, 1951), 133, 160. For an abridged version of the book, see pp. 195–230.

13. J. Webb, *The Mummy: A Tale of the Twenty-Second Century* (1827), ii, 221.

14. *Ibid.*, i, 190, 283.

15. *Ibid.*, 295, 64–5, 27.

16. *Ibid.*, i, 13.

17. *Ibid.*, i, 21, 137.

18. Mary Griffith, *Camperdown: Or, News from our Neighbourhood* (Philadelphia, 1836), 35.

19. John Webb, 'Translation of a French Metrical History of the Deposition of Richard the Second', *Archaelogia*, XX (1824), 270.

20. E. T. Gargan, 'Tocqueville and the Problem of Historical Prognosis', *American Historical Review* (1962–3), 332–45.

21. T. B. Macaulay, 'Von Ranke', *Edinburgh Review*, October 1840.

22. M. F. Lloyd Prichard (ed.), *A Voyage from Utopia*, by John Francis Bray (1957), 95.

23. *Ibid.*, 19.

24. *Ibid.*, 26–7.

25. *Edinburgh Review*, January 1830. He was criticising a book by the poet laureate Robert Southey called *Sir Thomas More, or Colloquies on the Progress and Prospects of Society*. In this Sir Thomas More is shown as appearing to Robert Southey to confirm Southey's view that the prospects of society had worsened since his time. With this Macaulay disagreed, summing up the issue between Southey and himself as 'rosebushes and poor-rates versus steam engines and independence'. Macaulay's prophecies about America seem to have caused far more stir. Though he had never seen the country, he wrote on 23 May, 1857, to Henry S. Randall, an early biographer of Thomas Jefferson. 'As long as you have a boundless extent of fertile and unoccupied land,' he said, 'your labouring population will be far more at ease than the labouring population of the old world.' But the time will arrive, he forecast, when Manchesters and Birminghams would grow up in America, affording ripe fields for the agitator. Then will come the demagogue, 'ranting about the tyranny of capitalists and usurers, and asking why anybody should be permitted to drink Champagne and to ride in a carriage, while thousands of honest folks are in want of necessaries'. He and his followers would then seize power, and one of two courses of action would be left open to Americans:

> 'Either some Caesar or Napoleon will seize the reins of government with a strong hand; or your republic will be as fearfully plundered and laid waste by barbarians in the twentieth century as the Roman Empire was in the fifth;—with this difference, that the Huns and Vandals who ravaged the Roman Empire came from without, and that your Huns and Vandals will have been engendered within your own country by your own institutions.'

First printed in the *Southern Literary Messenger* of March 1860 it was copied by the *New York Times* and some other northern journals. As A. M. Schlesinger (senior) wrote in the *Proceedings* of the American Antiquarian Society, LV (1947), 53–94.

> 'Macaulay's prophecy was a ghost that could not be laid. Every great economic upset in the years that followed redirected attention to it. His ominous words were cited either in a mood of resignation, or to underline the danger of entrusting power to the unpropertied, or to show why remedial action should be undertaken before it was too late.'

In the depression following the Panic of 1873 *Harper's Magazine* republished the letter in 1877 where it may have been seen by Henry George, who used it to reinforce his argument for the single tax in *Progress and Poverty* (1879). It was used by Josiah Strong in *Our Country: Its Possible Future and Its Present*

Crisis (1885) to argue for expansion into Latin America and Africa, by *Gunton's Magazine* to argue for social reform in 1896; and during the New Deal as a 'remarkable anticipation'. H. M. Lydenberg, *What Did Macaulay say about America* (New York, 1925).

26. Karl Marx and Frederick Engels, *The Communist Manifesto* (1848); F. Engels, *Ludwig Feuerbach* (1886).

27. This point is well brought out by an American Communist thinker Earl Browder in David Footman (ed.), *International Communism* (1960), 92–3.

28. Rudolf Schlesinger, *Marx, His Time and Ours* (1951), who said earlier (p. 83), that the Marxian synthesis had produced 'an external effect comparable only to the rise of Christianity'. See also John Strachey, *The Coming Struggle for Power* (1936), p. 276. 'More knew as well as Lenin all that either of them, or anyone else, can know of the general outline of the fully developed communist society to which mankind shall some day attain. But it took centuries of combined historical experience and technical achievement to discover the stages through which mankind had to pass on the way to that goal.' And again (p. 277), 'The continuity of communist and socialist thought, from its germ in More's *Utopia*, to its full maturity in the theory and practice of Lenin, is very extraordinary.' Most interesting, too, is the rise of Utopiology, or the collection of ideal models of society by German sociologists, e.g. Robert von Mohl, *Die Staatsromane* (Erlangen, 1855); Moritz Brasch, *Sozialistische Phantasiestaaten* (Leipzig, 1887); Friedrich Kleinwachter, *Die Staatsromane* (Vienna, 1891); Aron Kirchenheim, *Scharaffia Politica, Geschichte der Dichtungen vom besten Staate* (Leipzig, 1892); Rudolf Stammler, *Utopien* (1892); E. H. Schmitt, *Der Idealstaat* (1904); Andreas Voigt, *Die Sozialen Utopien* (Leipzig, 1906); J. Prys, *Der Staatsroman des 16 and 17 Jahrhunderts* (Wurzburg, 1917); Rudolf Alfred Doren, *Wunschraume und Wunschzieten* (Leipzig, 1927); Fritz Brueggamann, *Utopie und Robinsade* (Weimar, 1914); Robert Blüher, *Moderne Utopien* (Bonn, 1920); Hans Treyer, *Die Politische Insel, Eine Geschichte der Utopien von Platon bis zur Gegenwart* (Leipzig, 1936); A. Hahn, *Grenzenloser Optimismus, die biologischen und technischen Möoglichkeiten der Menscheit. Utopiologie* (Prague, 1939); Hubertus Schulte-Herbruggen, *Utopie und Antiutopie, von der Strukturanalyse zur Strukturpsychologie* (Bochum, 1960); B. D. Wolfe dedicated his *Marxism: One Hundred Years in the Life of a Doctrine* (London, 1967), 'to the cartographers and travellers—and those who have lost their way—on the journey to Utopia'.

29. Sir Francis Galton, *Essays in Eugenics* (1909), 42; The year in which the *Origin of Species* appeared also saw H. Lang's picture, in *The Air Battle: A Vision of the Future* (1859), of Britain defended by Africans. This was one of a number of foreboding military prophecies that were to be thrown up with increasing frequency. An outstanding example was that of a British engineering officer, the president of the Royal Indian Civil Engineering College at Staines, Sir G. T. Chesney. He set the contemporary world by the ears by describing the successful invasion of Britain by Prussia. His imaginative exposure of British technical backwardness, published in *Blackwood's Magazine* for May 1871, caught European as well as English ears. Rapidly translated into French, Dutch, German, and Italian, it provoked a rush of pamphlets, some humorous, others serious: Anon. *After the Battle of Dorking: or What*

became of the invaders (1871), *The Battle of Dorking: A Myth* (1871); *Our hero: or who wrote 'The Battle of Dorking'* (1871); *What happened after the Battle of Dorking: or, the Victory of Tunbridge Wells* (1871); M. Mottruhn (pseud.), *The Other Side at the Battle of Dorking* (1871), and A. Sketchley, *Mrs. Brown on the Battle of Dorking* (1871).

'These apprehensions of wars to come,' writes I. F. Clarke in *History Today*, XV (1965), 110, 'by their very number, must have sharpened expectations if they did not modify its strategy.' Certainly as he wrote 'it became common practice to describe imaginary defeats—or victories—in some future period in order to demonstrate the need for appropriate reforms in the armed forces, or to advertise the advantages of the measures and policies they recommended'. And as he has shown, the co-operation of writers with newspaper owners like Harmsworth and service chiefs, generated a hothouse atmosphere in which popular apprehension of Germany could ripen. The end of the second war against Germany transformed the role of apprehensive fantasy to the new conditions of a deterrence world. A new type of war philosophy emerged, plotting the strategy of a nuclear war like a chess game, to prepare a state of mind which would convince 'the enemy' that it was futile and useless to employ their own weapons, for fear of swift primitive sanctions. For a fuller treatment of this type of predictive fantasy see I. F. Clarke, *Voices Prophesying War 1763–1984* (Oxford, 1966).

30. The Earl of Lytton, *The Life of Edward Bulwer, First Lord Lytton* (1913), ii, 465. Earlier, at the age of thirty-nine, he had told Forster, 'I do believe in the existence of what used to be called magic.' (*Ibid.*, ii, 48). Now, in 1871 Forster thought Vril was mesmerism, but Bulwer-Lytton insisted it was electricity. 'If you can suggest any other idea of carrying out that idea of a destroying race, I should be glad. Probably even the notion of Vril might be more cleared from mysticism or mesmerism by being simply defined to be electricity and conducted by those slaves or rods, omitting all about mesmeric passes, etc. Perhaps, too, it would be safe to omit all reference to the power of communicating with the dead.' *Ibid.*, 11, 467.

31. *The Coming Race* (1871). A good edition, with *The Haunted and the Haunters*, was edited by F. J. Harvey Darton for the World's Classics (1932). A good appreciation is by Geoffrey Wagner 'A Forgotten Satire: Bulwer-Lytton's *The Coming Race*', *Nineteenth Century Fiction*, xix (1964–5), 379–85.

32. Curtis Dahl, 'Bulwer-Lytton and the School of Catastrophe', *Philological Quarterly*, XXXII (1953), 428–42; S. B. Liljegren, *Bulwer-Lytton's novels and Isis Unveiled* (Uppsala, 1957).

33. Lives by T. F. G. Coates and R. S. Warren-Bell (1903); George Bullock (1940) and Eileen Bigland (1953).

34. *Erewhon, or Over the Range* (1872). With a Preface. The second edition had a new preface and not until the fifth edition (1873), did Samuel Butler's name appear. Translated into Dutch (1873), German (1879 and 1928), French (1920), Braille (1926), Spanish (1926 and 1942), and Italian (1945). Two good editions exist, one with an introduction by Lewis Mumford (1927), another with an afterword by Kingsley Amis (1960). Two stimulating views are worth looking up, E. M. Forster in the *New Statesman and Nation*, 15th July 1944 (Vol. XXVIII, p. 43), and Robert Graves, 'A Galileo of Mare's Nests',

Spectator, 15th December 1923 (No. 4981, 949–50). H. Festing Jones, *Samuel Butler: A Memoir* (1919) and R. F. Rattray, *Samuel Butler: A Chronicle and an Introduction* (1935) and Malcolm Muggeridge, *The Ernest Atheist* (1936), destroyed his image but it is slowly being built up again by P. N. Furbank, *Samuel Butler* (1948); Philip Henderson, *Samuel Butler the Incarnate Bachelor* (1953); and Stanley B. Harkness, *The Career of Samuel Butler (1835–1902). A Bibliography* (1955).

35. In the spring of 1873 Butler asked his parents' approval to acknowledge his paternity of *Erewhon*. His father said he could do as he pleased but because he had written *Erewhon* he could never visit home again. Later, at his mother's funeral, his father said that the publication of *Erewhon* had killed her. Daniel F. Howard, *The Correspondence of Samuel Butler with his Sister Mary* (Berkeley, 1962).

36. Samuel Butler, *Erewhon Revisited, Twenty Years Later, both by the Original Discoverer of the Country and by his Son* (1901). Translated into French (1924), Spanish (1928). The Edition used here is that issued by the Travellers' Library in 1928.

5   THE OTHER SIDE

1. In an imaginary series of letters written from Britain to the Professor of History at the University of Auckland in the year 3867 (hence its title; *Two Thousand Years Hence* (1868)), Hugh O'Neil, an Irishman, born in St. Petersburg, criticised the politics of his day as certain to lead to those ruins. In his *Satirical Dialogues Dedicated to Anthony Trollope* (1870), 'a philosopher' points out (p. 19):

> *As science prospers, Energy decreases;*
> *And each invention, whatsoe'er the gain,*
> *Produces equal loss in hand and brain.*
> *The more machines can do the work of man:*
> *You make the latter valueless.*

The 'Liberal' argues:

> *The present not ignoring, we may better*
> *The future, making it a grateful debtor.*

Whilst the Conservative replies:

> *In that respect, I'd rather be a creditor,*
> *And of our present glories be the editor.*

His third satire, *The Age of Stucco* (1871), also dedicated to Trollope, could be regarded as a utopiate; for a substantial part of it is a mannered 'invocation' to his pipe.

For all the triteness of his thought O'Neil is important in that he had the idea of staging a predictive dialogue between particular parties.

2. J. H. Niau, *The Phantom Paradise* (Sydney, 1936).

3. For a complete list see I. F. Clarke, *The Tale of the Future* (London, The Library Association, 1961).

4. E. Maitland, *By and By. A Historical Romance of the Future* (1873), iii, 138.

Edward Maitland (1824–97 educated Morris' school, Brighton and Caius College, Cambridge, went to California in 1849, then Australia and returned to England in 1857. He joined Mrs. Anna Kingsford (whose life he subsequently wrote), in her crusade against materialism, animal food, and vivisection, and with her he founded in 1891 the Esoteric Christian Union. He joined the Theosophical Society, seceding in the following year to found the Hermetic Society. He was a Blakeian mystic, a large man of great spiritual sensitivity.

5. Edward Maitland, *Anna Kingsford* (1913), i, 26.

6. *Ibid.*, i, 116.

7. Harvey Cushing, *The Life of Sir William Osler* (1925), 1, 664–72.

8. A. O. J. Cockshutt, *Anthony Trollope. A Critical Study* (1955), 91–2; cf. Hugh Walpole's verdict: 'Trollope's attempts at prophecy are too unconvincing to be absorbing,' *Anthony Trollope* (1928), 138, and Bradford A. Booth: 'Just what Trollope intended by his fantasy is not always clear, but it seems to be a satire on social planning, a kind of modest proposal for the continuance of the status quo,' *Anthony Trollope. Aspects of his Life and Art* (1958), 129.

9. Rev. W. Tuckwell (1829–1919). Schoolmaster and town rector of Stockton, Warwickshire, 1878–93, later of Waltham, Lincolnshire 1893–1905. Author of *Reminiscences of a Radical Parson* (1905), *Nuggests from the Bible Mine* (1913).

10. Delivered on 8th February 1885, under the title *The New Utopia or England in 1985* it was subsequently reprinted in his *Christian Socialism and Other Lectures* (1891), 33–58. This is from page 56. Tuckwell was not the first clergyman to be transported by a vision of the future of Ireland. Earlier Cardinal Newman in his *Historical Sketches* (1873) iii, 32, had been so carried away by his vision of what a Catholic University in Ireland would do that in a 'hundred years hence' he professed to see Ireland 'become the road of passage between two hemispheres, and the centre of the world. . . . Thither, as to a sacred soil, the home of their fathers, and the fountain-head of their Christianity students are flocking . . . with the ease and rapidity of a locomotion not yet discovered.' This could be read, if nothing else, as an accurate prophecy of the Shannon airport, at present (1967) in the centre of a great development area.

11. *Ibid.*, 57–8. Awareness of the genre was such that James T. Presley began publishing a 'Bibliography of Utopias' in *Notes and Queries*, 4th Series, XI (1873), 519–21. With continuations it ended in 6th Series, IX (1884), 84.

12. Morley Roberts, *W. H. Hudson* (1924).

13. G. F. Wilson, *A Bibliography of the Writings of W. H. Hudson* (1922).

14. Written by Edmund Boisgilbert (Ignatius Donnelly), *Caesar's Column* was so disturbing that five publishers refused to touch it. For though he envisaged many technological wonders, he foresaw that these would only confirm the control of society by the rich and reduce the labouring classes to quasi-barbarian poverty, whilst the class war between them would virtually destroy civilisation. Donnelly was an espouser of stranger causes. Not only was he the author of a work on *Atlantis*, but he made the first attempt to disprove the authorship of Shakespeare's plays by cryptography.

15. Maxwell Geismar, *Rebels and Ancestors* (1954), 142.

16. A Russell Wallace, *The Scientific Aspect of the Supernatural* (1866). See also D. D. Horne, *Incidents of My Life* (1863).

17. Rene Sudre (trans. C. E. Green), *Treatise on Parapsychology* (1960), 370.

18. L. C. Robinson, *Journal for Psychical Research*, XXXIX, No. 693.

19. Rosalind Heywood, *The Sixth Sense* (1959).

20. L. L. Whyte, *The Unconscious before Freud* (1962), 171. For more recent speculations see F. Russell Stannard 'Symmetry of the Time Axis', *Nature*, 13th August 1966, and Martin Gardner 'Can Time Go Backward', *Scientific American*, January 1967, 98–108.

21. M. P. Shiel, *Science, Life and Literature* (1950), 168–9, 208, 211.

22. Charles Grant Blairfieldie Allen published *The Evolutionist at Large* (1881), *Charles Darwin* (1886), *Force and Energy* (1888), *Falling in Love* (1889), 'Natural Inequality', in *Forecasts of the Coming Century* (1897), *Flashlights on Nature* (1889), as well as editing H. T. Buckle in 1885. 'The Child of the Phalanstery' appeared in the *Backslider* (1901), 315–42.

23. Frederic Harrison, *Autobiographic memoirs 1870–1910* (London, 1911), ii, 275.

24. George Griffith also wrote under the name of Stanton Morich. Other works of his include *The Outlaws of the Air* (1895); *The Great Pirate Syndicate* (1899); *The Lake of Gold* (1903); *A Woman against the World* (1903); *The World Masters* (1903); *The Mummy and Miss Nitocris: A Fantasy of the Fourth Dimension* (1906); *Weather Syndicate* (1906); *The World Peril of 1910* (1907); *A Criminal Croesus* (1904); *The Lord of Labour* (1911).

25. Karl Pearson, *The Life and Letters and Labours of Francis Galton* (1930), iii, A, 412.

26. *Ibid.*, 416.

27. *Ibid.*, 265.

28. *Ibid.*, 260.

29. Lewis Carroll, *Sylvie and Bruno* (1889), i, 64: Roger Lancelyn Green, (ed.), *The Works of Lewis Carroll* (1965), 408. The 'companion' significantly enough had 'all the innocent frankness of some angelic visitant, new to the ways of earth and the conventionalisms—or, if you will, the barbarisms—of Society'.

30. See e.g. Elizabeth Sewell, *The Field of Nonsense* (1952), 31 ff. Himself a writer of science-fiction, E. T. Bell considers Carroll as a mathematician in his *Men of Mathematics* (1937). This should be supplemented by articles like William Garnett in the *Mathematical Gazette*, ix (1918–19), 237–41, 249–52, 293–8; R. B. Braithwaite, *ibid.*, xvi (1932), 174–8, and D. B. Eperson, *ibid.*, xvii (1933), 92–100; Warren Weaver in *Scientific American*, April 1956, and Martin Gardner, *ibid.*, March 1960. See S. H. Williams and Falconer Madan, revised by Roger Lancelyn Green, *The Lewis Carroll Handbook* (1962) and Martin Gardner (ed.) *The Annotated Alice* (Penguin Books, 1965).

31. Lewis Carroll, *Works, op. cit.*, 109.

32. Warren Weaver, *Alice in Many Tongues* (New York, 1964).

33. William Empson, *Some Versions of Pastoral* (1950), 264.

34. Florence Becker Lennon, *Lewis Carroll* (1947), 274. She also points out (p. 225) that he 'seems to have theosophy'.

35. *Works* (1965), 136.

36. Brian L. Aldiss (ed.), *Penguin Science Fiction* (1961), ii.

37. Edward S. Lauterbach and Thomas D. Clareson, 'Major Trends in American Science Fiction: 1880–1915', *Extrapolation*, I (Wooster, Ohio, 1959), 1–20; Mark R. Hillegas, 'The First Invasion from Mars', *The Michigan Alumnus Quarterly Review*, February 1960, 107–12; William B. Johnson and Thomas D. Clareson, 'The Interplay of Science and Fiction: The Canals of Mars', *Extrapolation*, V (1964), 37–48.

38. Originally published in the magazine *All-Around* and republished in 1963. See Remi Maure 'A la rédecouverte d'Edgar Rice Burroughs', *Mercury* V (Montferrand, 1965), 44–50.

39. Ben W. Fuson, 'A Poetic Precursor of Bellamy's "Looking Backward" ', *Extrapolation*, V (1964), 31–6.

6 BELLAMY AND THE MECHANICAL MILLENARIANS

1. I. O. Evans, *Jules Verne and his Work* (1965), 10.

2. Jules Verne, *In the Twenty Ninth Century: The Day of an American Journalist in 2889* (in *Yesterday and Tomorrow*, 1910).

3. It appeared in the American magazine *The Forum* in 1889.

4. W. D. Howells, 'Edward Bellamy', *Atlantic Monthly*, LXXXII, 1898, 253–6.

5. 'How I came to write *Looking Backward*', *The Nationalist*, I, 1889, 2–3.

6. V. L. Parrington, *Main Currents in American Thought*, iii, 1930, 308.

7. W. Arthur Boggs, '*Looking Backward* and the Utopian Novel, 1888–1900', *Bulletin of the New York Public Library*, LXIV, 1960, 329.

8. Parrington, *op. cit.*, 303; A. E. Morgan, *Edward Bellamy* (New York, 1944), 264 ff.

9. *Ibid.*

10. Four 'predecessors' of Bellamy can be identified: Radical Free Lance (pseud.), *The Philosopher of Foufouville* (1868); Edward Everett Hale, *Sybar* (1869); Alfred Denton Cridge, *Utopia; or the History of an Extinct Planet* (1884), and Henry F. Allen (anon.), *The Key of Industrial Co-operative Government* (1886).

11. Edward Bellamy, *Looking Backward, 2000–1887* (1888), 56.

12. Parrington, *op. cit.*, iii, 303.

13. John Bakeless in *Dictionary of American Biography*, ii (1929), 163.

14. *Looking Backward*, 90.

15. *Ibid.*, 94.

16. Review by William Morris in *The Commonweal*, June, 1889.

17. William Morris, *News from Nowhere or an epoch of rest, being some chapters from a Utopian Romance* (1891), 7.

18. *Ibid.*, 76.

19. *Ibid.*, 109.

20. *Ibid.*, 142–3.

21. *Ibid.*, 97 and 147.

22. *Ibid.*, 237.

23. Tennyson's symbolic use of the Arthurian legend was that Merlin is the intellect (whose disastrous affair with Vivien symbolises the corruption of the intellectual by the sensual), Sir Galahad the spirit divorced from earth who withdraws into spiritual realms, while Sir Arthur is the ideal soul, who attempts to realise himself in the world of sense (Guinevere), and to elevate humanity by 'liberal institutions' (The Round Table). R. W. Barber, *Arthur of Albion An Introduction to the Arthurian Literature and Legends of England* (1961), says (p. 151) that 'the story is that of man's Utopian dreams coming into contact with practical life and the warring elements of the flesh, and being ruined by one sin'.

24. *Letters of Henry James* (New York, 1920), 30–1.

25. C. M. Kirk and R. Kirk, *Criticism and Fiction and other Essays by W. D. Howells* (New York, 1959), 165; Van Wyck Brooks, *Howells. His Life and World* (1959), 184, 186; G. N. Bennett, *William Dean Howells. The Development of a Novelist* (Norman, Oklahoma, 1959).

26. Kirk and Kirk, *op. cit.*, 251. 'The Brick Moon' appeared in the Oct., Nov., and Dec. numbers of the *Atlantic Monthly* (1869) with a sequel 'Life in the Brick Moon' in the following Feb. issue. Republished in his *Collected Works* (Boston, 1899), Vol. iv. For his connection with Payne see R. V. Hines, *California's Utopian Colonies* (New Haven, 1966), 101–3.

27. Mark Twain published 'The Curious Republic of Gondour', a sardonic three-page sketch of a disillusioned democrat in the *Atlantic Monthly* of October 1875, but anonymously since he feared that 'the world might refuse to take him seriously over his own signature, or *nom de plume*'. Vernon Louis Parrington, Jr., *American Dreams. A Study of American Utopias* (Providence, 1947), 48; H. N. Smith and William N. Gibson, *Mark Twain—Howells Letters. The Correspondence of Samuel L. Clemens and William D. Howells, 1872–1900* (Cambridge, Mass., 1960), ii, 622.

28. *Writings of Mark Twain* (New York, 1929), XIV, 5.

29. *Ibid.*, 76

30. *Ibid.*, 65.

31. *Ibid.*, 47.

32. *Ibid.*, 109.

33. *Ibid.*, 211.

34. Kenneth S. Lynn, *Mark Twain and South Western Humour* (New York, 1954), 254.

35. Lewis J. Budd, *Mark Twain. Social Philosopher* (Bloomington, 1962), 117; Roger B. Salomon, *Twin and the Image of History* (New Haven, 1961), 103.

36. A. E. Morgan, *op. cit.*, 264 ff.; Bellamy influenced Howells's *A Hazard of New Fortunes* and told him: 'You are writing what everyone is thinking and all the rest will have to follow or lose their readers.' C. M. and R. Kird (ed.), *Criticism and Fiction and other Essays by W. D. Howells* (New York, 1959), 249.

37. Mrs. Marie Adelaide (Brown) Shipley in *The True Author of Looking Backward* (New York 1890), tried to prove he took the idea from August Bebel's *Die Frau und de Socialismus*. She also pleaded in 1888 before a select committee of the U.S. Senate for recognition of the discovery of America by Lief Erikson: itself a striking anticipation of modern views. Others should be added like Mrs. C. H. Stone, *One of Berrian's Novels* (1890); Ernst Müller's

Ein Rükblick aus dem Jahre 2037 auf das Jahr 2000 aus dem Erinnerungen des Herrn Julian West (1891) and Konrad Wilbrandt's *Herrn Friedrich Ost Erlebnisse in der Welt Bellamy's* (1891). The last two represented German objections to his socialism, a particular variant of which Germany was going through at the time. Le Vicomte Combes de Lestrade, a French sociologist, made a translation of *Looking Backward—Seul de son siècle en l'an 2000* (1891) and carried the debate to France.

38. Solomon Schindler (1842–1915) was a Jewish rabbi whose interest in messianism had been reflected in *Messianic expectation and Modern Judaism* (1886) and *Dissolving Views in the history of Judaism* (1888) before he wrote *Going West* (1894).

39. Extracts from this have been published by Glenn Negley and J. Max Patrick in *The Quest for Utopia. An Anthology of Imaginary Societies* (New York, 1952), 82–105.

40. King Camp Gillette, *The Human Drift* (1894), *The Ballot Box* (1897), *World Corporation* (1910), *The People's Corporation* (1924), and Melvin Linwood Severy, *Gillette's industrial solution: world corporation; an account of the evolution of the existing social system together with a presentation of an entirely new remedy for the evils it exhibits* (Boston, 1908).

41. Negley and Patrick, *op. cit.*, 137–54.

42. Allyn B. Forbes, 'The Literary Quest for Utopia 1880–1900', *Social Forces*, VI (December 1927), No. 2 lists forty-eight utopian romances and studies in collectivism during this period, while over a hundred and forty are listed in 'An Annotated Checklist of American Science-Fiction 1880–1915' in *Extrapolation* 1. No. 1 (1959), 5–20.

43. 'Mellonta Tauta' appeared in Godey's 'Lady's Book' in 1849. Also from Poe's macabre fancy came the *Unparalleled Adventures of Hans Pfael* (1835), which inspired Jules Verne; *The Facts in the case of M. Valdemar* (1845) a Gothic horror of mesmerism arresting a man at the moment of death.

44. A. E. Morgan, *op. cit.*, 241.

45. V. L. Parrington, Jr., *American Dreams: A Study of American Utopias* (2nd Edn., 1964) comments (p. 61), 'perhaps she was annoyed by John Macnie's *A Far Look Ahead* or by the Fourieristic experiments'.

46. J. J. Astor, *A Journey in Other Worlds* (1894), British Museum copy.

47. By Martin I. J. Greffen, *Frank R. Stockton* (Philadelphia, 1939), 104. Earlier science-fiction stories of this prolific author include 'A Tale of Negative Gravity', *Century*, XXIX (1884), and *The Great War Syndicate* (1890).

48. George Farrell, *Rev. Josiah Hilton. The Apostle of the New Age* (1898); Albert Adams Merrill, *The Great Awakening. The Story of the Twenty-Second Century* (Boston, 1899); [Edward A. Caswell] myself and another *To it and Self* (Chicago, 1900); Milan C. Edson, *Solaris Farm. A Story of the Twentieth Century* (Washington, 1900); [E. O. Gregley] Jack Adams, *Nequa or the Problem of the Ages* (Topeka, 1900); C. E. Persinger, *Letters from New America* (Chicago, 1900); P. Devinne, *The Day of Prosperity a Vision of the Century to Come* (1901); E. E. Mills, *The Decline and Fall of the B.E.—approved for use in national schools in Japan* (1908); J. I. Brant, *The New Regime A.D. 2202* (1909); Anon. [Colonel G. M. House]—*Philip Dru: Administrator: A Story of Tomorrow 1920–1935* (1912); Jeff. W. Hayes, *Portland, Oregon, A.D. 1999*

(Portland, 1913); Upton Sinclair, *The Millennium. A Comedy of the year 2000* (1912), also: I. *Governor of California, and how I Ended Poverty; a True Story of the Future* (Los Angeles, 1933); 1. *Candidate for Governor; and How I got licked* (New York, 1935); *Co-op; a Novel of Living Together* (New York, 1936). See *My Autobiography* (1963), 153.

49. For a recent picture see H. Bruce Franklin, *Future Perfect. American Science Fiction of the Nineteenth Century* (1966).

50. Walter Fuller Taylor, *The Economic Novel in America* (Chapel Hill, 1942), 325.

51. Roger B. Saloman, *Twain and the Image of History* (New Haven, 1961), 34.

52. Arthur F. Beringause, *Brooks Adams* (1955), 143.

53. Francis Lacassin, 'Gustave Le Rouge ou le naufrage de la S.F.', *Fiction* 155 (1966), 137–49 (French edition of the *Magazine of Fantasy and Science Fiction*).

54. Gustave le Rouge, *Le mystérieux Docteur Cornélius* (Paris, 1913, re-published 1966).

7   SUPERMAN AND THE SYSTEM

1. Harris Wilson (ed.), *Arnold Bennett and H. G. Wells* (1960), 73–4.

2. Eric Bentley, *The Cult of the Superman* (1947), 131, 88.

3. Nietzsche wrote to his sister in December 1888: 'You have not the slightest idea what it means to be next-of-kin to the man and destiny in whom the question of epochs has been settled. Quite literally speaking: I hold the future of mankind in the palm of my hand.'

4. Nietzsche's sister moved to Paraguay with her husband Bernard Forster where they founded a Colony: Nueva Germana.

5. Thomas Carlyle, *The History of Friedrich II of Prussia called Frederick The Great* (1885), I, i, iii.

6. *Ibid.*, xxi.

7. Edwin M. J. Kretzmann, 'German Technological Utopias of the Pre-War Period', *Annals of Science*, iii (1938), 417–30.

8. Hans-Jüngen Krysmanski, *Die utopische Methode Eine literatur-und wissenssoziologische Untersuchung deutscher utopischer Romane des 20. Jahrhunderts* (Koln, 1963), 31–74.

9. Bernard Bergonzi, *The Early H. G. Wells. A Study of the Scientific Romances* (1961), 1–61, gives a good account of the genesis of these stories in the *fin de siècle* atmosphere of the time. Bergonzi suggests (pp. 47–8), that the Eloi of *The Time Machine* with their overtones of elfin, eloigne, élite, and eld (aged), were in fact a decadent race. Their buildings were ruinous, they spent all their time in playing gently, in bathing in the river, in making love in half-playful fashion, in eating fruit and sleeping.

10. H. G. Wells, *The First Men in the Moon* (1901), Chapter 24.

11. *Ibid.*

12. C. S. Lewis, *Out of the Silent Planet* (1962), 81–2.

13. H. G. Wells, *In the Days of the Comet* (1906), 4.

14. *Ibid.*, 1, 2.

15. *Ibid.*, Epilogue.

16. G. B. Shaw, *Pygmalion*, conclusion.

17. *New York Herald*, 15th April, 1906.

18. *A Modern Utopia*, 327.

19. *The Discovery of the Future* (1901), Works, IV, 374.

20. *Ibid.*, 380.

21. *Ibid.*, 377.

22. H. G. Wells, 'An Apology for a World Utopia', in F. S. Marvin (ed.), *The Evolution of World Peace* (1921), 159, 160.

23. *A Modern Utopia*, 10.

24. R. M. Alberes, *L'Aventure Intellectuelle du XXe siècle. Panorama des Littératures Européennes 1900–1959* (Paris, 1961).

25. *When the Sleeper Wakes* (1899).

26. Anthony West, 'H. G. Wells', in *Encounter*, February 1957.

27. G. B. Shaw, *Man and Superman* (1901–3), Act III.

28. *Back to Methuselah*, Part III.

29. *Ibid.*, Part IV.

30. *Ibid.*, Part V.

31. Maurice Benn, 'An Interpretation of the Work of Hermann Hesse', *German Life and Letters*, Vol. iii (1949–50), 202–11, and W. H. Rey, 'Ernst Jünger and the Crisis of Civilisation', *German Life and Letters*, N.9. 5 (1951–2), 249–54.

32. Armin Arnold, *D. H. Lawrence and German Literature* (1963).

33. D. H. Lawrence, *Phoenix* (London, 1936), 304.

34. D. H. Lawrence, *Fantasia of the Unconscious* (London, 1931), 16.

35. *Ibid.*

36. Marvin Mudrick, 'The Originality of the Rainbow', in Mark Schorer (ed.), *Modern British Fiction* (1961), 250. Eugene Goodheart, *The Utopian Vision of D. H. Lawrence* (Chicago, 1963), 6, quoting from *Fantasia of the Unconscious*.

37. W. B. Yeats, *On the Baler* (1939), 25.

38. *A Vision* (1925), 215.

39. Ursula Bridge, *W. B. Yeats and T. Sturge Moore: Their Correspondence 1901–1937* (1953), 105. The excellent critical estimate of *Oswald Spengler* (1952) by H. Stuart Hughes should be read by all interested in historians and the future.

40. T. R. Henn, *The Lonely Tower: Studies in the Poetry of W. B. Yeats* (1965), 193.

41. Morton Irving Seiden, *William Butler Yeats. The Poet as Mythmaker 1865–1939* (Ann Arbor, Michigan, 1962). In his own attempt to 'rip the old veil of the vision across' W. B. Yeats joined a Hermetic Society in Dublin, and later joined Madame Blavatsky's Lodge, trying to conduct seances, experimenting with ritual magic and becoming obsessed by occult symbols like the wheel, the sphere, the cone, and the interpenetrating triangles. Later he joined the Isis-Urania Temple of the Hermetic Students of the Golden Dawn—a Rosicrucian Society of ardent social reformers who wished to use magic and alchemy to transmute or regenerate the modern world by destroying the present and ushering in a Golden Age. Finally, he married a medium almost as learned as himself.

Yeats prophesied that the 'latest results of that psychical research founded by William Crookes' would be combined with some Asiatic philosophy so as to prepare 'all to face death without flinching, perhaps even with joy. As according to their philosophy the dead will not pass to a remote Heaven, but return to the Earth, it would seem as though the soldier's dead body manured the fields he himself would till.' Quoted from MS in possession of Mrs. W. B. Yeats by Hazard Adams, *Blake and Yeats: the Contrary Vision* (Ithaca, 1955), 30.

8 THE DISENCHANTED MECHANOPHOBES

1. G. K. Chesterton, *The Napoleon of Notting Hill* (1904, Penguin Books, 1946), 70.

2. *Ibid.*, 157. Compare his 'In Defence of Nonsense':

That it is good for a man to realise that he 'the heir of all the ages' is pretty commonly admitted; it is a less popular but equally important point that it is good for him sometimes to realise that he is not only an ancestor, but an ancestor of primal antiquity; it is good for him to wonder whether he is not a hero, and to experience ennobling doubts as to whether he is not a solar myth.

G. K. Chesterton, 'In Defence of Nonsense', *Stories, Essays and Poems* (1946), 123.

3. G. K. Chesterton, *Heretics* (1908), 29, 70–5.

4. *Ibid.*, 79.

5. G. K. Chesterton, 'The External Revolution', in *Orthodoxy* (1908, 15th Reprint, 1957), 207.

6. G. K. Chesterton, *Orthodoxy* (1908), 2–6.

7. 'With the Night Mail: A Story of 2000 A.D.', *Actions and Reactions* (1909), 111–69.

8. Rudyard Kipling, 'As Easy as A.B.C.', in *A Diversity of Creatures* (1917), 21. *The Kipling Journal*, XXIX, No. 143, 2–3 discusses its debt to Bulwer-Lytton's *The Coming Race*.

9. *Ibid.*, 21.

10. *Ibid.*, 27.

11. Rose Macaulay, herself the author of a Utopian novel, considered it 'the least Forsterian of his writings. It has a Forster moral, but lacks charm, humour and style; it might have been written by someone else.' *The Writings of E. M. Forster* (1938), 31, whereas Lionel Trilling (*E. M. Forster* (1944, 1962 edn, pp. 42–3), though he finds a remote quality in Forster's elder heroines) which 'must check our natural tendency to find in them a symbol of the Earth which man has deserted', agrees that 'the Earth–Mother identification is explicit in "The Machine Stops"'. Rex Warner, another predictive fantast defends 'The Machine Stops' in his *E. M. Forster* (1950), but H. J. Oliver, *The Art of E. M. Forster* (Melbourne, 1960), criticises it for taking 'a long time to make its point about dominance of the machine, and in its lack of continuous narrative interest' and suggests 'that Forster is not quite at home in projecting himself into a future brave new world'. 'Its moments of poignancy are enhanced by the fact that they do not have to contend with a

charming or humorous context.' New Symbols, especially those of Orion whose nebula sword is 'the golden seed of world to be' (p. 93), and of the hideous long white worms which suck the hero back from the earth's surface into the Machine (p. 145), attract J. B. Beer, *The Achievement of E. M. Forster* (1962).

12. E. M. Forster, 'The Machine Stops', in *Collected Short Stories* (1947), 140–1. This has become a paradigm of the computerised city of the future. It has been recently reprinted, together with ten similar stories in, Damon Knight (ed.) *Cities of Wonder* (New York, 1966). In this, two other British stories, James Ballard's 'Billenium', and Brian Aldiss's 'The Underprivileged', appear together with the Macaulayesque fantasy of Stephen Vincent Benét, 'By the Waters of Babylon', which tells the story of a future exploration of the ruins of New York.

13. *Ibid.*, 157.

14. Forster confessed to a strong temperamental affinity with Butler—see his talk on 'The Legacy of Samuel Butler', in *The Listener*, XLVII, 12th June 1952, 955 ff.

15. E. M. Forster, *Goldsworthy Lowes Dickinson* (1934), 167.

16. Frederick Gutherm, *Frank Lloyd Wright on Architecture. Selected Writings (1894–1940)*, (New York, 1941), 67. Ashbee visited Wright in 1908 and again in 1918 (p. 85).

17. *Ibid.*, 101. Written in 1927.

18. *Ibid.*, 169.

19. Frank Lloyd Wright, *The Future of Architecture* (New York, 1963), 21.

20. *Ibid.*, 306.

21. Alice Mary Hadfield, *An Introduction to Charles Williams* (1959), 126.

22. Charles Williams, *Arthurian Torso* (1942).

23. Desirée Hirst, *Hidden Riches: Traditional Symbolism from the Renaissance to Blake* (1964), 308.

24. In *Another Time* (1940).

25. Monroe K. Spears, *The Poetry of W. H. Auden* (1963), 184.

26. *Ibid.*, 211.

27. Rex Warner, *The Wild Goose Chase* (1937). Reprinted in uniform edition 1947, 116.

28. *Ibid.*, 80–2.

29. *Ibid.*, 386.

30. Aldous Huxley, *Brave New World* (1932), 30.

31. *Ibid.*, 184.

32. Preface to 1946 edition.

Huxley's concept of a future society can be seen in *Chrome Yellow* (1922) and in other writings to 1931. John Atkins, *Aldous Huxley* (1956), 212–16; Rudolf B. Schmerl, 'The Two Future Worlds of Aldous Huxley', *P.M.L.A.*, LXXVII (1962), 330. He seems also to have been influenced by D. H. Lawrence, the first edition of whose letters he edited, for he also drew him as Mark Rampion in *Point Counter Point*. Lawrence had at one time considered founding a community, it never materialised, and Lawrence went to Australia and Mexico. Huxley stayed at home, joining in 1931 an organisation known as P.E.P. (Political and Economic Planning), but resigning soon afterwards to write *Brave New World* (1932). As Huxley said in the preface: 'All things considered, it looks as though Utopia were far closer to us than anyone, only fifteen years ago, could have imagined. Then, I projected it six hundred years into the future. Today it seems quite possible that the horror may be upon us within a single century.'

33. Aldous Huxley, *The Perennial Philosophy* (1946), 231 ff. Huxley inspired others like John Kendall (a pseudonym for Margaret Maud Brash, an author of numerous other novels), to write *Unborn Tomorrow* (1933) and John Palmer to write *Hesperides* (1936). The World State of 1995, as visualised in John Kendal's *Unborn Tomorrow* was organised from Moscow. After a great world war—in 1938—an economic collapse and an epidemic, the Slav State of the United World spreads, controlling breeding, reading, and behaviour by the most scientific means. But one scientist, Hayek, a Grade II man, is human enough to lose his temper and his heart. He falls in love with an undergraduate. They meet secretly, in the ruins of an old town, where they find an old man tending his wife's grave and worships in the old church. He awakens them to their bondage to the state—for Hayek was not allowed to breed, being of tubercular stock. As a punishment for his anti-social behaviour, Hayek becomes the subject of scientific experiments by the Slav biologist Kale, who is also in love with the heroine. After many adventures the hero and heroine escape to a game reserve in the Lake District where they find other refugees from the world state and beget five children. A satiric picture of the industrial centre Menin (on the planet Hesperus and reached by a time machine), was given by John Palmer in *Hesperides* (1936). Its seven echelons of citizen—administrators; technical experts; teachers; technicians; engineers; architects and economists; foremen; clerks and manual labourers —all have grades of initiative, the rest are servile. All live such functional lives that mere conversation between the sexes (as opposed to mating), has to take place in Houses of the Red Pennon. Leisure is unknown, since everyone works on shifts. The races of the interior, kept servile by control of their supply of water, revolt. Admitted to the 'benefits' of the constitution they still have to learn how to live.

34. Aldous Huxley, *Ape and Essence* (New York, 1948).

35. See W. H. Auden, *The Enchafed Flood: or, the Romantic Iconography of the Sea* (1951).

36. C. B. Cox, 'Lord of the Flies', *The Critical Quarterly*, 11 (1960), 112–17, considers it to be probably the most important novel to be published in England in the 1950s, and details two levels in the story: one, how intelligence and commonsense will always be overthrown by sadism and the lure of totalitarianism; the other, the power of original sin.

37. Frank Kermode, 'William Golding', in *Puzzles and Epiphanies* (1962), 205.

38. William Golding, *Lord of the Flies* (1954), Penguin edn., 1960.

39. Robert Graves, *Seven Days in New Crete* (1949).

40. Robert Graves, 'Nine Hundred Iron Chariots', in *Mammon and the Black Goddess* (1965), 51.

Earlier, in his poem 'Virgil the Sorcerer', Graves claimed that only poetry can release men from captivity. Virgil, wrongly imprisoned, draws a ship on the walls of the cell and urges his fellow captives (who gazed at him 'in a quick despair, knowing him mad; yet gently humoured him') to bring sticks for oars. 'They brought them at his call "up then and row!"'. They stepped from solid ground'. Graves believed that 'what Virgil did can yet be again done', as 'Poetry is a spell of furious power'.

Graves saw his age as Alexandrine and decadent, 'the square-headed merchants of practical parts' have deserted the old religion.

> *We serve a lost cause! does any pride remain*
> *In prolonging tradition beyond its due time,*
> *Morning and evening our ancient bells chime,*
> *Yet the whole congregation could sit in one pew,*
> *The sexton, the verger, and old folk one or two*

9 VIRGILS OF THE DYNAMO

1. M. DeWolfe Howe (ed.), *Holmes-Laski Letters* (1953), ii, 103.

2. Brooks Adams, *The Law of Civilisation and Decay* (1896), ed. Charles A. Beard, New York, Vintage Books, XI.

3. C. W. Ford, *Letters of Henry Adams 1892–1918* (1938), 301.

4. Max I. Baym, *The French Education of Henry Adams* (New York, 1951), 51.

5. Edmund Wilson, *The American Earthquake* (New York, 1958) and Frederick J. Hoffman, *The 20's* (New York, 1962), 225–243; L. Moholy-Nagy, *Von Material zu Architektus* (1929), trans. as *The New Vision. Documents of Modern Art*, iii (1949).

6. Rice also wrote a Utopian novel, *A Voyage to Purilia* (1930).

7. Barrett H. Clark, *Eugene O'Neill* (1947), 120.

8. Howard Scott in *The North West Technocrat*, XXVIII, No. 220 (1965), 13.

9. Sam Moskowitz, *Explorers of the Infinite. Shapers of Science Fiction* (1963), 116–17.

10. Howard Scott, *op. cit.*, who calls him Gernsbeck.

11. Sam Moskowitz, *Seekers of Tomorrow* (Cleveland World Publishing Company, 1966), 358.

12. Henry Elsner, Jr., *The Technocrats: Prophets of Automation* (Syracuse, 1967), 37, and Luther Whiteman and Samuel L. Lewis, *Glory Roads: The Psychological State of California* (New York, 1936).

13. Sam Moskowitz, *The Immortal Storm: A History of Science Fiction Fandom* (Atlanta, 1954). The English equivalent was *Science Fiction*; *Explorers of the Infinite: Shapers of Science Fiction* (1957); Robert Bloch (ed. Earl Kemp), *The Eighth Stage of Fandom* (Chicago, 1962). In a 'way of life' Bloch sketched a fan-oriented political and social system (*Fantastic Universe*, Oct. 1956). He believes that fanzines are the 'only remaining outlet for a free exchange of personal opinion in America'. There were 20 fanzines in the U.S.A. in 1967 according to Lin Carter, 'Fan Clubs U.S.A.' in *Worlds of If*, XVI, No. 6, Issue 103, (April 1967), 51–55.

14. Here the pioneer seems to have been Walter H. Gillings with his *Tales of Wonder* (1937) and *Science Fantasy Review* followed by *Science Fantasy* (1950); *Science Fiction* (London, 1939, printed in the U.S.A.); *Science Fiction Fort-*

nightly, February 1951, which became *Authentic Science Fiction*, 1952; *Science Fiction Adventures*, 1958. *Science Fantasy* (which became *Impulse* in March 1966) and *New Worlds* (which celebrated its 150th number in May 1965) are the two post-war British monthlies. The British Science Fiction Association also issues *Tangent*. See also Walter Gillins, 'The Glamorous Dreamers: The Story of British Science Fiction Fandom', *The New Futurian*, 1, 4–6; No. 2, 2–8; No. 3, 4–8; No. 4, 4–8; No. 5, 4–8 (Leeds 1954–5).

15. E.g. *The Futurian*, The Bulletin of the Leeds Science Fiction League began in 1937. Others like *Triode* (Cheltenham), *B.E.M.* (Bradford), followed. Most of these were cyclostyled ventures. After the Second World War such journals increased. *Zenith Speculation* (Birmingham) and *S.F. Horizons* (Sunningdale) leap to mind in 1966, as well as *Vector*, the journal of the British Science Fiction Association.

16. Aidan Reynolds and William Charlton, *Arthur Machen* (1963), 73.

17. E.g. E. S. Strauss, *The Blackdex* (Cambridge, Mass., 1965). An index, compiled on a computer, of stories in the eight leading science-fiction magazines from 1951–64.

18. I. Asimov (ed.), *The Hugo Winners* (1962).

19. J. Campbell, *Astounding Science Fiction*, July 1949, 4.

20. S. Finer, 'A Profile of Science Fiction', *Sociological Review* N.S., ii, (1954), 240–1.

21. *Ibid.*, 243.

22. *New Worlds S.F.*, Vol. 47, April 1964, No. 141.

23. James A. Harrison, *The Complete Works of Edgar Allen Poe* (New York, 1902), VI, 208–9, 212–13. Burton R. Pollin, 'Poe and Godwin', *Nineteenth Century Fiction*, XX (1965), 252–3; Patrick F. Quinn, *The French Face of Edgar Allen Poe* (Carbondale, Illinois, 1953).

24. Hesketh Pearson, *Conan Doyle* (1943), 1964 edition p. 176, cites Doyle as saying that Professor Challenger 'has always amused me more than any other I have invented'.

25. William E. Harkins, *Karel Căpek* (New York, 1962), 52.

26. Karel Căpek, 'The Meaning of R.U.R.', *Saturday Review*, CXXXVI (1923), 79.

27. B. R. Bradbrook, 'Letters to England from Karel Căpek', *Slavonic and East European Review*, XXXIX (1960), 65.

28. Harkins, *op. cit.*, 96.

29. Sam Moskowitz, 'John Wyndham', *Amazing Stories*, XXXVIII, June 1964, 33.

30. G. K. Chesterton, quoted A. E. Murch, *The Development of the Detective Novel* (1958), 10. See also W. H. Auden, *The Dyer's Hand* (1963).

31. Warren French, 'The Cowboy in the Dime Novel', University of Texas, *Studies in English*, XXX (1951), 219–34; Don Russell, *The Lives and Legends of Buffalo Bill* (Norman, Oklahoma, 1960).

32. Sam Moskowitz, 'The Saga of "Skylark" Smith', *Amazing Stories*, XXXVIII (April 1964), 52–65.

33. Isaac Asimov, *The End of Eternity* (1955), Chapter 1.

34. *The Naked Sun* (1957), Chapters 10 and 12. Because of his many parables, Isaac Asimov almost qualifies as the Homer of the automated

state, the Moses of the Robots. As the robot psychologist remarks in his short story *Evidence*, 'I like robots. I like them considerably better than I do human beings. If a robot can be created capable of being a civil executive, I think he'd make the best one possible. By the Laws of Robotics, he'd be incapable of harming humans, incapable of tyranny, of corruption, of stupidity of prejudice.' For Asimov's theory is that by following the Rules of Robotics, one may be a robot, but one can also be a very good man. For Rule one is that he's to risk his life to save another; Rule two that he's to defer to proper authority—doctor, psychiatrist, and follow rules even when they interfere with his comfort or safety; Rule three that he must have the instinct of self preservation. See W. F. Nolan (ed.) *Pseudo-People* (1967), 109 and 99.

35. A. Koestler, *The Trail of the Dinosaur* (1955), 147.

36. L. Sprague de Camp, *Lost Continents: The Atlantis Theme in Literature, Science and Adventure* (New York, 1954).

37. Preface to Robert Heinlein, *The Man who Sold the Moon* (1955 Pan Edition). This book, originally published in 1950, together with its successors *The Green Hills of Earth* (1951), *Revolt in 2100* (1953), and *Methuselah's Children* (1958), have been gathered together and republished as *The Past Through Tomorrow* (New York, 1966), which also gives his 'time chart' of the future on pp. 530–1. See also Chapter 11 note 41.

38. James Blish, *They Shall Have Stars* (1956), 173. Blish's preoccupation with theology is also visible in *A Case of Conscience* (1958), which shows the moral dilemma posed by a paradise free from original sin—Lithia—for a Jesuit biologist, Father Ruiz-Sanchez.

39. John W. Campbell (ed.), *Analog Anthology* (1964), intro.

40. Pat Williams, 'The Man Who Drives Minds to the End of their Tether', *Sunday Times Magazine*, 3rd October 1965.

41. H. Meyer, 'On the Heuristic Value of Scientific Models', *Philosophy of Science*, XVIII (1951), 114.

42. R. L. Schanck, *The Permanent Revolution in Science* (New York, 1954), Hans Vaihinger, *The Philosophy of 'As If'*, translated by C. K. Ogden (1925); O. Shaftel, 'The Social Content of Science Fiction', *Science and Society*, Spring 1953; S. Spriel, 'Sur la Science-Fiction', *Esprit*, May 1953; Basil Davenport, *Inquiry into Science Fiction* (1955).

43. R. P. Mills (ed.), *A Decade of Fantasy and Science Fiction* (1963), 9–32.

44. Ray Bradbury, *The Silver Locusts* (1951), 105.

45. Clifton Fadiman's introduction to *The Silver Locusts* (Corgi Edition, 1965), x.

46. Clifford Simak, *Time is the Simplest Thing* (1961), 114.

47. *Ibid.*, 180.

48. *Ibid.*, 190.

49. Polak, *op. cit.*, 27.

50. Brian W. Aldiss (ed.). *Introducing S.F. A Science Fiction Anthology* (1964), 10–11. Frederick Pohl and C. M. Kornbluth show more cynically in *The Space Merchants* (1953) a world run by business men with modern conveniences. More fancifully, and elegantly, Ray Bradbury's wry story of a book-burning fireman's slow awakening to the accidie of universal earhole

radios and four-way television in *Fahrenheit 451* (1954) warns readers against the electronic coma into which they may fall. The question is re-posed in *The Case Against Tomorrow* (1956) in which Frederick Pohl tells the story of The Midas Plague—Everyone works so hard to consume his share that no one gets any pleasure. Therefore robots have to be built to help them consume, just as earlier robots were built to help them produce.

51. J. Isaacs, 'The Nature and Function of Phantasy', *Analysis*, XXIX (1948), 73–97.

52. For a study of whom see Richard Gordon, 'Russell. An Evaluation', *Zenith Speculation*, I (1966), No. 11, 4–9.

53. See an account of this movement in the *Daily Mail*, 14th February, 1966. Science 'cults' are not new. In 1818 John Cleves Symmes, an American Army Chaplain, sent a letter to, amongst others, all members of Congress outlining a number of solid, concentrick spheres; one within the other, and it is open at the poles twelve or sixteen degrees. For the next eleven years Symmers lectured on his theory and was even offered a place on a Russian governmental expedition to Siberia: 'Captain Adam Seaborn' claimed in a satirical novel, *Symzonia*, to have made a trip through the interior. Edgar Allan Poe's *Arthur Gordon Pym*, though unfinished, was working up to a similar voyage. Forty years after Symmes died, W. F. Lyons' *A Hollow Globe* (1868), continued the illusion.

A second fantasy more geared to the future was outlined by Cyrus Reed Teed in 1869. He saw the world as the inside of a rocky shell some 1,000 miles thick. He founded a colony of the Koreshans—as his cult was called—in Florida. He supplemented geodesy by prophecy. In *The Great Red Dragon* (1909), written under the pseudonym of Lord Chester, he described how the Japanese, having destroyed the U.S. navy, invaded the United States, only to be destroyed by a Koreshan Air Force.

A third fantasy was put forward in 1913 by Austrian engineers, Hans Hörbiger and Philipp Fauth. They maintained that the Star Mother—300 million times bigger than the Sun—was struck by a dead star—4,000 times bigger than the Sun. The frozen dead star penetrated the Star Mother, and then exploded creating our present solar system with its planets. These planets, they predicted, will ultimately be swallowed up by the sun just as Earth has swallowed up five small ones. The largest of these, Lura, was swallowed 12,000 years ago, and caused a major flood, which drowned Atlantis.

A fourth, that of Orgonomy or the Religion of Energy was developed by William Reich. To him, modern man was imprisoned by 'The Trap' and 'Armoured' by repressions. He advocated experimental sex in adolescence to divest parents of their authority and train a new generation for freedom. As a Freudo-Marxist, excluded from the international psychoanalytic movement in 1933, he looked for 'genital characters' or new men, and as a result of work in his therapeutic community at Rangeley, Maine, he devised his theory of cosmic orgone energy based on the genital embrace (orgasm). This acquired, in his mind, a cosmic significance: matter embraced and created more matter. Thus the science of Orgonomy *unified* physics, biology, and morals instead of separating them. Every new galaxy or astronomical discovery was incorporated into it. His *Orgone Energy Bulletin* and his book *The Sexual*

Revolution (1936) show that he had converted Henry Adams' dream into a nightmare. Orgone energy could become deadly if the mechanistically-minded scientists in the pay of politicians had their way, so he transformed himself into a Cosmic Orgone Engineer, making fertility devices and combating people from other worlds who were themselves Orgone Engineers. These aliens, 'CURE' men he called them in 1954, were visiting earth because they were concerned about the far-reaching effects of atomic energy explosions on their own planets. He believed their intentions were benign and that they were impelling us towards health and good sense. He was soon afterwards imprisoned for selling Orgone Energy Accumulators and died in prison in 1957.

54. Alfred Korzybski, *Manhood of Humanity* (1921) (2nd edition 1950, Lakeville, Connecticut), 143–5.

55. Pierre Teilhard de Chardin, *The Future of Man*, translated by Norman Denny (1964), 82, 267, 296.

56. John Betjeman, *New Bats in Old Belfries* (1945).

57. Sir G. H. Knibbs, *The Shadow of the World's Failure* (1928), 5–6.

58. *Ibid.*, 122.

59. A. L. Pullar, *Celestalia. A Fantasy A.D. 1975* (1933), 64.

60. *Ibid.*, 241.

10 SECTARIAN SCIENTISM

1. K. E. Harper and B. A. Booth, 'Russian Translations of 19th Century English Fiction', *Nineteenth Century Fiction*, VIII (1953–4), 158 and 197

2. K. E. Tsiolkovsky, 'Beyond the Atmosphere: A 1923 Essay', *Spaceflight*, 9 (1967), 9–11; *Beyond the Planet Earth* (1960).

3. Robert Milch, 'Science Fiction in Russia Today', *Riverside Quarterly*, ii (1966), 175–6. See also Don K. Price, *The Scientific Estate* (Cambridge, Mass., 1962), 6, Peter Yershov, *Science Fiction and Utopian Fantasy in Soviet Literature* (New York, 1954), and Rufus W. Mathewson Jr., *The Positive Hero in Russian Literature* (New York, 1958), 203.

4. Nonna D. Shaw, 'The Only Soviet Literary Peasant Utopia', *Slavic and East European Journal*, VII (1963), 279–89.

5. Written in 1920, it was translated into English (1924), Czech (1927), and French (1928). The novel appeared in 1929, and the first English translation published in 1924. Translations in B. Guerney *Anthology of Soviet Stories* (New York, 1959) and by G. Zilboorg, *We* (New York, 1959). See also D. J. Richards, *Zamyatin, a Soviet Heretic* (1962), and Christopher Collins 'Zamyatin, Wells and the Utopian Literary Tradition', *The Slavonic and East European Review*, XLIV (1966), 351–60.

'The first novel of literary importance to present a relatively complete vision of the negative results of the realisation of Utopia'. George Woodcock, *The Crystal Spirit. A Study of George Orwell* (London, 1967), 170, who also (*167*) insists that Huxley 'borrowed copiously' from it.

6. Vladimir Mayakovsky, *The Bedbug and Selected Poetry*, translated by Max Haywood and George Reavey, ed. Patricia Blake (1961). Earlier in 1912 he had written, 'We alone are the *Face of our Time*. Time's trumpet blares in our

art of words. The past is stifling. . . . Throw Pushkin, Dostoevsky, Tolstoy, etc., overboard.'

7. B. Russell, *The Impact of Science on Society* (1952). See also his *Icarus or the Future of Science, The Prospects of Industrial Civilisation, Freedom and Organisation, 1814–1914* (1934). *The Scientific Outlook* (1931), discusses the future of societies managed by a scientifically minded bureaucracy.

8. B. and D. Russell, *The Prospects of Industrial Civilisation* (1923), 267.

9. Alan Wood, *Bertrand Russell. The Passionate Sceptic* (1957), 131.

10. J. B. S. Haldane, *Possible Worlds* (1927), 310–11. His and his wife's views, together with those of some other scientists of the inter-war years, are explored in Neal Wood, *Communism and British Intellectuals* (1959), 121–51.

11. An élite of 'intellectuals' ruling over normals by the twenty-second century was envisaged in the same year by M. Jacquer in *The Question Mark* (1926).

12. J. D. Bernal, *The World, the Flesh and the Devil: An Inquiry into the Future of Three Enemies of the Rational Soul* (1929), 94–5.

13. *Ibid.*, 53. Ten years later in *The Social Functions of Science* Bernal modified his ideas. Reporting on the visit in July 1931 of a Russian delegation consisting of Bukharin, Joffe, Vavilov, Hessen, and Rubinstein amongst others, to the Second International Conference of the History of Science and Technology, he described it as 'the most important meeting of ideas that has occurred since the revolution', and commented:

> 'just as the growing free thought of English Dissent in the eighteenth century had been frightened into emotional Methodism by the French Revolution, so the mechanistic Darwinism of the triumphant capitalism of the nineteenth century was being frightened by the growing strength of the Soviet Union into the popular scientific mysticism of Jeans and Eddington, of J. S. Haldane and Julian Huxley.'

Bernal also posed the problem as to whether it was 'better to be intellectually free but socially totally ineffective' or 'to become a component part of a system where knowledge and action are joined for one common social purpose'.

Whilst shrinking from Bernal's rigorous scientism, many of his professional colleagues were, nevertheless, impressed by the appearance in England of the redoubtable Russian dialectical materialist Bukharin, and by the rapid publication of the delegation's contributions in *Science at the Cross Roads* (1931), with its challenging presentation of the 'entirely new phenomenon' in the Soviet Union of 'the collective organisation of scientific research planned on the scale of an enormous country'. *The Spectator*, July 1931, reprinted J. D. Bernal, *The Freedom of Necessity* (1949), 336.

14. Olaf Stapledon, *Last and First Men. A Story of the Near and Far Future* 1930, Penguin edition, 1963), 15; Richard Gerber, *Utopian Fantasy* (1955), describes *Last and First Men* as 'probably the only fully developed evolutionary Utopia, and . . . by far the most ambitious and sustained attempt to create an "evolutionary bible" '.

15. Olaf Stapledon thought that Wells's humanistic idea was trivial, his view of human nature superficial, and that he had not realised the full implica-

tions of it. He himself was influenced by G. Duhamel, *Scènes de la Vie Future* (1931). It is significant that Stapledon was educated at Abbotsholme School (founded by the Utopian Fellowship of the New Life), and at Balliol College, Oxford. He worked in a shipping office in Liverpool and took his Ph.D. at the local university, and acknowledged: 'Science, though I lacked scientific training, was first a sort of gospel, and later something the fundamental principles of which must be carefully criticised. It took me a long time to realise both its true value and its mischief,' *Saturday Review of Literature*, 18th July 1936, quoted S. J. Kunitz and Howard Haycroft, *Twentieth Century Authors* (1956), 1325.

16. *Last and First Men* (Penguin edition, 1963), 226.

17. *Ibid.*, 252.

18. *Ibid.*, 277–80.

19. *Ibid.*, 303.

20. *Ibid.*, 316. H. G. Wells was much influenced by this, e.g. *Star-Begotten* (1937), 81.

21. C. S. Lewis, *The Abolition of Man* (1944), 19–20. I owe this reference to Professor John Lawlor of Keele.

22. C. S. Lewis, *Out of the Silent Planet* (1938, Pan edition, 1962), 120.

23. *Ibid.*, 160–1.

24. C. S. Lewis, *That Hideous Strength* (1945, Pan edition, 1955), 23.

25. *Ibid.*, 26–7.

26. *Ibid.*, 109.

27. *Ibid.*, 243.

28. *Ibid.*, 157.

29. J. B. S. Haldane, *Everything has a History* (1951), 252.

30. *Ibid.*, 263.

31. In Gordon Wolstenholme (ed.), *Man and His Future* (1963), 337–61.

32. Bertrand Russell, *Nightmares of Eminent Persons* (1954).

33. 'Second Thoughts on James Burnham', in *Collected Essays* (1961), 572–6.

34. E.g. his essay 'Politics versus Literature', *ibid.* (1950).

35. George Orwell, *Collected Essays* (1961), 164.

36. George Orwell, *The Road to Wigan Pier* (1937).

37. *Collected Essays* (1961), 353.

38. *Animal Farm* (1945).

39. George Orwell, *Nineteen Eighty Four* (1949, Penguin Book edition, 1962), 214.

40. *Ibid.*, 51.

41. This argument for 'behavioural engineering' was put forward by Professor B. F. Skinner, a professor at Harvard, and he endows the 'reporter' of the experiment—Burris—with a version of his own first name. The name of the experimental community, Walden Two, was chosen:

in honour of Thoreau's experiment, which was in many ways like our own. It was an experiment in living, and it sprang from a similar doctrine of our relation to the State. Several ambiguities in the name amused us. Thoreau's was not only the first of the Waldens, it was an experiment with *one* life, and social questions were neglected. Our problem was to build a 'Walden for Two'. There's also a pun on t-double-o- 'All this and Walden too'. B. F. Skinner, *Walden Two* (1948), 185.

Frazier protested that to 'get away from life as we know it, either in space or time' was the first rule of the Utopian romance, and insisted: 'The one fact that I would cry from every housetop is this: the Good Life is waiting for us —here and now!' (*Ibid.*, 160–1). 'We can,' he said '*make* men adequate for group living—to the satisfaction of everybody. We look ahead, not backwards, for a better version . . . No industrialist ever strove harder to get rid of an unnecessary worker. The difference is, we get rid of the work, not the worker.' (*Ibid.*, 61.)

42. *Ibid.*, 247.

43. Augustine Castle, who had 'once given a course in the Utopias from Plato and More and Bacon's *New Atlantis* down to *Looking Backward* and even Shangri-La', and is 'the grand inquisitor', comes with a party consisting of Burris, two ex-servicemen, and their girl-friends, to see Walden Two. They find its only government to be a board of Six Planners—three men, three women—serving for ten years, allowed only two labour credits per day for their pains. They had to earn two more credits per day, one in straight physical labour. New planners were selected by the Board from names submitted by the Specialist Managers of Food, Health, Play, Arts, Dentistry, Supply, Labour, Nursery School, Advanced Education, and various industries. As trained and tested personnel, appointed on ability, they have, as helpers, Scientists, who receive the same labour credits as the managers—two or three hours a day—for conducting research in plant and animal breeding, infant behaviour, educational processes, and the use of raw material. None of these three groups was a 'leisure class' since all had to engage in manual work as well so that the problems of the 'big-muscle user' would be forgotten. The rest of the community work four hours a day, and if they happen to be writers or to work on anything which sold in the outside world, the money so earned went to the community.

44. *Ibid.*, 196.

45. *Ibid.*, 211–12.

46. As in a beehive, behavioural engineering begins with the birth of every child, by the elimination of all spurious motives—fear of one's family, honours, and snob value. The natural motivating force of babies—exploration—was reinforced by housing them in air-conditioned cubicles where a tune, a pattern of lights or some similar reward could be obtained by pulling a ring.

'It's possible to build up fantastically perseverative behaviour without encountering frustration or rage,' said Frazier. 'We appeal to that drive to control the environment which makes a baby continue to crumple a piece of noisy paper and the scientist continue to press forward with his predictive analyses of nature.' B. F. Skinner, *Walden Two* (1948), 102.

Since the interests, school records, and health of the husband and wife have already been examined by the Manager of Marriages before the parents marry, children escape being born with the more obvious physical handicaps. With such 'reinforcement-training' to keep them happy, energetic, and curious, teaching can be cut to a minimum, since 'education' takes place in workshops, laboratories, and fields.

'Many of our children,' continued Frazier, 'naturally study more and more advanced material as they grow older. We help them in every way short of teaching them. We give them new techniques of acquiring knowledge and thinking . . . an excellent survey of the methods and techniques of thinking, taken from logic, statistics, scientific method, psychology and mathematics. That's all the 'college education' they need. They get the rest by themselves in libraries and laboratories.'

One library so absorbed Professor Burris that he 'forgot his mission to ferret out signs of psychological insufficiency'. The technical books, formularies and so on, apparently for the use of the various managers and applied scientists, were quite new to him 'having supposed that that sort of knowledge existed only in the heads of craftsmen, who imparted it to apprentices'. The laboratories were the slaughter house, the field, the dairy and poultry house, the medical centre and the kitchen.

'Happiness,' says Frazier, 'is our first goal, but an alert and active drive towards the future is our second. We'll settle for the degree of happiness which has been achieved in other communities or cultures, but will be satisfied with nothing short of the most alert and active group-intelligence yet to appear on the face of the earth.'
'The science of behaviour,' he continues, 'is the science of science—a special discipline concerned with talking about talking and knowing about knowing. . . . Science in general emerged from a competitive culture. Most scientists are still inspired by competition or at least supported by those who are. But when you come to apply the methods of science to the special study of human behaviour, the competitive spirit commits suicide. It discovers the extraordinary fact that in order to survive, we must in the last analysis *not* compete.' (*Ibid.*, 248.)

So effective had Walden Two become that Waldens Three, Four and Five were patterned after it. So big did they grow that Walden Six was founded from it some seventy miles away. The hiving-off process took place vertically: Assistant Managers in Walden Two becoming Managers of Walden Six and even the Board of Planners sub-dividing:

'Suppose it's possible to grow and sub-divide once every two years,' Frazier continued, 'then in ten years Waldens Two and Six will give birth to some sixty odd communities. . . . In *thirty* years,' he continued with increasing determination, 'we could absorb the whole country many times over.'

The prospect was so frightening that an Office of Information was set up, not to create, but to control publicity. No one person could set up another Walden since he couldn't pass along the technical information and skill needed in all the departments:

'As the science of behavioural engineering advances,' continued Frazier, 'less and less is left to personal judgment. More training and apprenticeships are needed. At present we must proceed carefully and train a complete crew of competent managers for each new Walden.' (*Ibid.*, 191.)

47. George R. Stewart, *Earth Abides* (1950, Corgi edition, 1965), 157.

48. E. C. Large, *Dawn in Andromeda* (1956), 265–79. A similar theme—a small community based on a sharing of specialised knowledge, with external constraint replaced by self-discipline and mutual dependence—characterises the work of Simone Weil who tried to replace Marxism by a more intelligible theory of social change. See her *Oppression et Liberté* (Paris, 1955). Translated by Arthur Wiles and John Petrie as *Oppression and Liberty* (1957), and Roy Pierce, 'Sociology and Utopia: The Early Writings of Simone Weil', *Political Science Quarterly*, LXXVII, 1962, 505–23.

49. Ivan Yefremov, *Andromeda: A Space Age Tale* (translated by George Hanna) (Moscow, 1960), 336.

50. *Ibid.*, 62, 236. Thirty years later J. D. Bernal was insisting (p. 228) 'The need for conscious foresight is now becoming really important in a way in which it never was in the past.' In *World Without War* (1958, 2nd ed. 1961). ('not a Utopia or even science-fiction' p. 266) he writes 'the more we have of people, the better'—on condition that 'everyone has the fullest possibility of developing under the best conditions' (p. 278). To him the possibility of thinking together as well as by ourselves would transform mankind and he wrote:

It is by no means impossible that man may succeed, by a combination of electronic devices reacting with brain cells, in communicating thoughts directly from one mind to another, without the use of language. This would probably mean that not only thoughts but also emotions and memories could be transmitted with the vividness of actual experience. Such a method of communication would enlarge immensely, in content and immediacy, the picture and the book. It would permit mankind to pass on from generation to generation the essentials of personal contributions and not only a few relics which is all we can do now. It is not only for this perhaps pious purpose of preserving the best in every human spirit that we wish to be able to improve the immediate quality of our communication. Perhaps this is the least of reasons, because if we could improve that quality of communication it would alter the whole pattern of social co-operation. Even now we realize that for reasons deep laid in history and custom we manage to co-operate with each other extremely badly on the whole, hence indeed come many of the troubles of our time. (pp. 280–1.)

51. 'Soviet and Other Science Fiction', *Time Literary Supplement*, 2nd March 1967.

52. D. K. Price, *The Scientific Estate* (Cambridge, Mass., 1955).

53. Isaac Asimov (ed.) *Soviet Science Fiction* (New York, 1962) and *More Soviet Science Fiction* (New York, 1962); Robert Magidoff, *Russian Science Fiction* (New York, 1964); as well as *Destination Amalthea* and *A Visitor from Outer Space* (Foreign Languages Publishing House, Moscow).

54. *Times Literary Supplement*, 2nd March 1967, 172.

55. Alexander S. Balinky, 'The Proclaimed Emergence of Communism in the USSR' in Harry G. Shaffer (ed.) *The Soviet Economy* (1964), 107.

56. See K. R. Popper in *British Journal of the Philosophy of Science* (1950), 117 ff., 173 ff.

57. Karl Popper, *The Poverty of Historicism* (1961), 141.

II SURMISING FORUMS

1. J. G. Crowther, *The Social Relations of Science* (1942), 575.

2. *Lancet*, 2nd January 1966.

3. Fairfield Osborn, *Our Plundered Planet* (1948); and *The Limits of the Earth* (1953); William Vogt, *The Road to Survival* (1948); Roderick Seidenberg, *Post Historic Man* (1950); E. P. Hanson, *New Worlds Emerging* (1951); J. Rosin and M. Eastman, *The Road to Abundance* (1953); Harrison Brown, *The Challenge of Man's Future* (1954); Marston Bates, *The Prevalence of People* (1955); Richard L. Meier, *Science and Economic Development* (1956); William L. Thomas (Jr.), *Man's Role in Changing the Face of the Earth* (1956); J. Murray Luck, 'Man against his environment. The Next Hundred Years', *Science*, CXXVI, 1957, 903–7; 'The Futurists: Looking Toward A.D. 2000', *Time*, 25th February 1966, 22–3; Margaret Mead, 'Towards more Vivid Utopias', *Science*, CXXVI, 1957, 957–61. 'Forecasting the Future', *Science Journal* 3, No. 10, Oct. 1967. 'Towards the year 2000: work in progress', *Daedalus* vol. 96, No. 3 (1967).

4. Reprinted in Morton Grodzins and Eugene Rabinowitch, *The Atomic Age. Scientists in National and World Affairs* (1963), 47–52, 177; Harrison Brown, James Bonner, and John Weir, *The Next Hundred Years* (1957), 7.

5. Herman Kahn, *On Thermonuclear War* (1960), 9.

6. *Ibid.*, X.

7. *Op. cit.*, 525.

8. *Ibid.*, p. 586. See also p. 568 where he wrote:

I believe that in any world short of Utopia—and I am not willing to include in this term worlds greatly improved over our current one—we will have an important and expensive national security problem . . . it is a combination of irresponsibility and wishful thinking to look to large cutbacks in the national security programme.

9. Max Lerner, *The Age of Overkill* (1962), 27.

10. H. A. Simon, *The Shape of Automation for Men and Management* (1965), XV, 96; *The New Science of Management Decision* (1960), 27.

11. Ronald Brech, *Britain 1984: A Report Prepared for Unilever* (1963), 39–40.

12. Ronald N. Michael, *Cybernation. The Silent Conquest* in Andrew Hacker (ed.), *The Corporation Take-over* (1964), 193, 220–1.

13. R. V. Chase, 'The Heard-Huxley Paradise', *Partisan Review*, March–April 1943.

14. C. H. Sisson, *An Asiatic Romance* (1953).

15. Geddes MacGregor, *From a Christian Ghetto: Letters of Ghostly wit A.D. 2453* (1964).

16. David Karp, *One* (1954), 54.

17. John Iggulden, *Breakthrough* (1960), Four Square Edition, 1963, 41.

18. Robert Heinlein, *Orphans of the Sky* (1963), Mayflower paperback edition, 1965, 18.

19. William Tenn, 'Null-P', in Kingsley Amis and Robert Conquest (ed.) *Spectrum: An Anthology of Science Fiction* (1964), 125–36.

20. Kurt Vonnegut, *Player Piano* (Mayflower edition, 1962).

21. For a critical treatment of Camus' interpretation of the myth of Prometheus see Richard H. Cox: 'Ideology, History and Political Philosophy: Albert Camus' *L'Homme Révolté*', *Social Research*, XXXII, 1965, 70–97.

22. A. Camus, *L'Homme Révolté* (Paris, 1951), 44. An English translation exists by Anthony Bower (1953).

23. C. M. Kornbluth and Frederik Pohl, *Wolfbane* (1959), 200–2.

24. Mircea Eliade, *Patterns in Comparative Religion*, translated by Rosemary Sheed (London, 1958), 407.

25. Kurt Vonnegut, 'Tomorrow and Tomorrow and Tomorrow', in Tom Boardman (ed.), *Connoisseurs S.F.* (1964), 65–6.

26. George R. Stewart, *Earth Abides* (1950).

27. Earlier in *Utopia 239* (1955) Rex Gordon describes father, daughter, and daughter's lover leapfrogging the imminent atomic holocaust by taking a voyage to the future in a metal cylinder. They land in one part of Britain that has not been devastated—a holiday camp in South West Devon that has become a true Utopian colony in a world deprived of coal and oil. It relies on corn to fight the all invading sand. The three time-travellers find it extremely difficult to adjust to the high degree of civilisation that was brought about by applied psychology.

28. Rex Gordon, *The Time Factor* (1965), 64–5, 69.

29. Groff Conklin (ed.), *Great Science Fiction by Scientists* (New York, 1962); Clifton Fadiman (ed.), *The Mathematical Magpie* (New York, 1962); Frederick Pohl, *The Expert Dreamer* (1962); a number of science-fiction authors use pseudonyms: Eric Blair (George Orwell); N. S. Norway (Nevil Shute); M. Foot (Cassius); J. B. Harris (John Wyndham); H. St. G. Saunders (J. L. Palmer F. Beeding); N. Bell (S. Southwold); R. B. Montgomery (E. Crispin); P. Wilding (J. R. Haynes); J. R. Fearn (V. Gredban, V. Statten, V. Magroon); F. S. Eldershaw and M. F. Barnard (M. B. Eldershaw); H. V. Yorke (H. Green); J. A. Vlasto (J. Remenham); V. Cory (V. Cross); D. McIlwain (C. Maine); E. H. Waldo (Theodore Sturgeon); W. F. Jenkins (Murray Leinster); H. C. Stubbs (H. Clement); H. Hart (P. Frank); F. C. Robertson (R. Crane); I. Asimov (P. French); J. W. Wall (Sarbon); John Taine (E. T. Bell). For criticism see 'Science in Science Fiction' by G. S. Robinson, W. T. Williams, D. M. A. Mercer, and A. R. Manser in *The Advancement of Science*, XXII (1965), 195–207.

30. Fred Hoyle, *Ossian's Ride* (1959), 250.

31. Leo Szilard, 'The Mark Gable Foundation', *The Voice of the Dolphins. Five Stories of Social and Political Satire* (New York, 1961). Szilard served the Metallurgical Laboratory of the Manhattan Project at Chicago as chief physicist, and subsequently became professor of physics at the University. He drafted the historic letters which Einstein sent to President Roosevelt in 1939 and 1945. Both appealed to the immediate future and both underestimated it. The 1939 appeal envisaged a single bomb 'carried by boat and

exploded in a port, might very well destroy the whole port together with some of the surrounding territory. . . . Such bombs might very well prove to be too heavy for transportation by air'. The 1945 appeal referred to the possibility of such bombs being 'smuggled into the United States for subsequent detonation'.

32. Fred Hoyle, *Man and Materialism* (1957), 149.

33. Henry Adams, *The Degradation of the Democratic Dogma* (1919, Putnam edition, New York, 1958), 277.

34. Ritchie Calder, *The Inheritors* (1961), 273–382.

35. Teilhard de Chardin, *The Phenomenon of Man* (1959), 183. This has in turn been criticised by P. B. Medawar in *The Art of the Soluble* (1967) for amongst other things its 'tipsy euphoric prose which is one of the more tiresome manifestations of the French spirit' (p. 72).

36. Daniel Callahan (ed.), *The Secular City Debate* (London, 1966), 202.

37. W. A. Visser, 't. Hooft, 'Humanising the Future', *The Listener*, LXXVII (1967), 397; Jurgen Moltmann (trans. J. W. Leitch), *Theology of Hope* (London, 1967).

38. Arthur C. Clarke, 'The Awakening', in *Reach for Tomorrow* (1963), 89–94.

39. A. Koestler, 'The Boredom of Fantasy', *The Trail of the Dinosaur* (1955), 45.

40. Charles Galton Darwin, *The Next Million Years* (1952), 124.

41. See Alexei Panshin 'Heinlein in Dimension', and 'The Execution', *The Riverside Quarterly* (Saskatoon, 1966), ii, 35–51 and 193–209; 'The Non Fiction of R. A. Heinlein', *Zenith Speculation*, i, No. 12 (1966), 4–10, and Heinlein in Dimension', *ibid.*, ii, 2–37.

42. Ayn Rand, *Anthem* (1946). His influence can be seen in Keith Laumer's *The Great Time Machine Hoax* (1965), where the hero oscillates through time at the instance of his great-grandfather's computer, rescuing two time-stranded computers and being the instrument for the ventilation of Ayn Rand-style lectures in the process.

43. James Joyce, *A Portrait of the Artist as a Young Man* (1928), 296.

44. James Joyce, *Ulysses* (1934), 682.

45. James Joyce, *Finnegan's Wake* (1955), 186.

46. *Paris Review*, Autumn 1965. See also Richard Kostelanetz, 'From Nightmare to Serendipity; A retrospective look at William Burroughs', *Twentieth Century Literature* II (1965), 123–30.

47. William Burroughs, 'The Hallucinatory Operators are Real', *S.F. Horizons*, 2 (1965), 6.

48. J. G. Ballard, Guest Editorial, *New Worlds*, No. 118.

49. J. G. Ballard, *The Drowned World* (1962, Penguin edition, 1965), 14.

50. *Ibid.*, 23.

51. Quoted Brian Aldiss, 'British Science Fiction Now', *S.F. Horizons*, 2 (1965), 31.

52. Aldous Huxley, *Island* (1962, Penguin edition, 1964), 59. Farnaby tells the doctor who tends him after climbing the cliff, 'Remember the beginning of *Erewhon*' (p. 22). See also 201.

53. *Ibid.*, 150.

54. *Ibid.*, 195.
55. *Ibid.*, 150.
56. *Ibid.*, 152.
57. *Ibid.*, 152.
58. *Ibid.*, 197.
59. *Ibid.*, 93.
60. *Ibid.*, 253, see also 99:

No Billy Grahams or Mao Tse-tungs or Madonnas of Fatima. No hells on earth and no Communist pie in the twenty-second century. Just men and women and their children trying to make the best of the here and now, instead of living somewhere else, as you people mostly do, in some other time, some other home-made imaginary universe.

61. F. le Gros Clark and N. W. Pirie, *Four Thousand Million Mouths: Scientific Humanism and the Shadow of World Hunger* (1951), 26.

62. United Nations, *The Future Growth of World Population* (1958); Notestein, Frank W., Irene B. Taeuber, Dudley Kirk, Ansley J. Coale, and Louise K. Kiser, *The Future Population of Europe and the Soviet Union* (1944); Calvert, G. N., *The Future Population of New Zealand* (1945); Pascal K. Whelpton, *Forecasts of the Population of the United States: 1945–1975* (U.S. Bureau of the Census, Washington, 1947); Royal Commission on Population, *Report*, H.M.S.O. (1949), 80–90. Frank W. Notestein *et al.*, *The Future Population of Europe and the Soviet Union* (Geneva, 1944), 199–211.

63. H. S. Pritchett, 'A Formula for Predicting the Population of the United States', *Transactions of the Academy of Science of St. Louis*, December 1890, p. 12; and 'The Population of the United States during the Next Ten Decades', *Popular Science Monthly*, LVIII (1900–1901), 49–53; J. J. Spengler, 'Population Prediction in Nineteenth-Century America', *American Sociological Review*, I (1936), 905–21; Harold F. Dorn, 'Pitfalls in Population Forecasts and Projections', *Journal of the American Statistical Association*, XLIV (1950), 311–34.

64. Gorden Wolstenholme, *Man and His Future* (1963), 1.

65. P. B. Medawar, *The Future of Man* (1960), 12, 97, and 102.

66. B. de Jouvenal, *L'Art de la conjecture* (Monaco, 1964). An English translation by Nikita Lary was published in 1967.

67. 'The Futurists, Looking Towards A.D. 2000', *Time*, 25th February 1966, 22–3.

68. Groff Conklin and Noah Fabricant (ed.), *Great Science Fiction About Doctors* (New York, 1963), 164.

69. *Ibid.*, 108.

70. A. C. Clarke, *Profiles of the Future* (1962, Pan edition, 1963), 7; see also his *Voices from the Sky* (1966) and *Time Probe: the Sciences in Science Fiction* (New York, 1966).

71. In a celebrated article in a British radio journal, *Wireless World*, October 1945.

72. In his first science-fiction novel *Prelude to Space* (1953) but written in 1947.

73. With the exception of *Islands in the Sky* (1952) there have followed since

then, at less than yearly intervals—*Prelude to Space, The Sands of Mars, Against the Fall of Night, Childhood's End, Expedition to Earth, Earthlight, Reach for Tomorrow, The City and the Stars, Tales from the 'White Hart', The Deep Range, The Other Side of the Sky, A Fall of Moondust, Tales of Ten Worlds, Dolphin Island, Glide Path*. Most of these can now be bought in paperback editions.

74. Nigel Calder (ed.) *The World in 1984*, 2 vols. (1965).

75. 1990 *Week-End Telegraph*, No. 126, 3rd March 1967, 45. Compare this with 'Britain in the 1990's. Special Issue of *Esso Magazine*, Winter 1966/7.

76. Kingsley Amis, *New Maps of Hell* (1961), 63.

77. Axel Jensen, *Epp*, translated by Oliver Stallybrass (1967), 13.

78. Events with a high probability-rating are:

a tenfold increase of annual investment in automated equipment; urbanisation of 75 per cent of the U.S. population and the wide use of ultra-light metal substitutes. Amongst the low possibilities are: effective world-wide anti-poverty program is carried out; annual wage of $6,000 is guaranteed to all bread-winners; the growth of new limbs and organs can be artificially induced; staggered work week replaces Monday-to-Friday standard; economic and military alliance exists between the U.S. and the U.S.S.R.; per capita Gross National Product of U.S.A. is up 100% since 1966; limited weather control is carried out globally; private U.S. investment in foreign countries is doubled since 1966; agricultural production is increased by direct genetic manipulation; standing international police force exists; elements manufactured to order from sub-atomic 'building blocks'; substantial synthetic protein production is economically feasible; human brains linked to computers extend man's intelligence; effective physical treatment of mental illness is possible; unemployment rate in the U.S. is lower than in 1966; hereditary defects can be controlled through genetic manipulation; substantial increase in food supply is obtained through ocean farming; most business is conducted by picture-phone; most people in the world are immunised against common diseases; regular commercial transportation by rocket has been instituted; individual intelligence is raised by drugs and average life span of people reaches 100 years.

79. Nigel Calder, *The Environment Game* (1967), 171–3.

80. *Ibid.*, 185–6.

81. *Ibid.*, 210. Compare this with the earlier suggestion of Miles Walker put forward at the British Association for the Advancement of Science in 1932 and Olaf Stapleton's views as outlined *ante* Chapter 10 Section IV.

82. Francois Perroux, *The IVth French Plan* translated Bruno Leblanc (London, 1965, xi).

83. V. Dupont, *L'Utopie et la Roman Utopique dans la Litterature Anglaise* (Paris, 1941). See also R. Ruyer, *L'Utopie et les Utopies* (Paris, 1950); Rita Falke, 'Versuch einer Bibliographie der Utopien', *Romanistiches Jahrbuch* (1953–4), 92–109; G. Duveau, *Sociologie de l'Utopie et autres essais*, Paris, 1961; Regis Messac, *Esquisse d'une Chronobibliographie des Utopies* (Lausanne, 1962); W. de Spens, 'Les royaumes d'Utopie', *Table ronde* (1962); J.-M. Domenach, 'sur le bon usage de l'avenir', *Esprit*, Fevrier 1966; and Jean Meynaud, 'A

Propos des Spéculations sur l'Avenir: Esquisse Bibliographique' *Revue Francaise de Science Politique*, XIII (1963), 666–88.

12 OPERATIONAL ESCHATOLOGIES

1. Wilbert E. Moore, 'The Utility of Utopias', *American Sociological Review*, XXI, No. 6 (1966), 770. The point was made earlier by Paul Valéry in *Œuvres* (Paris, 1957), 1025.

> The mental process of foresight is one of the essential bases of civilisation. It is both the source and the means of all undertakings, whether they be large or small; it is also the assumed basis of politics.

2. Wilbert E. Moore and Eleanor Bernet Sheldon, 'Monitoring Social Change: A Conceptual and Programmatic Statement', American Statistical Association, *Proceedings of the Social Statistics Section*, 1965, 144–9.

3. Moore, 'Utility of Utopias', 772.

4. R. K. Merton, *Social Theory and Social Structure* (1949), 179.

5. Joseph M. Goldsen (ed.), *Outer Space in World Politics* (1963), 173.

6. David Lewin, 'Disney's Last and Greatest Dream is Coming True', *Daily Mail*, 14th February 1967.

7. Dorothy Emmett, *Rules, Roles and Relations* (1966), 117. See also S. I. Dockx and Paul Bernays, *Information and Prediction in Science* (New York, 1965).

8. *Esso Magazine*, Winter 1966–7, Special Issue on Britain in the 1990s, 41.

9. Pierre Masse, 'Prévision et prospective', *Prospective*, Novembre 1959, p. 107, see also Robert E. Lane, 'The Decline of Politics and Idealogy in a Knowledgeable Society', *American Sociological Review*, XXI, No. 5 (1966), 649–62.

10. 'Prospect of World Hunger', *Manchester Guardian*, 28 November, 1966, p. 9.

11. C. Wright Mills, *The Sociological Imagination* (1959), 190; Emile Grunberg and Franco Modigliani, 'The Predictability of Social Events', *The Journal of Political Economy*, LXII (1954), 465–78; William J. McGuire and Demetrius Papageorgis, 'Effectiveness of Forewarning in Developing Resistance to Persuasion', *Public Opinion Quarterly*, XXVI, 1962, 24–34.

12. David Riesman, 'Some Observations on Community Plans and Utopia', in *Individualism Reconsidered* (Glencoe, Illinois, 1954), 70. He quotes

> 'Make no little plans; they have no magic to stir men's blood and probably themselves will not be realised. Make big plans: aim high in hope and work, remembering that a noble logical diagram, once recorded, will never die, but long after we are gone will be a living thing, asserting itself with ever growing insistency.'

See also Erich Jantsch, *Technological Forecasting in Perspective* (OECD Paris 1967) and Olaf Helmer, *Social Technology* (New York, 1966).

13. As C. S. Lewis suggests in *Of Other Worlds* (1966), 68.

14. *Ibid.*

15. See for instance Edgar W. Boss, 'The Theology of C. S. Lewis' (Ph.D.

Chicago, 1948); Chad Walsh, *C. S. Lewis. Apostle to the Sceptics* (New York, 1949); Charles Moorman, *Arthurian Triptych* (University of California Press, 1960); Marjorie Wright, 'The Cosmic Kingdom of Myth: Charles Williams, C. S. Lewis, and J. R. R. Tolkien' (Ph.D. University of Illinois, 1960); Edmund Fuller, *Books with Men Behind Them* (New York, 1962) and Clyde S. Kilby, *The Christian World of C. S. Lewis* (Grand Rapids, Michigan, 1964).

16. C. Wright Mills, *The Sociological Imagination* (New York, 1959), 190. In *Change and Habit: the Challenge of our Time* (1966), Arnold Toynbee envisages a further 2,000 million years of further existence on earth in which life, if we survive, will be mechanised, leisured, urban, and dull.

17. A term used by Gérard Klein in *Fiction* 136 (Paris, March 1965), 132.

18. I. F. Clarke, *The Tale of the Future* (1961); See also for instance R. A. Peddie, *Subject Index of Books published up to and including 1880* (1933–48), adopts the heading 'Utopias and Forecasts' in his third volume and New Series, pp. 898 and 827 respectively.

19. Daniel Bell, 'The Post-Industrial Society', in Eli Ginzberg (ed.), *Technology and Social Change* (New York, 1964), 58–9.

20. Daniel Bell, 'Twelve Modes of Prediction', *Daedalus*, XCIII (1964), 873.

21. Frederick J. Hoffman, *Freudianism and the Literary Mind* (Baton Rouge, 1957), 323–4.

22. Thomas Mann, 'Freud and the Future', first published in 1936 and reprinted in *Essays of Three Decades* (1947), 427.

23. S. Freud, *Basic Writings* (1938), 549.

24. N. O. Brown, *Life Against Death. The Psychoanalytical Meaning of History* (1959), 167, 253. See also Herbert Marcuse, *Eros and Civilisation* (1956).

25. Bernard Wolfe, *Limbo '90* (1952, Abridged edition, Penguin Books, 1961), 367.

26. *New introductory Lectures on Psycho-analysis*, 248. 'Leonardo da Vinci', 43; cited David Riesman, *Individualism Reconsidered* (1954), 340.

27. Tenth Anniversary number, *American Journal of Psychoanalysis*, XI, (1951), 7.

28. Munroe K. Spears, *The Poetry of W. H. Auden* (1963), 178.

29. E. H. Carr, *What is History?* (The George Macaulay Trevelyan lectures, 1962).

30. Edward T. Gargan, 'Tocqueville and the Problem of Historical Prognosis', *American Historical Review*, LXVIII, 1962–3, 332–45; Hannah Arendt, *Between Past and Future* (1961).

31. H. R. Trevor-Roper, 'Arnold Toynbee's Millennium', *Encounter*, June 1957, reprinted in *Encounters* selected by Melvin J. Lasky (1963), 131–51.

32. E. P. Cheney, *Law in History* (New York, 1927); Henry Adams, *The Tendency of History* (1925); Leo Gershoy in Charles E. Boewe and Roy F. Nichols, *Both Human and Humane* (Philadelphia, 1960), 127–8.

33. Lewis Mumford, *The Transformation of Man* (1957), 121.

34. *Ibid.*, 124.

35. See Charles Moorman, *Arthurian Triptych: Mythic Materials in Charles Williams, C. S. Lewis and T. S. Eliot* (Berkeley, 1960), 145.

36. T. S. Eliot, *The Four Quartets*.

37. William Hubben, *Dostoievsky, Kierkegaard, Nietzsche and Kafka: Four Prophets of our Destiny* (New York, 1962), 1–49.

38. W. S. Smith (ed.) *The Religious Speeches of Bernard Shaw* (Pennsylvania, 1962), 33.

39. *Ibid.,* xxii.

40. H. G. Wells, 'God the Invisible King', in *Collected Works,* XI (1925), 502.

41. *Ibid.,* 511.

42. H. G. Wells, *ibid.*

43. Olaf Stapledon, *Last Men in London* (1932), 63–4. 'It is my task to tell you of your own race as it appears through the eyes of the far future; but first I must help you to reconstruct in imagination something of the future itself, and of the world from which we regard you.'

44. A. Koestler, *The Trail of the Dinosaur* (1955), 245.

45. Edmund Crispin, *Best Sf* (1964), 10–14.

46. A. W. Derleth (ed.), *Beach-heads in Space* (New York, 1952); (ed.), *Portals of Tomorrow* (New York, 1954); (ed.), *Time to Come* (New York, 1954). Derleth also edited the best supernatural stories of H. P. Lovecraft (1930–37), in 1945.

47. C. S. Lewis, *Perelandra,* 153–4.

48. Teilhard de Chardin, *The Future of Man* (London, 1964), 267.

49. George Woodcock, 'Utopias in Negative', *The Sewannee Review,* LXIV, 1956, 83.

50. George Knox, 'Apocalypse and Sour Utopias', *Western Humanities Review,* XVI, LI, 1962, 11; Judith Shuklar, *After Utopia* (Princeton, 1957); F. E. Manuel (ed.) *Utopias and Utopian Thought* (Boston, 1967).

51. Teilhard de Chardin, *op. cit.,* 72.

52. Teilhard de Chardin, *op. cit.,* 82, 296.

53. Max Brod (ed.), *The Diaries of Franz Kafka, 1914–1923* (translated Martin Greenberg and Hannah Arendt, New York, 1949), 86; Max Brod (ed.), *The Diaries of Franz Kafka, 1910–1913* (translated Joseph Kresh, New York, 1948), 27.

54. Jean Paul Sartre, *Being and Nothingness* (translated Hazel E. Barnes, New York, 1956), 129.

55. Margaret Church, *Time and Reality. Studies in Contemporary Fiction* (Chapel Hill, 1963), 260.

56. See, for example, *Nausea* (translated by Lloyd Alexander, Norfolk, Conn., 1959); *The Age of Reason* (translated by Eric Sutton, New York, 1959); *Troubled Sleep* (translated by Gerald Hopkins, New York, 1961).

57. Rollo, May, *Existence: A New Discussion in Psychiatry and Psychology* (1953). He worked with H. S. Sullivan after being a student of Paul Tillich's with whom he conducted a dialogue: May's *The Meaning of Anxiety* (1950), was met by Tillich's *The Courage to Be* (1952).

58. Vikter Frankl, *The Doctor and the Soul* (1958), 113.

59. G. Bernard Shaw, *Back to Methuselah,* Part IV, Act. 1.

60. Ernst Cassirer, *An Essay on Man* (New Haven, 1944), 62.

61. Kenneth Boulding, *The Meaning of the Twentieth Century: The Great Transition* (New York, 1964), 167, 192.

62. H. G. Wells, *A Modern Utopia* (1905).

63. D. H. Lawrence, *Studies in Classic American Literature* (1924), 1964 edition, 9.

64. G. F. Von Weizäcker, *The Relevance of Science: Creation and Cosmogony* (1964), 164–7.

65. S. G. F. Brandon, *Man and His Destiny in the Great Religions* (1962), 385.

66. Reinhold Niebuhr, *Moral Man and Immoral Society* (1947), 276–7.

67. Arnold W. Green, *Recreation, Leisure and Politics* (1964), 40.

68. Paul Tillich, *The Courage to Be* (1952).

69. Karl Jaspers, *Tragedy is not Enough* (1953).

70. Julian Huxley, *The Uniqueness of Man* (1941), 290. Another defence of ideal types as conceptual tools for understanding the future or the past has been made by Ludwig von Mises in *Theory and History* (1958). He suggests the development of 'Thymology' (from the Greek Θυμός = the source of willing, thinking, and feeling) and defines it as 'on the one hand an offshoot of introspection and on the other a precipitate of historical experience' (p. 266). As a historical discipline, he argues, 'we must take recourse to it if we want to anticipate other people's future actions and attitudes' (p. 313).

71. John Dewey, *Philosophy and Civilisation* (New York, 1931), 330. He argued that Democracy has 'to be constantly discovered and rediscovered, remade and reorganised'. *The Public and its Problems* (New York, 1927), 206–7.

72. Dennis Gabor, *Inventing the Future* (1963), 18–19.

73. J. O. Bailey, *Pilgrims Through Space and Time. Trends and Patterns in Scientific and Utopian Fiction* (New York, 1947), 187.

74. *Ibid.*, 259–60.

75. Gabor, *op. cit.*, 168.

76. E.g. J. Murray Luck, 'Man against his Environment: the Next Hundred Years', *Science*, CXXVI, (1957), 903–9.

77. Ralf Dahrendorf, 'Out of Utopia: Toward a Reorientation of Sociological Analysis', *American Journal of Sociology*, LXIV (1958), 115–25.

78. Arthur Koestler, *The Trail of the Dinosaur* (1955), 251.

79. D. K. Price, *Government and Science* (1954), 1962 edition, 192.

80. F. L. Polak, *The Image of the Future* (Leyden, 1961), ii, 114–15.

81. Martin Meyersen, 'Utopian Traditions and the Planning of Cities', *Daedalus*, XL (1961), 182–3.

82. John Rader Platt, 'Can we foresee the Future?', *The New Republic*, 8th December 1958, 9–12.

83. G. W. Leibniz, *Theodicy. Essays on the Goodness of God, the Freedom of Man and the Origin of Evil*, translated by E. M. Huggard and edited by Austin Farrar (1952), 129.

84. R. Latta, *Leibniz, The Monadology and Other Philosophical Writings* (1898), 44.

85. Claude Cuénot, *Teilhard de Chardin* (1965), 384.

86. P. Teilhard de Chardin, *Letters from a Traveller* (1962), 277.

87. Cuénot, *op. cit.*, 302.

88. R. Bultmann in *Kerygma and Myth*, ed. H. W. Bartsch and translated by R. H. Fuller (1962), 10.

89. John Macquarrie, *The Scope of Demythologising* (1960), 234–5.

90. L. L. Leshan, 'Time Orientation and Social Class', *Journal of Abnormal Society Psychology*, XLVII (1957), 589–92.

91. F. A. von Hayek in *Economica XIII* (1933), 133.

92. See for instance Robert Boguslaw, *The New Utopias: A Study of System Design and Social Change* (Engelwood Cliffs, New Jersey, 1965).

93. Paul Fraisse (translated by Jennifer Leith), *The Psychology of Time* (London, 1964), 172.

94. *Ibid.*, 173.

95. *Ibid.*, 177.

96. See Lewis Padgett (the pen-name of Henry Kuttner and Catherine Moore), 'Mimsy were the borogroves' in *A Gnome there was and other tales of Science Fiction and Fantasy* (New York, 1960) and Frederic Brown, *Night of the Jabberwock* (New York, 1950).

97. Alice has also warned us against relying too much on games techniques, and against shrinking problems down in scale. For the balls in the Wonderland croquet game turned over and out into hedgehogs, the hoops moved around like soldiers, whilst the poor players found themselves under threat of decapitation.

As a modern exegete of the moral of this croquet game Norbert Weiner noted that the concepts of cybernetics pose the same kinds of problem as were originally posed by theologians. To him 'the future offers very little hope for those who expect that our new mechanical slaves will offer us a world in which we may rest from thinking. Help us they may, but at the cost of supreme demands upon our honesty and our intelligence. The world of the future will be an ever more demanding struggle against the limitations of our intelligence, not a comfortable hammock in which we can lie down to be waited upon by our robot slaves'. Norbert Weiner, *God & Golem Inc.*, (1964), 73–4.

INDEX